D1174638

Ancient Panama

The Texas Pan American Series

Ancient Panama

Chiefs in Search of Power

Mary W. Helms

University of Texas Press
Austin and London

The Texas Pan American Series is published with the assistance of a revolving publication fund established by the Pan American Sulphur Company

Some of the material in Chapter 1 is excerpted, by permission of the publisher, from Mary W. Helms and Franklin O. Loveland, eds., *Frontier Adaptations in Lower Central America.* Copyright © 1976 by ISHI, The Institute for the Study of Human Issues, Philadelphia.

Library of Congress Cataloging in Publication Data

Helms, Mary W
Ancient Panama.
(Texas Pan American series)
Bibliography: p.
Includes index.
1. Indians of Central America–Panama–History.
2. Panama–History–To 1903. I. Title
F1565.H44 972.78'004'97 78-26906
ISBN 0-292-73817-X

Printed in the United States of America

Contents

Tables

Figures

Preface

This study of ancient Panamanian chiefdoms as they appeared on the eve of European discovery developed by accretion more than by formal design. It began with a general survey of the distribution of rank societies in pre-Columbian Panama, which necessitated a review of ethnohistoric materials relating to the isthmus at the time of initial Spanish contact in the early sixteenth century. In order to develop further certain points which were only briefly mentioned by the conquistadors, I sought ethnographic analogies with nonisthmian chiefdoms, particularly those in Polynesia, that might be structurally comparable with the ancient Panamanian polities. I also sought ideas and information in the contemporary ethnographic literature pertaining to the descendants of the ancient isthmian societies, most notably the San Blas Cuna, and to native peoples of Colombia, particularly the Desana. These lines of investigation ultimately led me to explore aspects of ancient Panamanian chiefship that heretofore had not received explicit study or that were amenable to reinterpretation.

Consideration of long-distance contacts among Panamanian elites and between these elites and Colombian rulers is a major focus of this work. I was led by ethnographic analogies to interpret such contacts largely in terms of a search for politically useful knowledge, that is, as intellectual quests that then paid political dividends. I suspect that the pursuit of esoteric knowledge by the ruling elite.

particularly about supernaturally and geographically "distant" peoples, places, and events, is a common phenomenon in chiefdoms. Consideration of long-distance contacts within this perspective might yield interesting results if examined crossculturally.

In developing this and other lines of investigation, I frequently have been forced by the limitations of the primary ethnohistoric data to offer suggestions and inferences rather than firm conclusions. I have tried at all times to separate that which is speculative from that which rests on more substantial grounds and have attempted to keep to the rather narrow middle road of controlled interpretation that separates unwarranted speculation from a too hesitant or too constrictive use of ethnohistoric evidence. I hope that by proceeding in this fashion I may have raised some questions and suggested useful perspectives and that this volume may contribute to our understanding of the cultural processes operative in the so-called Intermediate Area of Nuclear America.

A few words should be said concerning Cuna orthography. There is great variety in spelling among the ethnographic sources pertaining to the Cuna, but two systems of spelling conventions predominate, differing mainly in the designation of stops. Wherever a Cuna word first appears in the text I have tried to indicate both spellings. Some inconsistency remains, however, particularly in quotations from various sources. I have also followed English convention by rendering Cuna plurals with *s*, rather than with the suffixes used by Cuna speakers.

In preparing this volume I benefited greatly from the commentary of several colleagues. It is a distinct pleasure to thank James Howe, who read the manuscript with great care and a considerable investment of time and energy, for his detailed criticism and excellent advice concerning my handling of Cuna materials. Excerpts from *Village Political Organization among the San Blas Cuna*, by Howe (1974), are quoted with his permission. I am grateful, too, to Heather Lechtman, who reviewed portions of the manuscript and offered valuable commentary upon metallurgical issues. Janet Wojnicki provided assistance with typing and Alan Teller with photography. I greatly appreciate their help.

Ancient Panama

1

Panama in the Early Sixteenth Century

Theories and Hypotheses

The native peoples and cultures of lower Central America have been cited more frequently for their apparent failings in pre-Columbian cultural development than for their achievements. The region from northeastern Honduras through Panama (see Fig. 1) has been commonly viewed by scholars as an isolated hinterland that did not participate in the early dynamics of cultural growth exemplified by Mesoamerican Olmec and Peruvian Chavín and as a conservative backland where pre-Columbian high civilization, as evidenced by intensive agricultural techniques, dense population, urbanism, and state forms of political organization, did not evolve. This negative orientation undoubtedly has been encouraged by the paucity of archaeological and ethnographical data available for the area when compared with the rich resources at hand for Mesoamerican and Central Andean studies.[1]

This monograph presents a reconstruction and analysis of select aspects of the political systems of pre-Columbian Panamanian societies at the time of initial European contact, that is, about A.D. 1500. I examine in particular the relationships between chiefly status and power, regional and long-distance exchange networks, and the acquisition of esoteric knowledge. These considerations also focus attention upon various sumptuary items of chiefly display, particularly the

Fig. 1. Lower Central America

fabricated gold pieces and, to a lesser extent, the polychrome ceramic wares for which ancient Panama is justly famous.

The study was undertaken initially to explore implications of the conclusion reached by Carl Sauer in his volume *The Early Spanish Main* (1966) that, contrary to general opinion, such sophisticated metallurgical processes as casting and alloying probably were not practiced in Panama at the time of European contact, although raw gold occurred in moderate supply and simple goldworking techniques, such as hammering and gilding, were probably used by isthmian craftsmen in the early sixteenth century. If this is so, then many of the elaborate gold pieces found in the ownership of the inhabitants of Panama by the Spanish conquistadors (and a significant percentage of the artistic pieces unearthed through archaeological excavations from the "chiefdom period" or found in private collections) must have been crafted in regions beyond Panama and received by isthmian peoples through some form of exchange.[2]

The analysis also proceeds from the argument that by A.D. 1500 many of the Panamanian polities, most of which were organized as rank societies, or chiefdoms, had achieved a particularly dynamic form of chiefdom system characterized by intense status rivalry and competition for power. It is further proposed that, under circumstances of strong chiefly competition and rivalry, exchange of valued high-status goods, such as elaborate gold pieces, and competition among chiefs for advantageous positions in the exchange networks that made these goods available would be highly significant means (though not the sole means) to affirm chiefly status and to give evidence of chiefly efficacy, thereby bolstering the personal power and credibility of individual chiefs. Common ground is further sought between the chiefly pursuit of esoteric contacts with geographically distant peoples and the development by elite leaders of esoteric contacts with cosmologically and cosmographically "distant" supernatural forces.

Physiography

The narrow Isthmus of Panama, with its close juxtaposition of mountain ranges, coastal plains, river systems, and seacoasts (see Fig. 2), presents excellent natural resource diversity and the concomitant potential for subsistence production and redistribution generally associated with the maintenance of chiefdoms. Two major mountain ranges are on either side of the low-lying transisthmian Chagres river

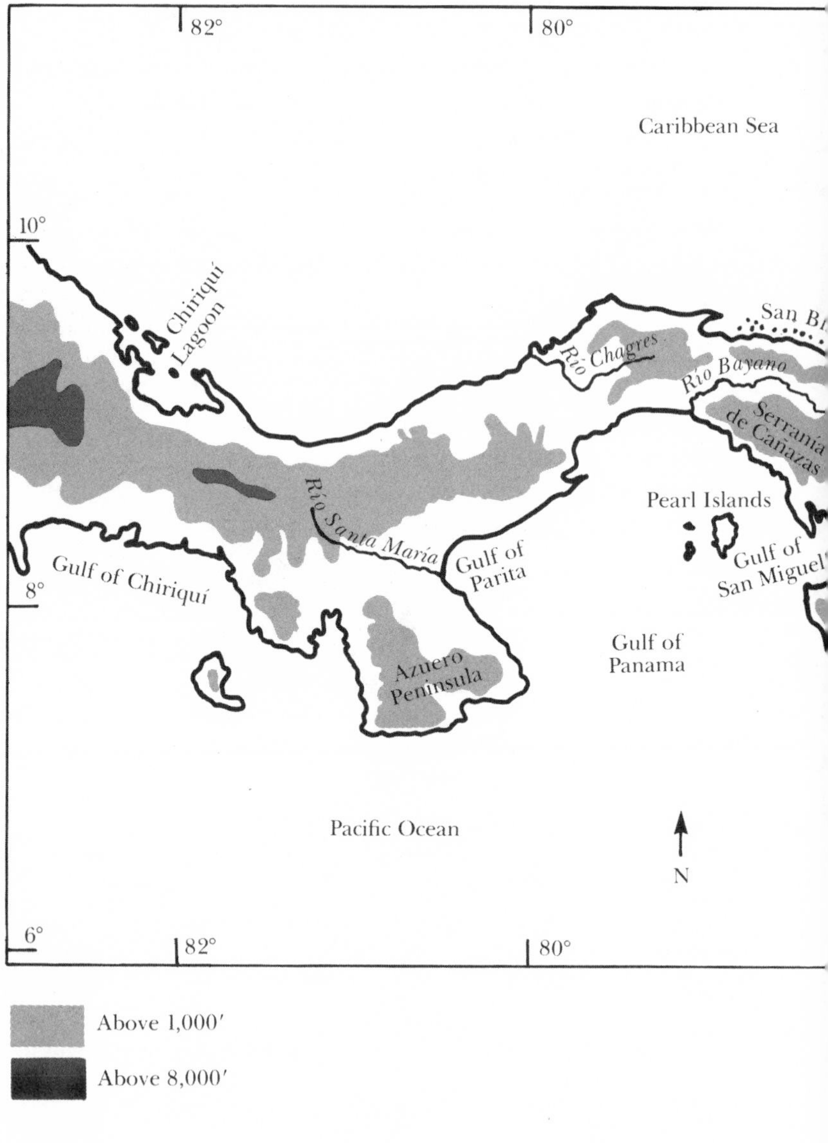

Fig. 2. Panama and northern Colombia: physiographic features.

78°
76°
74°
Sierra
Nevada
de Santa
Marta
10°
hipelago
Gulf of
Urabá
Río Sinú
Río Tuira
8°
Río Cauca
Río Magdalena
Western Cordillera
Central Cordillera
Eastern Cordillera
Río Atrato
78°
76°
74°
6°

system, now channeled as the Panama Canal. The volcanic range to the west is the higher, generally averaging three thousand to five thousand feet altitude, with individual peaks rising to over nine thousand and eleven thousand feet (Bennett 1968: 1, map 1; Holdridge and Budowski 1956: 93). Some twenty or more short, swift rivers flow north from this western sierra to the Caribbean Sea, creating a series of narrow but richly alluvial riverine valleys that reach inland from the rugged cliffs and narrow coast of the Caribbean littoral to the foothills and higher mountain slopes of the cloud-covered interior peaks. These Caribbean slopes, which receive a great deal of moisture throughout the year, have been classified as Tropical Moist Forest (Holdridge and Budowski 1956: 95, 96; Bennett 1968: 4–5).

Tropical Moist Forest is also characteristic of the Caribbean slopes to the east of the Panama Canal Zone (Holdridge and Budowski 1956: 95). Here the major mountain system is lower, averaging elevations between one thousand and two thousand feet (Bennett 1968: 2). This Caribbean coastline lacks the rugged cliffs found to the west. But numerous streams and rivers again traverse the short distance between mountains and sea, providing numerous narrow alluvial strips and opening narrow valleys into the highlands where a number of convenient passes provide ready access to the land beyond.

To the south, on the Pacific side of the central mountains, eastern and western Panama show more contrast. The southern slopes of the eastern *serranías* are drained by tributaries of the Río Bayano, flowing west and south to the Gulf of Panama, and the Río Chucunaque, flowing east and south to a confluence with the Río Tuira, which also empties into the Gulf of Panama via the Gulf of San Miguel. The Río Bayano and the Río Chucunaque together create a longitudinal lowland depression which crosses the interior of eastern Panama approximately from the present-day Canal Zone to the Tuira river system. Another highland, the Serranía de Cañazas, rises to an elevation of over forty-five hundred feet between this interior lowland basin and the Gulf of Panama. The Tuira river system drains a continuation of the central mountain backbone that trends east and south into Colombia. Headwaters of some of its major tributaries again provide convenient access across these mountains toward the Gulf of Urabá and the mighty Río Atrato, gateway to northern Colombia.

West of the Panama Canal the southern, or Pacific, slopes of the western sierras merge into low foothills which then open onto fairly broad coastal plains, again crossed by a multitude of rivers, some small, some more prominent. Coastal lowlands also extend along the eastern, or gulf, side of the mountainous Azuero Peninsula. Compared with the Caribbean versant, the lands on the Pacific side of the central mountain ranges show a more diversified pattern of moist and dry subregions. Nonetheless, Tropical Moist Forest is characteristic of much of the eastern section and of portions of the western. An extensive area of Tropical Dry Forest predominates, however, in the north of the Azuero Peninsula and around the Bay of Parita (Holdridge and Budowski 1956: 94–96, 105). Although generally drier than the Caribbean slopes, the entire area receives quite adequate supplies of rainfall for cultivation and contains extensive areas of rich alluvial soils (Bennett 1968: 5; Holdridge and Budowski 1956: 96, 106; West and Augelli 1966: 451–452; Linares 1977*a*: 308).

Settlement Pattern and Resources

At the present time much of Panama is covered with tropical forest, deciduous woodlands, and stands of bush. In A.D. 1500, however, the country was largely open savannah with secondary growth, particularly along rivers, of grasses, canes, shrubs, and trees.[3] The land was fertile and tillable, and agriculture, together with hunting and fishing, provided the basic subsistence for the populations of dozens of small chiefdoms (Sauer 1966: 244, 285, 287–288).[4]

The first observational information regarding the native inhabitants of Panama is found in the accounts of Columbus' fourth voyage in 1502–1503, which describe briefly the inhabitants of the Caribbean coast west of the Canal Zone (Colón 1959: 241–261; see also Sauer 1966: 120–146). Balboa's letter of 1513 to King Ferdinand contains additional information concerning the lands and peoples of eastern Panama, the Gulf of Urabá, and northern Colombia (Andagoya 1865: i–xix; see also Sauer 1966: 222–223). Useful material is contained in the narrative of conquistador Pascual de Andagoya (1865; see also Trimborn 1952) and in the reports by Gaspar de Espinosa (1864, 1873). Various accounts are also found in the compilations by Pietro Martire d'Anghiera (Peter Martyr d'Anghera) (1912) and by Bartolomé de las Casas (1927). The fullest accounts, however, are available in Gonzalo Fernández de Oviedo y Valdés' *Historia general y natural de las Indias* (1853) and his *Sumario de la natural historia de las Indias* (1959), which include data accumulated during Oviedo's residence in Panama as a government official. The ethnographic data contained in these and other sixteenth-century records and reports have also been carefully extracted and organized by contemporary scholars, including Lothrop (1937: 1–48), Sauer (1966: chaps. 6, 8, 11–14), Romolí (1953, 1960), Anderson (1914), Torres de Araúz (1977), and Linares de Sapir (1968). These primary and secondary sources are those on which I have relied most heavily for information regarding native conditions in early sixteenth-century Panama.

The Spanish records are noteworthy primarily for the generalness of their descriptions and for the lack of detailed data on many topics of interest to scholars today. They have been criticized by other investigators as shallow, ethnocentric, and full of inconsistencies. There is no doubt that these reports contain errors and exaggerations and must be analyzed carefully and interpreted judiciously. Nonetheless, when subject to the controls of ethnohistorical methods, many useful data emerge which can directly or indirectly shed much light on indigenous cultural patterns. On the other hand, there are limitations in coverage which cannot be corrected. Decimation of the native population after the arrival of Pedro Arías de Avila (Pedrarias Dávila) as governor in 1514 and the Spaniards' loss of interest in Panama after the first quarter of the sixteenth century as the riches of Mexico and Peru drew fortune hunters and colonists to north and south prevented fuller investigation into some of the less obvious aspects of native social, economic, and political life.[5]

According to the Spanish reports, extensive portions of the lowlands and mountain slopes of early sixteenth-century Panama were open savannah with canebrakes and groves of shrubs and trees (*montes*) along rivers (Espinosa 1864: 512, 519; Sauer 1966: 244, 285–286). These open lands and bordering sections of cane and *montes* were extensively cultivated by slash-and-burn techniques, probably using digging sticks. Scattered dwellings were located here and there near waterways, about the valleys, and on the mountain slopes probably near cultivated plots (Oviedo 1853: bk. 29, chap. 27, p. 131, and 1959: 29, 41; Sauer 1966: 240, 242; Romolí 1953: 108). In a few cases more nucleated "towns" are described—Natá and Darién, for example—but evidence suggests that "towns" such as Natá were simply the dwelling places of the family and personal servants of a chief, while the common people lived abroad in dispersed settlements (Anghera 1912: I, 309; Lothrop 1937: 14; Young 1971: 39–41). The Darién settlement, however, may have included both elites and commoners (see Sauer 1966: 174).[6]

This population distribution has been cited by Sauer as evidence that, in spite of frequent references to warfare, there apparently was little need for the general populace to live defensively in larger communities (1966: 240). Warfare, in fact, seems to have been oriented toward the *bohíos*, or dwelling compounds, of the high chiefs, which were protected with stone walls (as at Comogre) or enclosed by timber and a large moat or by columnar cactuses (recorded for Panama west of Escoria) (Anghera 1912: I, 219; Espinosa 1864: 510, 515; Sauer 1966: 221, 271). Some of this defense construction may have been raised for protection against wild animals (Andagoya 1865: 18; Enciso 1932: 179).[7]

Since the Spaniards generally traveled from one chiefly *bohío* to another, knowing that control of the high lord and his family generally yielded control of the populace, we have a few more detailed records of these chiefly residences, or elite centers.[8] The dwelling of Comogre, one of the most prestigious rulers, was estimated by the Spaniards at 150 paces long by 80 paces wide (in measuring distance a pace may be estimated as three feet). It was formed of timber beams securely fastened together and further strengthened by stone walls. The ceilings were carved and the floors "artistically decorated." A storehouse and cellar were well stocked with provisions. The chiefly residence apparently contained several rooms, for in the innermost apartment the Spaniards were shocked to find a chamber containing the dessicated bodies of the chief's deceased ancestors, richly dressed and suspended with ropes in order of the rank they held in life (Anghera 1912: I, 219). A very brief description of the headquarters of the chief Tubanama (Tumanama) also notes two long houses, each 220 paces by 50 paces, built to shelter warriors (Anghera 1912: I, 309; cf. Wafer 1934:lviii).

The thatch-roofed homes of the common populace, although substantially built of canes tied with lianas and plastered over with earth (Oviedo 1959: 39; Lothrop 1937: 14; Wafer 1934: 89), were surely smaller than the elaborate elite centers. In this contrast of dwelling places the chiefly *bohío* probably stood forth as overt evidence of the high status and authority, prestige, and power of the ruler. The significance of the *bohío* as a visible symbol of the chiefly estate may be all the more noteworthy since Panama gives little evidence so far of distinctly ceremonial structures, such as temples or pyramids, that would also have served this purpose, although sacred shrines in interior mountains may have existed (see Espinosa 1864: 505).[9]

This interpretation of the symbolic significance of the chiefly *bohío* gains some support from ethnographic reports of the twentieth-century Cuna currently living on islets of the San Blas Archipelago of northeastern Panama. The Cuna, descendants of the pre-Columbian societies of eastern Panama (see Torres de Araúz 1974), use the concept of house construction, particularly of the larger meeting house (probably the contemporary form of the ancient *bohío*) in which chiefs and populace periodically assemble, as metaphor for communal solidarity and for the strength and support of the chiefship. The structural main post and secondary vertical posts and roof-support poles are associated with chiefs and other ritually and politically significant "men of importance." These timbers, like community leaders, are firmly placed and enduring; the posts work to support the building just as the community leaders work to support society. The ordinary populace, in contrast, corresponds to the walls of the building, which are composed of thin lengths of cane that provide little or no support and require frequent replacing (Howe 1977: 154, and 1974: 83).[10]

The ethnohistorical data offer no complete enumeration of the chiefdoms established in Panama at the time of European contact. However, some three dozen are directly indicated in one context or another and there are passing references to more. The data also indicate directly and by implication that the general range or extent of chiefdom holdings provided access to a diversity of local natural resources. In some cases, chiefdoms extended from mountain heights to seacoast (frequently with a river valley as central focus) or, in comparable manner, reached from mountain heights to interior river basin lowlands (again with a waterway as defining feature). Such domains included varied resources of ocean and coastal littoral (or river basin lowlands), cultivated plains and slopes, waterways, and forest. In other cases, these diverse ecological zones appear to have been divided between two adjacent chiefdoms, one located in the lowlands so as to command coastal and cultivated savannah lands, the other situated in the more mountainous interior to include hillsides and mountain heights. In these circumstances exchange of resources between coast and interior occurred. The Spaniards noted, with reference to precious metals, their favorite natural resource, that "it usually happens that a country rich in cereals is devoid of gold. On the other hand, where gold and other metals are common, the country is usually mountainous, rocky and arid; it is by exchanging products that commercial relations are established" (Anghera 1912: I, 202–203; see also Oviedo 1853: bk. 29, chap. 28, p. 140).

Ocean and littoral, rivers, savannahs, and mountain heights provided a wealth of foods and other resources. The Spani mented frequently on the abundance of sea turtle, mana and, especially, freshwater and ocean fish; on the diversit cultural products, including sweet manioc, sweet potatoes roots, maize, pineapples, mamey, coconuts, and citrus fruits; and on the abundance of white-tail (Virginia) deer, collared peccaries, iguanas, and various fowls and birds, including pheasants and ground-feeding doves that were hunted by drives and with traps and nets, the meat to be dried by smoking and salting, as were fish (see, e.g., Oviedo 1853: bk. 29, chap. 28, p. 136, chap. 29, pp. 142–143, and 1959: 29, 110–118; Espinosa 1864: 512, 519; Lothrop 1937: 15–18; Sauer 1966: 133, 241–244, 272–274).

Quantities of all these foods were stored in the *bohíos* of the chiefs. The storerooms of the powerful lord Comogre contained multicolored piles of maize, quantities of roots, peanuts, green and red chili peppers, coconuts, pineapples and other fruits, smoked venison and pork, dried fish, baskets of corn meal, bundles of herbs, jars of maize beer, and a considerable assortment of red and white "wines," that is, various fermented drinks, or *chichas*, made not only from maize but also from starchy roots, palm fruits and sap, pineapples, and other fruits (see Romolí 1953: 98–99; Sauer 1966: 241–244). The Spaniards themselves were sometimes feasted from these supplies by high-ranking hosts who placed quantities of meat and *chicha* and lumps of salt before them in calabashes and on leaves (see Romolí 1953: 99).

Complexity of Stratification

Although general features of settlement pattern and subsistence are provided in the Hispanic accounts, the ethnohistorical materials are deficient on many topics relevant to sociopolitical structure and function. Furthermore, what data are available are fragmentary and incomplete. Some insights can be gleaned, however, if this evidence is compared with characteristics of chiefdoms from other areas where data are more satisfactory. This methodology assumes that, while details may be expected to vary, a measure of regularity and predictability exists with respect to the *general* structural and functional characteristics of rank societies wherever they appear (see Service 1971: chap. 5; Fried 1967: chap. 4; Goldman 1970: chaps. 1, 20–23).

If this assumption be granted, let us compare the available information regarding the general characteristics and operation of pre-Columbian Panamanian rank societies with comparable features of

Polynesian chiefdoms, which are particularly useful for this comparative analysis because of two detailed studies (Goldman 1970; Sahlins 1958) that treat the Polynesian material from complementary methodological and theoretical perspectives. It must be clearly understood, however, that I do not intend a direct correlation between all the Polynesian criteria and all the data available for Panama. There is no reason to expect that Panamanian adaptive strategies were identical in all details and particulars to those that evolved in Polynesia. Therefore, a complete extrapolation from Polynesia to Panama is unwarranted and unintended. Nonetheless, by comparing the chiefdoms of Panama with those of Polynesia, even in a most general manner, we may derive insights into the degree of stratification and the modes of chiefly operations that may have characterized early sixteenth-century isthmian societies.

Let us begin by considering the criteria of stratification set forth by Sahlins in his comparative study of social stratification in Polynesia (1958: 11–12, 248–249). They include the following items: number of status levels in society, relative degree of access to strategic resources by nobility and commoners, amount and type of control of production by nobility, nature of the redistribution hierarchy, amount of emphasis on insignia of rank, degree of chiefly control over socioregulatory processes, nature of chiefly marriages, forms of obeisance toward chiefs, and distinctions in life-crisis rites between chiefs and nonchiefs. Let us consider the information available for Panama on each of these topics.

Panamanian society contained two basic social levels, elite and commoner, with finer distinctions within these broad categories. The highest-ranking members of the elite were the *quevís*, or high chiefs, termed *caciques* by the Spaniards (Oviedo 1853: bk. 29, chap. 26, pp. 129–130, chap. 27, p. 131; Andagoya 1865: 12). Next in rank were those termed *sacos*, also called *caciques* by the Europeans.[11] Oviedo defines a *saco* as a principal personage who has vassals but is inferior in rank to a *cacique* (1853: bk. 29, chap. 26, pp. 129–130, chap. 27, p. 131, and 1959: 28). The literature occasionally makes reference to *sacos* who were brothers of the *quevi* or who were chiefs subordinate to the *quevi* by virtue of defeat in battle. Possibly the term also held affinal connotations, although no primary data exist on this likelihood for pre-Columbian society (but see Oviedo 1959: 28). There are hints of such associations, however, in ethnographic observances among the contemporary (twentieth-century) San Blas Cuna. David Stout suggests that the Cuna term *saka*, meaning "father-in-law" and "mother-in-law" (i.e., wife's parents), is related to or derived from the aboriginal term *sako* (*saco*), which, he suggests, also connoted father-in-law and contained implications of affinal obligations via bride service by daughters' husbands (1947: 81; see also Nordenskiöld 1938: 30).[12] (The term *queví* is no longer used.)

In ancient Panama, male members of the lowest echelons of the elite status level were known as *çabras*. *Çabras* were men originally of commoner status (either directly by birth or by more distant family ancestry) who achieved the rank of *çabra* by virtue of outstanding bravery in battle. The honored warrior, granted title by his ruler, was also given gifts of women and slaves and frequently was assigned to be the local administrator of a given population and territory. The *çabras* then lived apart from commoners and were "more honored," directing land and villages "something like gentlemen or grandees, separated from the common people, and . . . superior to others of the ordinary people whom they command" (Oviedo 1959: 28, 29). The sons of *çabras* inherited the father's title and position but were allowed to keep it only if they, too, became professional warriors, thus providing the chief with a constant force of fighters. Those honored as *çabras* apparently fell under the political (and perhaps affinal) direction of *sacos* (Oviedo 1853: bk. 29, chap. 26, pp. 129–130, and 1959: 28–29; Romolí 1953: 109; Lothrop 1937: 22).

Oviedo also notes a territorial referent for the various grades of elite: "The *cacique*, the *saco* and the *çabra* have their own names, and likewise the provinces, rivers, valleys, and places where they live are named" (1959: 28, and 1853: bk. 29, chap. 26, p. 130). In other words, *çabras* and *sacos*, men of lower and higher elite status, respectively, may have held overlapping stewardship (see Sahlins 1958: 6) over the various territorial villages and districts that, in sum, composed the total domain, or "province," of a *queví*. Judging from all available evidence, the ties connecting this hierarchy of command and political responsibility were forged by a combination of interpersonal associations, including consanguineal and affinal bonds, rewards for valorous military service, and defeat and incorporation of rivals.

Very little information is available concerning commoners, although the general populace was distinguished from the elite by dress, by status endogamy, and by differences in life-crisis rites, which will be discussed in more detail below. Lionel Wafer provides some information concerning family and household organization in the late seventeenth century which possibly may be illustrative of the precontact domestic life of the ordinary Panamanian: ". . . the Indian houses . . . were very large and well built . . . with many interior divisions. These were the typical family dwellings of the Cuna, where the patriarch exercises control over all the group, consisting of his wife and daughters with their husbands and children, and, often, grand-daughters with their families" (1934: xviii–xix).

The Spanish records also identify *pacos,* war prisoners who served the elite as "slaves." *Pacos* were branded, or tattooed, on the face with identification marks signifying the lord who was served; they often also had a front tooth knocked out. Such persons served as hammock carriers for the *queví* when traveling and some were used as homosexual partners (*camayoa*).[13] War captives possibly may have been utilized as agricultural laborers, too (cf. Fernández Guardia 1913: 236). They were also an exchange resource, for captive "slaves" were given to the Spaniards by the *quevís* as gifts of alliance. They further served as baggage carriers or bearers both for the Spaniards and in native society (Oviedo 1853: bk. 29, chap. 2, p. 8, chap. 26, pp. 126, 129, chap. 27, p. 134, chap. 28, pp. 138, 140; Lothrop 1937: 22, 23).

In accordance with general theory regarding the operation of rank societies (and continuing our consideration of Sahlins' stratification criteria), the high chief, or *queví,* should have been politically and economically supported in his office by contributions in kind or labor from the populace, while reciprocal services and goods should have been rendered by the chief to his people. The data indicate that no regular chiefly tribute was collected in Panama, but that personal services and labor were expected when the chief required house building, planting, or fishing and at times of war. In return for services and labor, food and drink were distributed by the lord (Andagoya 1865: 13). Oviedo comments: ". . . many houses and much land belong to a *cacique* who is obeyed, served, and respected by his people. When he eats in the field or in the village, all the food is placed in front of him and he distributes it to the people, and gives to each one what he cares to. He also has certain men who farm for him, others who hunt and fish. Sometimes the *cacique* takes part in these activities or in some pursuit that pleases him, unless he is at war" (1959: 41–42, and 1853: bk. 29, chap. 27, pp. 132–133). Espinosa implies that members of the populace took turns planting maize for the lord (1864: 491).

No information is available concerning other aspects of local production and redistribution. It is likely, however, that *sacos* and, especially, *çabras* were charged with overseeing the technicalities of food production (cf. Goldman 1970: 483) and with accumulating whatever contributions of goods and services were required to support and enhance chiefly activities. We are told, for example, that a brother of the *queví* of Careta and a brother of the *queví* of Escoria, who were *sacos* of their respective chiefs, lived on the sea and/or directed fishing ports; we can assume that produce of the sea and activities of the ports fell under their jurisdiction as representatives of their *quevís* (Lothrop 1937: 8; Andagoya 1865: 8, 9). Espinosa describes how a group of natives came to the elite compound at Natá to barter crabs and fish for maize, which may be indicative of specialized gathering of sea resources by coastal groups (1864: 491).

Nor is there direct indication whether production of craft items was controlled by the chief or other members of the elite. Indeed, information on craftsmen or specialists is very limited. Oviedo noted that one who excelled in any special skill, be it hunting, fishing, netmaking, song and dance direction, supernatural contact, and so forth, received recognition as a *tequina,* or "master" (1853: bk. 29, chap. 26, p. 127, and 1959: 33; cf. Goldman 1970: 491–495).[14] The ethnohistoric literature also mentions skilled divers trained from infancy to gather shellfish in the Bay of Panama (Anghera 1912: I, 295); potters and gold artisans, probably of the northern Sierra de Cañazas, who fashioned articles for barter (ibid., p. 221); and the expert armorers of Escoria in western Panama who were famous for the fine weaponry they fashioned (Espinosa 1864: 508; Andagoya 1865: 25).

The literature is more rewarding with respect to other aspects of chiefly status. Status endogamy seems to have existed, for Oviedo states that "the *caciques* and lords among these Indians take as many wives as they desire, if they can find handsome ones who please them and who are women of rank, daughters of lords, and of their own nation and language" (1959: 31, and 1853: bk. 29, chap. 27, p. 133; see also Romolí 1953: 109; Lothrop 1937: 24, 25). Specific incidents in the Hispanic accounts also record diplomatic marriages between *quevís* and high-ranking daughters of neighboring elite groups (see Oviedo 1853: bk. 29, chap. 27, p. 133).[15] Andagoya indicates, however, that only one wife was formally married, her sons to inherit the chiefship and property, while many other women were taken without this ceremony and their sons did not inherit (1865: 13).

By virtue of their high position and as expression of their chiefly perquisites, particularly their roles as guardians of the moral (behavioral) order and the peace, *quevís* also settled quarrels and disputes.

by putting to death any who were found to have lied to them (Oviedo 1853: bk. 29, chap. 29, p. 142, chap. 26, p. 129; Andagoya 1865: 13).

Chiefs and others of the elite also affected distinctive insignia indicative of rank and of chiefly powers and sanctity. Elite symbols were particularly observed in dress and ornamentation, house carving, and household utensils. The size and decoration of chiefly *bohíos* and the lavishness of chiefly feasts already have been described. With respect to attire, most women wore a cotton skirt or apron falling from the waist to at least the knees, but women of the nobility wore ankle-length skirts. Women generally wore gold rings in their ears and nose, but women of high status also wore an abundance of bracelets, anklets, and necklaces of shells and gold and used gold bars as breast supports (Oviedo 1853: bk. 29, chap. 26, p. 126, chap. 28, p. 138, and 1959: 44; Lothrop 1937: 13–14; Romolí 1953: 107). Men of the nobility were also clad in fine cloaks and ornaments, at least on formal occasions (see Romolí 1953: 97–98; cf. Wafer 1934: 84–89; Lothrop 1937: 13). (The nature and significance of this ornamentation, particularly of gold pieces, will be discussed in considerable detail below.) Oviedo describes how body paint served to distinguish persons of different ranks or social positions. For example, as was mentioned above, slaves were painted (or tattooed) with a mark that designated them as *pacos*, while free servants and "vassals" of a *queví* or other lord wore a painted mark which identified them as subject to that particular chief. The chief himself wore that mark, which he chose when he inherited the lordship from his father. The ordinary populace also wore painted patterns out of general respectability, as is discussed in Chapter 3 (Oviedo 1853: bk. 29, chap. 28, pp. 138, 139; Lothrop 1937: 13, 14, 22).

The practice of carrying the chief in a hammock when traveling was mentioned previously (see Oviedo 1853: bk. 29, chap. 26, p. 126), but there is no other information in the Spanish documents regarding gestures of respect or of obeisance to the elite. We do have considerable data, however, concerning the disposal of the dead and the admission to an afterlife. According to Oviedo, when commoners and slaves (and disgraced nobles) died, their existence ended, "their spirits die with the body," and they were "converted into air or into nothingness" (1959: 35, 36). Only to chiefs and other members of the nobility was eternal life assured, as it was also to those wives, retainers, and war captives who chose or were chosen to accompany the chief to the afterlife through sacrifice or suicide at the time of his death

(Oviedo 1959: 36, and 1853: bk. 29, chap. 31, pp. 154, 156; see also Espinosa 1873: 23–25; Lothrop 1937: 43–46). Andagoya indicates, however, that only concubines could be so sacrificed, not the legally married wife whose sons would inherit the chiefship and other benefits (see 1865: 15). Oviedo also says that only the elite and those who accompanied them in death were given a form of burial, while the remains of commoners and slaves were taken to the forests and abandoned to the elements and the wild beasts (1853: bk. 29, chap. 31, pp. 154, 156). Philip Young has suggested in a personal communication that Oviedo's description of commoners' fate was really a description of the first stage of secondary burial.[16] Additional interpretation of these practices is given in Chapter 3.

Lothrop has discussed the variety of burial techniques practiced in pre-Columbian Panama at some length (1937: 43, 46–48). He includes a description written by Espinosa of the mortuary preparation of the deceased chief Parita (Espinosa 1873: 23–25). The remains of chiefs were generally dessicated, wrapped in fine mantles, and dressed in jewelry. They then were either interred (as at the Sitio Conte) or preserved aboveground in a special chamber of the chiefly *bohío*, where they were placed with the bodies of previous rulers in the order of chiefly succession, as the Spaniards described for Comogre. Those sacrificed to accompany the chief were buried in either case, again dressed in elaborate finery and jewels (Oviedo 1853: bk. 29, chap. 31, p. 155; Andagoya 1865: 15–16).[17]

Let us now consider the data presented above from the perspective of Sahlins' study of social stratification in Polynesia. Sahlins has grouped Polynesian societies into four broad categories, Groups I, II*a*, II*b*, and III, indicating less-to-greater complexity of stratification. Although comparable information on Panamanian chiefdoms is fragmentary, it appears that the isthmian rank societies were not as complex structurally as those in Sahlins' Group I (Hawaii, Tonga, Samoa, Tahiti). Nor do the Panamanian chiefdoms appear as loosely structured as the societies in Sahlins' Group III (Pukapuka, Ontong Java, Tokelau) (see Sahlins 1958: 11–12). Panamanian rank societies appear to fit best the criteria of stratification listed in Sahlins' Groups II*a* and II*b* (Mangareva, Mangaia, Easter Island, Uvea, Marquesas, Tikopia, Futuna). In Table 1, the criteria for these two subdivisions of Group II, whose criteria of stratification Sahlins considers too similar to warrant distinction into two separate groups (see 1958: 10), are compared with the extant data from Panama. Where isthmian information is insufficient to form a definite opinion, dotted lines

Table 1. Panamanian Data Compared with Sahlins' Group II*a* and Group II*b*

*Sahlins' Group II*a	Sixteenth-Century Panama	*Sahlins' Group II*b
Two basic status levels with tendency to form third	←— Nobles (*quevís* and *sacos*) and commoners; *çabras* as potential third status?	Two status levels
Pre-eminent stewardship by high chiefs	←— *Queví* assigns administrative territory to *sacos* and *çabras*	Highest rights of access to strategic resources usually held by upper status level
Dispossession of lower-status members from land possible	? Insufficient data ?	No dispossessions
Punishments for violation of economic tabus usually supernatural	? Insufficient data, but note ceremony surrounding gold mining in Veragua ? - - →	Economic tabus carrying supernatural sanctions
Control of communal and craft production by upper level	? Insufficient data ? - - →	Communal production usually controlled by chiefs; craft production often so
No direct regulation of household production	? Insufficient data ?	No direct control over household production
A two-level redistributive hierarchy	← - - Postulated distribution of long-distance goods by elites of regional centers; further redistribution by elites of local centers	Chiefs often the foci of redistribution
Usually no ability of chiefs to confiscate goods by force	? Insufficient data ?	
Highest chiefs divorced from subsistence production	←— Labor services given chief as needed	Upper level usually not freed from subsistence production
Marked insignia of rank	* ←— *Queví* and other elites wear distinctive headdresses and elaborate gold ornaments in abundance; distinctive robes; *bohíos* carved and painted; gold utensils for	Few insignia of rank

		quevi; *quevi* carried in hammock by runners; descent group or polity has distinctive "mark" or emblem, associated with *quevi*	
Fair degree of arbitrary authority	←-- ?	Insufficient data ?	Limited chiefly authority
Control of socioregulatory process by chiefs	←—	Chiefs as judiciary	Chiefs consult with elders on important decisions
Chiefs could punish those who infringed their rights severely in some cases	←--	Those who lie to *quevi* during judiciary hearing are killed; warfare between *quevi* and brother at Acla; secular chiefly rivalries and warfare; but considerable supernatural protection postulated, too	Violent secular punishments inflicted by chiefs were few; chiefs' prerogatives supernaturally protected
Intrastatus marriages of chiefs but not too strictly enforced	←—	Chiefs marry within elite strata of own and other polities but take commoners as concubines	Only slight preference for intrachiefly marriages
Personal tabu system fairly elaborate		? Insufficient data ?	Nonelaborate personal tabu system of chiefs
Obeisance postures not marked	** ←—	Significant obeisance postures, including carrying of chiefs in hammocks; probable use of chiefly language on ceremonial occasions	Few to no forms of obeisance
Special life-crisis rites often exist in chiefly families	*** ←—	Burial of chiefs or preservation of remains of deceased chiefs in *bohío*; elaborate grave goods; sacrificed retainers vs. secondary burials with few grave goods for commoners	More difference in degree than kind in chiefly vs. nonchiefly crisis rites

* May approach Sahlins' Group I: "large range of clothes, ornaments, etc. serving as insignia of rank."

** May approach Sahlins' Group I: "elaborate obeisance postures and other forms of respect including developed chiefs' languages and carrying of chiefs on litters, etc."

*** May approach Sahlins' Group I: "unique rites for all life crises of high chiefs, held on a spectacular scale."

They assured the accuracy of the statements of the disputing parties indicate my impression of the criteria. Asterisks mark the few Panamanian characteristics which seem to go beyond Group II*a* criteria and approach those of Group I.

In Table 1 the data suggest that in overall terms the chiefdoms of Panama had achieved something akin to the Polynesian Group II*a* level of stratification, although a conservative judgment suggests that a number of criteria more characteristic of level II*b* also occurred, particularly with respect to local productivity controls and directives. This information may be interpreted in several ways. Conceivably, most Panamanian chiefdoms included characteristics of both Groups II*a* and II*b*. Yet it is quite possible that the chiefdoms of Panama had not all achieved an identical level of stratification by A.D. 1500. Some may have approximated most closely the Polynesian II*b* category, while others may have achieved criteria of stratification closer to the Polynesian II*a* category. Generally speaking, however, Panamanian chiefdoms may be safely assigned to a more or less intermediate position in the gradation of stratification proposed by Sahlins for Polynesia.

Competition and Power

The Panamanian data summarized in Table 1 suggest more than a tentative correlation of Panamanian chiefdoms with Sahlins' Group II Polynesian societies. They further imply that certain areas of elite sumptuary display—such as marked insignia of rank in dress, dwellings, and ornamentation; carrying of chiefs on litters; and special burial rites—may have gone somewhat beyond the general characteristics of Group II societies to approach elite sumptuary characteristics more commonly associated with Polynesian Group I chiefdoms. On the other hands, the admittedly sparse data pertaining to elite regulation of economic production in Panama do not point toward Group I criteria, but fall within Group II. In other words, elite sumptuary characteristics in Panama may have been somewhat more complex than would be expected from the characteristics pertaining to local production alone. This trend suggests in turn that factors other than control of local production may have been involved in the development and elaboration of the elite sector in Panama.

Investigation of this point requires closer consideration of the nature of elite power and authority in rank societies. Irving Goldman's study of aristocracy in Polynesia (1970) is helpful here. Goldman focuses on the hierarchical nature of Polynesian rank and status systems, emphasizing particularly the dynamics by which formal principles of rank and status organization are adjusted to harsh realities of power and politics. He considers ways and means by which official elite rankings, which are based on systems of genealogical seniority that ascribe highest honor and, theoretically, highest power to the firstborn (primogeniture) and to descendants of the line of firstborn (the senior descent line), are fitted to the hard fact that individual abilities to wield power do not necessarily accord to formal rank and status positions. Goldman notes the swirl of competitions and rivalries surrounding the actual allocation and application of power and the constant pressures on those in power positions to expand the range and effectiveness of chiefly controls so as to give overt evidence of their ability to rule.

Goldman classifies the rank societies of Polynesia into three categories, the Traditional, the Open, and the Stratified, according to the variety of status systems by which power is expressed (1970: 20–24). Briefly described, the Traditional system is one in which formal genealogical positions are given priority over any other claims to authority and are upheld by a religious system headed by a sacred chief. The Open system, in contrast, sees more intense rivalry for power between high-ranking elites regardless of the official directives regarding the allocation of controls via the gradations of genealogically defined status positions.[18] (Indeed, ambiguities over status positions can arise even within the genealogical structure so that there may be question regarding who is to rule by virtue of legitimate claims by birthright.) As a result, Open societies are more strongly militaristic and overtly "political" than are Traditional societies, although religious controls are still important. Finally, Goldman's Stratified system contains both highly influential formal status positions and effective allocation of controls by means independent of formal positions. In addition, those of high status not only rule but also possess all title to land, while commoners are both ruled and landless (ibid., pp. 20–24).

Once again the chiefdoms of Panama can be arranged within this framework, although there are virtually no direct ethnohistorical data from Panama regarding the actual operation of chiefly rule to assist in this placement. Therefore, Panamanian chiefdoms must be correlated with Goldman's Polynesian scheme indirectly by comparing the distribution of the various Polynesian societies in Sahlins' and Goldman's classifications. As Table 2 illustrates, Sahlins' Group I correlates rather well with Goldman's Stratified category, and the societies composing Sahlins' Group III are contained in Goldman's Traditional Category. Sahlins' Group II, with which we are most concerned, is distributed primarily between Goldman's Open and Traditional systems. Therefore, it would appear that the criteria defining Goldman's Open classification, and to a lesser extent those defining his Traditional system, might be most applicable to the Panamanian chiefdoms.

The major difference between the Traditional and the Open status systems as defined by Goldman centers on the intense competition and status rivalry among Open system elites. If we posit that Panamanian chiefdoms were organized in terms of the general interplay of status and power characteristic of Goldman's Open society and, to some extent, of his Traditional society, we would expect to find Panamanian social structure (at least the elite sector) composed of nu-

Table 2. The Classifications of Sahlins and Goldman Compared

Sahlins	*Goldman*
Group I	Stratified
Hawaii	Hawaiian Islands
Tonga	Tonga
Tahiti	Society Islands (including Tahiti)
Samoa	Mangareva
Group II	Open
Mangareva	Samoa
Mangaia	Mangaia
Easter Island	Easter Island
Marquesas	Marquesas
	Niue
	Traditional
Uvea	Uvea
Tikopia	Tikopia
Futuna	Futuna
Group III	
Pukapuka	Pukapuka
Ontong Java	Ontong Java
Tokelau	Tokelau
	Maori
	Manihiki-Rakahanga
	Tongareva

merous ranked status positions defined by genealogical principles of seniority that formally accorded degrees of honor and control, and thus power, to individuals according to their relative birth order vis-à-vis lines of primogeniture. The highest, chiefly positions would accrue to firstborns and descendants of lines of firstborns. This formal structure, however, would be modified by political realities that required an incumbent chief to actively express and expand the control of persons, natural resources, elements, skills, and information that was the primary measure of a chief's ruling ability (cf. Goldman 1970: 16–20). In other words, genealogical legitimacy notwithstanding, in actuality, chiefs would face challenge and competition for their office and for the public exercise of chiefly power from others of high genealogical status and would be compelled to seek modes of support other than formal inheritance in order to continue to function (cf. Goldman 1970: 24–26; Swartz, Turner, and Tuden 1966: 13; Burling 1974: 13–52).

We have very little primary data concerning chiefly power and elite competition from pre-Columbian Panama. However, I should like to briefly analyze within this context of challenge and rivalry the scant ethnohistoric data recorded by Oviedo describing procedures guiding succession to elite positions, including the office of *queví*. The relevant section reads as follows:

> The eldest son succeeds his father, and if there are no sons, the oldest daughter becomes the heir and is married to her leading vassal. But if the oldest son is survived by daughters and not sons, the daughters do not become his heirs, but the sons of the second daughter, because they know definitely that she is of their family. Just as my sister's son most certainly is my nephew [and, Oviedo adds in the version recorded in his *Historia general*, is the descendant of my father] and the son or daughter of my brother may be doubted to be his own. (1959: 31, and 1853: bk. 29, chap. 27, p. 133)[19]

In this passage, which appears rather confusing, Oviedo may be providing us with the possible moves or alternatives within the overall strategy of succession without specifying many of the underlying rules guiding these choices. The clearest key to understanding Oviedo's words appears in the final sentence, which stresses paternity (Lothrop 1937: 26; Stout 1947: 79). In fact, Oviedo explicitly indicates that the question of paternity among the elite was not entirely academic. "For the most part these women are virtuous, but there are some, especially among high-born ladies, who give themselves to any man who wants them, saying that noble and high-born women should never refuse to grant anything requested of them. Only low-born women refuse" (1959: 31, and 1853: bk. 29, chap. 27, pp. 133–134).

Yet the question of paternity as a factor in succession can be augmented with additional interpretations that take account of the whole of Oviedo's statement if his data are analyzed within the proposition that Panamanian chiefs frequently may have faced serious competition for power from high-status rivals and sought ways to circumvent or reduce this threat. It is also enlightening to view the several steps or possibilities indicated in Oviedo's remarks as comprising in sum a "single," technically patrilineal, succession of the lordship from authorized male to authorized male in situations when direct father-son patrilineal succession was broken. (Patrilineal inheritance of elite positions refers to the rule directing individual access to a specific privilege and should not be taken to mean that patrilineages were basic social units. Following Goldman [1970: 418–443], the term "status lineage" is used here to refer to the organization of social groups in Panama for which we have no evidence regarding lineality as an organizational principle.)

Very likely the several steps or alternatives differentiated by Oviedo or his informants reflect various concepts or distinctions of power and status that underwrote the dynamics both of chiefly efficacy and legitimacy and of rivalry for chiefly office by other elite competitors. Since in actual practice, as evidenced by general ethnography, succession patterns very often are indistinct and the competition easily escalated to violence, the specific directives on succession procedures indicated in Oviedo's statement suggest that this is the view of an incumbent chief hoping to minimize rivalry and to provide specific guidelines so that the chiefship may pass with as little difficulty as possible to his preferred heir (see Burling 1974: 258). In actuality, it is likely that serious rivalry among a number of high-status men, many of whom probably were immediate subordinates (*sacos*) of the previous chief, was impossible to avoid and that the death of a chief frequently heralded a period of elite struggle (see ibid., pp. 256–257). In fact, Oviedo mentions somewhat parenthetically that force of arms determined the succession more than did formal rules for inheritance (1853: bk. 29, chap. 27, p. 133).

One aspect of chiefly rule which also encourages elite rivalry emphasizes what we can call practical authority, that is, the *socially* recognized element of *effective* control and power held if possible in the Panamanian case by the line of firstborn *males* within the (presumably) highest-ranking status lineage, but potentially attainable by any capable high-status male. Another aspect of chiefly rule, however, emphasizes the *personal* element of power deriving from the high status accruing to the *firstborn regardless of sex* by virtue of being the firstborn in a line of firstborns (Fortes 1973; Goldman 1970: 14–16, 20–24). In chiefdoms where competition and status rivalry are actively pursued, chiefly legitimacy claimed *either* by practical authority *or* by personal status allows a measure of flexibility whereby the chiefly line may manoeuver to protect its position and maintain its control at times of stress and challenge by others (Goldman 1970: 14). Conversely, emphasis on one or the other of these principles of chiefly authority may also provide a contender with fuel for his challenge.

In the Panamanian data as recorded by Oviedo, the normal procedure for succession to chiefly office was direct patrilineal succession from father to eldest son who, presumably, held office by virtue of the socially recognized authority accruing to the line of firstborn males in the highest-ranking status lineage so long as they were acceptably competent in the performance of their duties (Fig. 3, step 1). If, however, the direct patrilineal line was broken by a lack of sons, then the oldest daughter became the heir to office and was married to her leading vassal (Fig. 3, step 2). I suggest that the oldest daughter was considered eligible to succeed to high chiefly office by virtue of the authority accorded her through her unique status as firstborn. However, though holding office, she was not socially authorized to actually exercise effective controls and power in the public sector, since socially, or "publically," significant power resided in males. It is likely that the oldest daughter's husband was expected to act as regent in this respect, and for this reason she had to marry her highest-ranking ("leading") male subject. But from the perspective of the status lineage claiming hold to the chiefly office through this oldest daughter, her high personal status by birthright preserved the formal claim of her status lineage to the line of legitimate rule until such time as a socially recognized heir was agreed upon, since no one else, including her husband, presumably stood higher in personal rank.[20]

On the other hand, the tenuousness of this claim to office via high personal status (a characteristic of Open societies in Polynesia) is expressed by the final step in Oviedo's report whereby the son not of

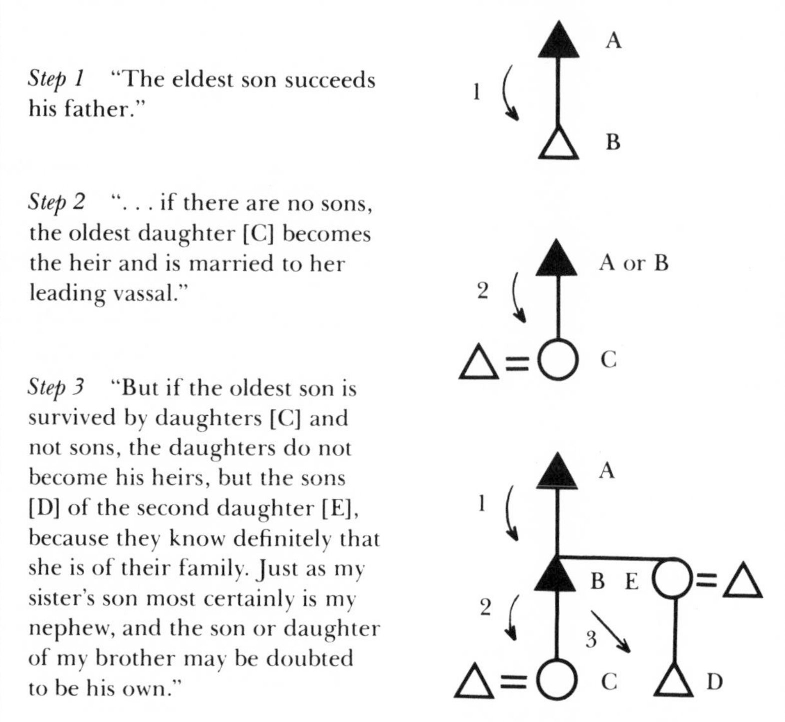

Fig. 3. Succession to office in pre-Columbian Panama as described by Oviedo. (From M. W. Helms and F. O. Loveland, eds., *Frontier Adaptations in Lower Central America,* Institute for the Study of Human Issues, 1976, p. 31; by permission of the publisher)

the oldest, incumbent daughter but of the "second daughter" is designated heir to the chiefly office (Fig. 3, step 3). Oviedo himself indicates that this line of succession is claimed by another characteristic of personal status, that is, by the link with the ruling-status lineage provided the son by the fact of his birth to a female of the group. This birth, regardless of paternity, indisputably established his genealogical relatedness to the ruling lineage (the son was thus also a descendant, specifically a grandson, of the deceased *queví*), a vital criterion for chiefship.

Andagoya's narrative gives additional evidence for the importance of birth as a legitimizing principle in Panamanian society: "They married one wife and they held a festival on the day of the wedding . . . The *sons of this woman* were those who inherited the lordship or house" (1865: 13, my emphasis). Other women were taken as concubines, but their children did not inherit (ibid.). The importance of the legitimacy provided by the mother also explains why (from the perspective of the chief) the chiefly office was not given (apparently) to his younger brother. Children of a younger brother could not be unreservedly considered genealogical members of the ruling-status lineage. In Oviedo's words, "just as my sister's son most certainly is my nephew, and the son or daughter of my brother may be doubted to be his own" (1959: 31). Since this factor of doubt could also be used by rival claimants to the chiefship, the emphasis on legitimacy by birth becomes even more understandable.

Yet why should succession to chiefly office be denied the son of the oldest daughter (she of highest personal status) and preferably be given instead to the son of the "second daughter," which is to say, the deceased male chief's sister's son (Fig. 3). The problem here, I propose, focused on the socially effective power or practical authority held by the oldest daughter's husband by virtue of his wife's office, and the potential genealogical challenge that could be launched at the incumbent ruling line in spite of the technicality of paternity if a son of this husband's household became chief. The nature of the challenge offered by this husband's effective power will be clarified in the discussion below regarding the competitive *krun* ceremony. Concerning the genealogical challenge, it could be logically argued by the husband's descent group that the status lineage containing the patriline of a male ruler (his legal father, or mother's husband; his father's father; and so on) becomes the ruling-status lineage by definition. In other words, if the son of the oldest daughter's household inherited the chiefship, the daughter's husband could claim, through his status as highest-ranking male and his role as father (social if not biological) to the new chief, legitimacy of ruling authority for his status lineage on grounds of the principle of patrilineal succession.[21] I suggest that it was in order to avoid this potential challenge that the line of succession was settled on the "second daughter's," or sister's, son. (Possibly, too, "second daughter's son" refers to a class of candidates, that is, all those men born to women of the ruling descent line other than the regent, or perhaps to women within a certain number of degrees of relationship to the rulership, for a system of priorities to restrict access to office is highly likely. From among this group of men the most able could emerge, perhaps by rivalrous trial as Oviedo suggests.)

We are told nothing regarding any prescribed husband for this sister, but we can assume that he would not be the highest-ranking male or in a position to acquire effective practical power to the degree of the oldest daughter's husband. Therefore, the personal status of the sister as a highly ranked member of the ruling family, together with the genealogical legitimacy accorded to her son by her status lineage, would be more likely to outweigh any claim to power by her husband's status lineage in terms of genealogically validated rank. With the assumption to office of a son of this sister, patrilineal succession within the ruling-status lineage (from deceased firstborn male to another legitimately born male of the ruling line) is officially and safely re-established (see Oviedo 1853: bk. 29, chap. 31, p. 156, for description of the activities that celebrated the succession of the new lord; compare the very similar succession patterns suggested for Tikal in Haviland 1977 and for other circum-Caribbean groups in Helms n.d.).

In spite of his genealogically validated legitimacy, the new chief would still face challenges to his power from high-status competitors, requiring him to constantly give overt evidence of his personal ability to wield effective power. Warfare and long-distance exchanges are suggested by the ethnohistorical literature as means of accomplishing this goal, and I will turn to these topics shortly. In later pages the importance of the acquisition of esoteric knowledge will be considered in this context, too. First, however, I should like to consider another forum for public expression of chiefly ability in a situation of competition and rivalry that is not clearly noted by the primary data from the sixteenth century but is indirectly evidenced by later information regarding the *krun* (in Spansh, *balsería*), a stick-throwing game mentioned by seventeenth-century observers and practiced by the Guaymí (Ngawbe) of western Panama as late as 1961.

Philip Young, who has discussed the activities surrounding the observance of *krun* and the significance of the event for contemporary Guaymí society (1971: 84, 169, 204–212, and 1976: 37–53), clearly indicates that many activities associated with *krun* are concerned with the public expression of personal strength, influence, and ability by competing "men of importance." It is likely, I believe, that *krun*, as it was described to Young by twentieth-century informants and as it is portrayed in colonial accounts, represents the enactment, by what is now a deculturated, egalitarian society that has lost much of the traditional elite subculture pattern through European contact, of a ceremony of competition that once served as a means of expressing rivalries and evidencing chiefly ability among the pre-Columbian Panamanian elite. Parenthetically, it should be noted that there is passing mention in the Spanish sources pertaining to the isthmus of a version of a rubber-ball game comparable to that known from the Greater Antilles, Mesoamerica, and portions of South America. Oviedo, for example, says that the game of *batey* played by natives in eastern Panama was like that described for the Antilles. Espinosa also mentions *batey* in the interior regions of western Panama near the Azuero Peninsula (1864: 515; see also Stern 1945: 33). The apparent function of this game as a ceremonial expression of competition and of personal prestige is comparable to that proposed for *krun*, although details of play contrast significantly.

According to Young, in addition to its purely enjoyable aspects, the enactment of *krun* in colonial and contemporary times constituted the final step "by which a man achieved great importance in Ngawbe society." The game, which lasted several days, was arranged between two men—a sponsor, or *kubudu*, who elected to hold the event, and his invited guest-competitor, or *edabáli*, the "man he chooses to challenge" (Alphonse 1956: 123). Initially, the sponsor first had to make certain of the support of kinsmen, for he could never provide all the necessary food and drink with his personal resources alone. Furthermore, "closeness of the kinship link and available resources were both taken into consideration in determining what was to be supplied by each household, but, in general, closely related households (e.g., those of brothers, sons, sisters) were expected to provide more than others" (Young 1971: 205). These preparations could involve a great many people. Young notes an account of a *krun* given about 1948 in which approximately one thousand persons, including some 250 households, were represented on the sponsor's side, most being relatives, with the rest "friends, and relatives of the relatives" (ibid., p. 208).

On the first day of the festivities the sponsor and his supporting families brought their contributions of food and drink to the site chosen for the game. When the invited *edabáli* and his supporters (in the 1948 event, another one thousand persons) arrived, general feasting began during which the sponsor and his *edabáli* competed in drinking (Young 1976: 44), and old grudges and fights readily erupted among supporters of both sides (Alphonse 1956: 123). After four days of feasting and gaming the guests departed. The following year the *edabáli* was expected to reciprocate by inviting the *kubudu* and his group to a *krun* in his area (Young 1971: 207).

In addition to the opportunity accorded the sponsor to give public evidence to another prominent man and to a combined group of several thousand persons of the size and strength of his own band of supporters and of his handsome generosity by distribution of food in great quantity (see Young 1971: 208–209), *krun* also served as a means to express potentially disruptive hostilities in a socially acceptable manner (see Balandier 1970: 111–113). Furthermore, in earlier times it may have provided an opportunity for trade and exchange between the two groups who, Young notes, generally lived at some distance from each other. (Distance minimized the overlap of kinship relations between host and guest and reflected the great number of persons involved on both sides.) In Fray Adrian de Ufeldre's early seventeenth-century account of *krun*, mention is made of a fair held after the games during which people exchanged various goods (Young 1976: 43, 48; see also Salcedo 1908: 95).[22]

Young further provides us with a valuable account of the means by which an individual in contemporary Guaymí society became sufficiently "important" to be able to stage such an event. Physical prowess, industriousness, intelligence, and generosity are all important qualities in a man's rise to prominence (1971: 209–210); we can probably add to Young's list an element of luck in having a wide circle of kinsmen. An ambitious man grows in social importance, first, by working diligently as a son-in-law providing services and food to parents-in-law and by laboring hard in his own gardens so as to be generous to kinsmen, thereby acquiring return obligations from them. He also seeks to gain a reputation for wise arbitration in dispute settlement, and, as his fame as arbiter spreads, people come from ever greater distances to seek his services. He also begins to participate in *krun*, demonstrating physical ability and courage in the games. Finally, a man may seek open recognition as the most important man in his area by sponsoring *krun*. Eventually, in his later years, as his strength begins to fail, the esteemed "man of importance," although still enjoying high personal prestige, will be replaced socially by a younger and more vigorous man. "A son may succeed to the leadership position of his father only if he also possesses the personal qualifications" (ibid.).

Young notes (1971: 212) that this "path to leadership" as described for contemporary Guaymí society is similar in many respects to the so-called big-man complex in Melanesia. I would further suggest that the steps and procedures underlying the rise of prominent men also are comparable to (and historically derived from) pre-Columbian patterns of chiefly competition and rivalry. The major difference between the factors leading to sociopolitical prominence in pre-Columbian Panamanian society and those involved in contemporary Guaymí society probably concerns the categories of persons who were eligible to acquire such prominence. In post-Columbian times, Young indicates, any man technically could attempt such a climb, though few would succeed. In pre-Columbian Panamanian society, in contrast, only those of ascribed elite status (that is, *sacos* and *quevís*) may have been eligible to compete. More specifically, it can be assumed that the greatest pressure to successfully cultivate the support of kinsmen and nonkin, to successfully arbitrate, to evidence outstanding physical prowess and courage, and, finally, to stage successful *krun* challenges would have fallen on those who, by the accident of birth, stood in the patrilineal line of succession to the office of high chief. It is likely that when such a chief or heir held the necessary personal capabilities to outperform others of the elite his hold on his office was strong. If, however, his personal abilities were not commensurate with the demands upon him, another, more capable member of the high elite could launch a successful challenge either by *krun* or perhaps by more dangerous forms of battle.

If the official office of chief was held by an oldest daughter, as in the example given by Oviedo, her high-ranking husband presumably assumed this burden of public expression of chiefly capability. If this man was of sufficient personal caliber to successfully meet challenges with potential rivals, however, he would also present a threat to the incumbent ruling-status lineage. Therefore, it is probable that a son of this couple would not be formally awarded the chiefship by the ruling-status lineage, not only for the genealogical grounds outlined above but also for reasons of practical politics.

Exchange and Warfare

In this attempted reconstruction of some of the political processes that may have been operative in pre-Columbian Panamanian societies, chiefs are seen as facing constant challenge or the threat of challenge by other, ambitious "men of importance." In order to meet this competition, a chief presumably not only had to constantly evidence personal strength and wisdom but also had to generously offer goods and services to his followers in order to reward loyalty, build reciprocal obligations, and hold a core of supporters, both kinsmen (the connotation of *sacos* as "in-laws" is relevant here, as are the many wives mentioned for chiefs) and nonkinsmen. Nonkin may have included defeated rivals and their followers, whose support may have been a most crucial element for chiefly success. Yet, in the absence of kin ties with the ruler, this support was probably also the most tenuous.

The sixteenth-century ethnohistorical data suggest that personal chiefly ability could be evidenced and material goods and rewards for kin and nonkin supporters could be acquired by warfare and by some mode of elite exchange. (We have already noted the role of the pre-Columbian chief as arbiter, another facet of chiefly ability.) Warfare may have functioned both as a chiefly "activity" and as a source of material goods and rewards for followers. Concerning warfare as "activity," the general tenor of the discussion by Balandier (1970: 64–65) is appropriate, even though his comments are intended to refer mainly to "segmentary" societies rather than to more strongly centralized groups. Political life, Balandier notes, can be rather diffuse, intermittent or nonvisible, being hidden within the more formal and nonpolitical (kinship) structures and institutions of society and emerging to full prominence and direct visibility only when distinctly political occasions or situations arise. It is by means of such occasions or situations that the essential dynamic quality of political life is emphasized and that persons holding power are most clearly revealed.

It follows from this line of argument that political leaders will seek or even actually create occasions or situations of a political nature that will openly reveal or emphasize their power positions and abilities and, in societies where political competition and rivalry are strong, also give opportunity for contest with opponents. Thus, it is possible that in ancient Panama chiefly warfare (as well as the exchange activities to be discussed shortly) was encouraged as a political occasion or activity in its own right that served to highlight the contenders as men of prestige and of "power," quite apart from booty or loot gained (see Oviedo 1959: 32, and 1853: bk. 29, chap. 26, p. 129).

Yet warfare had other benefits, too. It created the opportunity for commoners to achieve the lesser elite rank of *çabra,* a reward that probably attracted many young men to the cause of a prominent chief or high-status challenger. Warfare could provide new administrative territories for ambitious *sacos,* thereby, perhaps, reducing rivalries against the *quevi.* Warfare also may have yielded material goods, and in this context it can be viewed from two perspectives: as competitions over land and local subsistence resources or as competitions for exotic and scarce durable wealth for use and circulation at the high-elite level of society (cf. Goldman 1970: 476–482). First let us consider chiefly competition from the perspective of the availability of subsistence goods.

According to Oviedo, warfare was conducted in Panama for "power" and to acquire land (1959: 32, and 1853: bk. 29, chap. 26, p. 129); according to Andagoya, to obtain access to fishing and hunting territory (1865: 12, 17). However, the likely distribution of local resources in pre-Columbian Panama suggests that chiefly warfare to obtain control of additional territory for its subsistence resources was feasible only up to a point. The physiography and climate of Panama appear such that in any given region more or less the same *range* of ecological zones and thus presumably about the same *diversity* of local resources would be found in most of the numerous river valleys reaching from mountain to seacoast (see Bennett 1968). Admittedly, regions may have differed in terms of *amount* of various resources. For example, cultivated savannahs were much more extensive along the somewhat drier coastal plains of western Panama than on the wetter Caribbean versant, while ocean fish purportedly were more abundant in Caribbean than in Pacific waters (Wafer 1934: 71–72, 74). But warfare appears to have existed between more or less neighboring societies within a given region; there is no evidence of warfare between groups in different regions as, for example, between Caribbean and Pacific peoples. Furthermore, there is sufficient evidence (reviewed in the next chapter) to indicate that many chiefdoms centered on one or more river valleys. Each probably included in its territory a fairly complete range of the ecological zones and, therefore, of the natural and subsistence resources occurring from mountain to seacoast or interior lowland.[23]

Logically speaking, the high degree of regional "resource redundancy" proposed for basic subsistence and natural resources would appear to limit the benefits of territorial conquest except in terms of sheer increase in quantity of goods. To be sure, greater quantity of resources could have been a desirable goal: population growth may have placed increasing pressure on local resources; conceivably, grasslands were becoming more difficult to cultivate and/or desirable slash-and-burn land at the edges of wooded tracts was in increasingly limited supply. Similarly, resource acquisition was important if an institutionalized method of "conspicuous consumption" constantly removed subsistence resources from the system. It is quite possible that warfare for land and for access to fishing and hunting territory may have reflected one or another of these circumstances.[24] However, unless an unusual subsistence resource could be gained, one not commonly found yet highly valued, it would seem difficult for one chief to have maintained permanent control over extensive conquered territories simply in terms of production and redistribution of local subsistence resources. Of course, the chronic warfare reported for early sixteenth-century Panama could have reflected this very difficulty of permanent control of subsistence resources alone.

However, if we accept at least provisionally the likelihood of a significant degree of resource redundancy (but see n. 23), then the best opportunities for chiefs and other high-status challengers to obtain material rewards for their supporters and to evidence personal resourcefulness and ability lay not in controlling subsistence and utilitarian resources, or in apportioning territories among rivalrous *sacos*, but in establishing access to "scarce" nonutilitarian resources, including gold, pearls, and textiles.[25] The means to acquire these scarce items centered, I suggest, on chiefly participation in various regional and "long-distance" exchange systems linking Panamanian chiefs both with each other and with elites in distant regions beyond the isthmus.[26] Several methods by which chiefs could gain access to such exchange networks are suggested directly or indirectly in the ethnohistoric and ethnographic data. All these means derive from the likelihood that elites had unequal access to exchange networks. That is, some chiefs were located geographically closer to major exchange contacts or routes, while others were located in more distant regions.

One likely method for gaining access to exchange benefits was by military competition, and, as the next chapter will detail, it is noteworthy that warfare is frequently indicated between chiefs located at major junctions on long-distance exchange routes and groups on their immediate borders as well as among groups at a far distance from these routes. Alliance by marriage between chiefs well located in terms of exchange contacts and chiefs more distantly situated could also have facilitated access to scarce items for the latter and expanded the political base of supporters for the former (cf. Molloy and Rathje 1974). Willingness to support high chiefs with food and other resources for *krun*-like competitions in exchange for a share of scarce goods is yet another possibility, again materially benefiting elites located in territory more remote from major exchange routes and providing a broad support base for the centrally located "man of importance." The acquisition of scarce goods through participation in an elite educational system is another contingency of particular interest which is discussed in detail in Chapters 4 and 5.

Presumably, exchanges were facilitated even more if hinterland chiefs had access to local resources which were considered valuable scarce materials elsewhere and which they could inject into the system in exchange for the goods they desired. For example, many interior mountain regions yielded raw gold, which was collected and sent to coastal zones or to major regional chiefdoms in exchange for various fabricated goods (see discussion of Comogre in following chapter). In like fashion, chiefs of the pearl-rich Pearl Islands in the Bay of Panama may have contributed these valuables to the general flow of goods. The coast of Careta yielded fine sea shells widely exchanged as penis sheaths. Cotton hammocks and textiles, fine weapons, and ceramics are also mentioned in the documents as craft specialties and exchange items particular to certain groups. The uneven distribution of salt is also relevant in this context. Salt could be obtained in small amounts by a tedious process of boiling and evaporating salt water from sections of the Pacific coast, where a great rise and fall of tides creates extensive salt marshes, but it was not readily available on Caribbean coasts, where the extent of tides is much less (Wafer 1934: 77, 104 n. 1; see also Espinosa 1864: 519; Holdridge and Budowski 1956: 99). By preparing such condiments or craft specialties or by gathering valuable raw materials, hinterland chiefs could be linked into wider regional networks centering on chiefdoms with greatest access to long-distance contacts. The most strategically located polities would serve as collection points for regional raw materials and crafts and as redistribution points for valued scarce goods received from more distant exchange contacts outside the region. Figure 4 diagrams a hypothetical regional network of this sort, and the following chapter attempts to document the regional fields that may actually have existed in the isthmus about A.D. 1500.

The moderate variation in levels of stratification that may have obtained among Panamanian chiefdoms by A.D. 1500 may have been directly related to varying degrees of chiefly success in competition for long-distance exchange advantages. It is proposed that those chiefs or other high-status elites who participated most directly and actively in major long-distance exchange networks acquired both a greater quantity of scarce elite wealth items and a larger body of political supporters anxious to be affiliated with such a *quevi*. Both factors further provided a competitive edge against the constant pres-

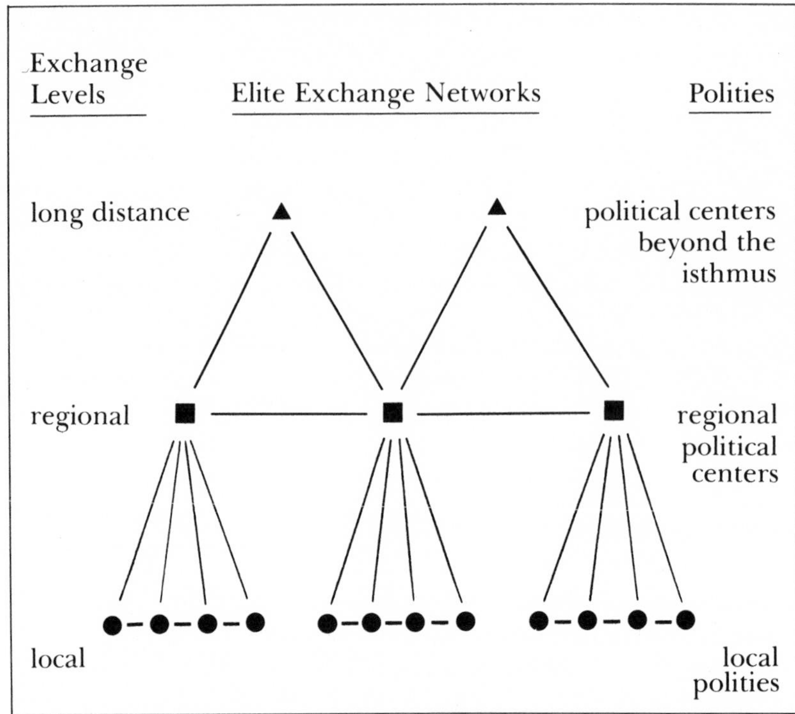

Fig. 4. Schematic diagram of elite exchange levels and networks.

sure of rivals. Those chiefs less directly associated with major long-distance exchange networks presumably received fewer goods, and even this reduced quantity required association with chiefs more favorably situated. Such associations could place the hinterland ruler in a position of potential or actual subordination (perhaps as a *saco*) to the more advantageously located *queví*.

Nor was this network of chiefly alliances and exchange confined to Panama. Indeed, this study suggests that the major chiefs operating as centralization points for regional "fields of influence" in Panama held this focal position precisely because they were units within still "higher-level" long-distance exchange networks which coordinated the major Panamanian chiefdoms with elite centers in northern Colombia, where many of the more elaborate exchange items, particularly gold pieces, were manufactured (see Fig. 4).[27] These larger exchange networks probably also extended to northern Central America with possible further connections to Mesoamerica, although these contacts are not considered in this work. It must be emphasized that

Panamanian participation in such far-flung exchange activities is viewed not simply as an adjunct to chiefly activities, interests, and affairs in Panama but as vital to the sociopolitical dynamics of Panamanian chiefdoms. It is probable that rank societies initially evolved from locally preceding conditions in the isthmus itself, but the data suggest that at least some Panamanian chiefs achieved higher positions of influence and power as a direct result of participation in the long-distance exchange patterns. It is likely that virtually all Panamanian chiefdoms were stimulated to at least some degree by the political dynamics generated by diplomatic and military alliances and competitions within the long-distance exchange system.[28]

2

Fields of Influence

Method and Interpretation

In the following pages some of the major regional exchange networks or politicoeconomic "fields of influence" that may have functioned in ancient Panama shortly before the time of European conquest are identified. As much information as possible was initially accumulated for every chiefdom mentioned by the Spanish documents, a task made infinitely easier by the prior work of Samuel Lothrop (1937), Kathleen Romolí (1953), and, especially, Carl Sauer (1966). The possible location and extent of most of these chiefdoms was then mapped on a large-scale (1:500,000) physical map of Panama. The results have proved interesting, although there is no doubt that a number of errors are included in the analysis.

The difficulties are due basically to the paucity and unevenness of the Spanish records available for study. For some stretches of territory we are told only that a "great many" chiefdoms existed, but names and even general locations are not provided. Some of the chiefs and chiefdoms actually named are accorded considerable discussion, but others are simply mentioned. In the absence of data for many chiefdoms, my judgments regarding the relative power, or "importance," of rulers are also subject to error. These judgments rest largely on Spanish observations, which cannot be considered completely accurate or objective. Spanish interpretations sometimes reflected the opinions of various *quevís* regarding neighboring chiefs, and it was not uncommon for *quevís* to extol the wealth and power of chiefs farther afield in order to entice the troublesome Spaniards to leave their own territory (see Anderson 1914: 164). The seeming insignificance of chiefs who appear to have held somewhat less power and general prestige may reflect gaps in the Spanish records rather than the actual status of the ruler, for many of these apparently "lesser" chiefs are those for whom we have the least data.

In addition, Spanish opinion concerning the "significance" of a chief or a region frequently reflects the conquistadors' judgment as to whether a particular lord was sufficiently wealthy (or cooperative) to suit their interests. In this respect, however, Spanish judgment may be a positive guide to the information we seek, for the Spaniards were vitally interested in gold, and gold ornamentation was a major "scarce good" indicating elite status and chiefly power in pre-Columbian Panama. Consequently, those chiefdoms where the conquistadors found significant quantities of gold may be considered as significantly more "important" in our model than those where the Spaniards were disappointed in their search for wealth.

Satisfactory map locations were also a problem in many cases. Although the Spanish accounts may provide the name of a *cacique,* or *quevi,* and sometimes a fair idea of the location of the chiefly *bohío,* the conquistadors did not usually record the territorial extent of a chief's domain. Therefore, in many cases I simply drew a boundary line approximately half-way between *bohío* locations. In some instances even this degree of guessing was not attempted. It is interesting, however, that these boundary guesses frequently coincide with a stream or river. There is reason to think that chiefs may have viewed their domains in terms of waterways and associated valleys, for these geographical features were also known by the chief's name (Oviedo 1853: bk. 29, chap. 10, pp. 44–45, chap. 26, p. 130). Waterways might also have been used as territorial boundaries, though there is no specific information on this point in the ethnohistoric literature.[1]

In spite of these reservations and inadequacies, when judgments concerning the relative "importance" of various chiefs were compared with suggested map placements the domains of chiefs considered most powerful or prestigious were found to be located adjacent to major transportation arteries, either rivers or land trails. These centrally located chiefs were surrounded by neighboring lords of no greater (and sometimes clearly lesser) power and prestige. Each centrally located—and possibly most powerful—ruler, together with his perhaps less significant elite neighbors, is seen as composing what I am terming a regional "field of influence."

Further support for this interpretation is found in the late seventeenth-century account by Lionel Wafer, who, during his sojourn in Panama, stayed with a chief who in fact held just such a central, commanding position. Wafer describes chief Lacenta, whose *bohío* was located at the headwaters of the Río Bayano (where a major pre-Columbian chiefdom, Comogre, had also been situated several generations earlier), as a "prince over all the South part of the Isthmus of Darien; the Indians both there and on the North side also, paying him great respect" (1934: 18). Elliott Joyce, commenting on Wafer's account, suggests that Lacenta was "Chief Paramount" over lesser chiefs and kin groups (ibid., pp. 17–18 n. 4). A somewhat comparable regional leadership still obtains among the San Blas Cuna. The famous Nele Kantule is probably the best known of these Cuna "high chiefs," of whom we shall say more later.

My interpretation of the Hispanic data identifies five major regional fields of influence in A.D. 1500 centering on the chiefs or chiefdoms of Comogre, Chape, Escoria, Parita, and Veragua, with Darién and Sacativa as additional possibilities. Two or three other fields of influence may have existed in areas for which there are few or no documentary data, such as the Río Tuira system, southeastern Panama, and the Pearl Islands.[2]

Eastern Panama

The fields of influence of eastern Panama include those of Darién, Comogre, and Chape (see Fig. 5). It is useful to begin with Darién because of its geographical location in the far eastern reaches of the Panamanian isthmus (within the national territory of the Republic of Colombia today). The "province," or territory, controlled by the *queví* of Darién is said to have included about thirty miles of Caribbean coast, from the Atrato delta to Cape Tiburón, and to have extended inland into the Serranía del Darién (Sauer 1966: 220, 238).[3] The major pre-Columbian community in this region, a town of long previous occupation (Parsons 1960) also known as Darién, is located by Sauer on a branch of a channel of the Río Atrato in the extensive swampy lowland surrounding the Atrato delta (1966: 165, 174 n. 19; see also Parsons 1960). The town itself stood on a low outlier of higher land above the swamp, with mountain slopes, foothills, and

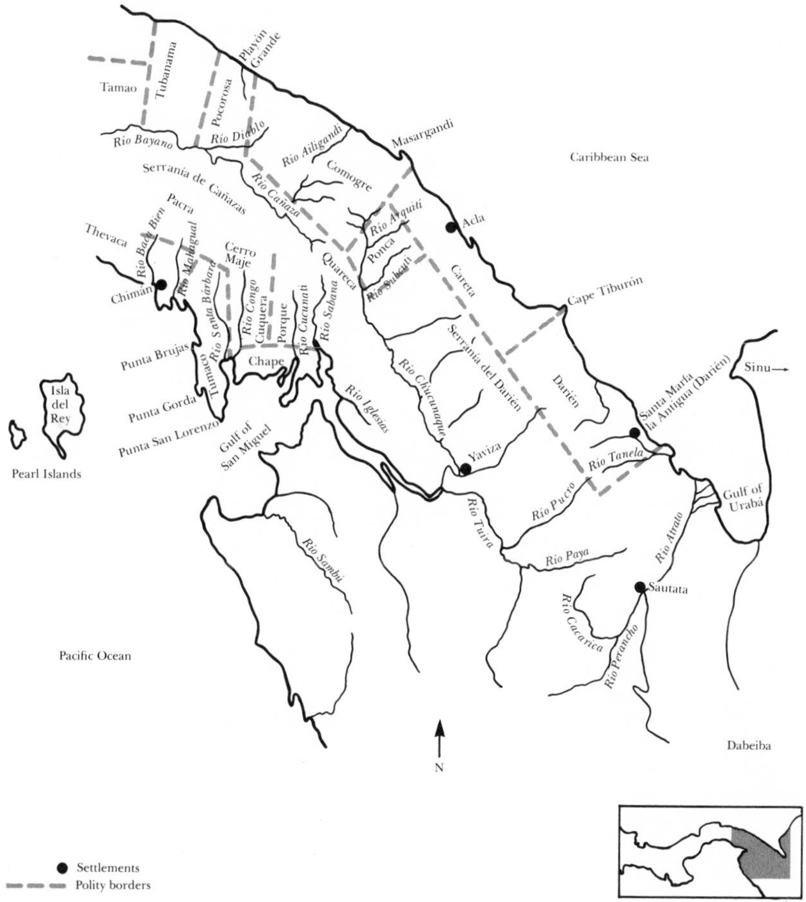

Fig. 5. Eastern Panamanian chiefdoms: proposed locations ca. A.D. 1500.

well-drained valley floor to the west. Strips of alluvium, sometimes flooded, lay between the slopes of the *serranía* and the swamps (Sauer 1966: fig. 22, p. 165). Fishing and hunting were well rewarded in the swamps and stream channels, while ridges, mountain slopes, and probably the sections of alluvium were suitable for agriculture. The Spaniards noted an abundance of root crops, maize, and cotton (Sauer 1966: 174). Two crops of maize were harvested annually (Anghera 1912: I, 225).

Other natural resources were locally available, too. The Spaniards found that the rivers and dry arroyos of the *serranía* a dozen or so miles west of the town yielded a modest quantity of gold (Anghera 1912: I, 413; Andagoya 1865: 8). According to the *queví* of Darién, smaller pieces of worked gold came from these sources, while larger gold pieces derived from a place twenty-five leagues away (Las Casas 1927: bk. 2, chap. 63, p. 351; Anghera 1912: I, 202).[4] This distant source in Colombia was called Dabeiba, a chiefdom where raw gold was processed into jewelry and figurines (Andagoya 1865: viii; see also Sauer 1966: 228; Chapter 5 below). Balboa indicates that the Gulf of Urabá was a point of dispersal for gold and that "all the gold that goes forth from this gulf comes from the house of the cacique Davaive" (Andagoya 1865: viii).

Looking at the map, it immediately becomes apparent that Darién was indeed well situated with respect to major travel routes leading in various directions (see Fig. 5). The intricate network of waterways composing the Atrato delta gave ready access by canoe to the gold-rich chiefdoms of the northern Colombian Andes via this river and its tributaries (Sauer 1966: 223). In the lowlands across the Gulf of Urabá from Darién was the wealthy gold-crafting elite center of Sinú (see Chapter 5). The Spaniards also could travel by land some seven leagues from Darién (which they called Santa María la Antigua de Darién) to the province of Abraime on the Río Atrato via the present village of Sautata. From Sautata another tributary of the Atrato, the Río Perancho, and its tributary, the Río Cacarica or Cauco, allowed access by canoe to the base of a saddle that marks the divide between the Atrato and Tuira drainage systems (see Fig. 5). Six miles across the saddle a tributary of the Tuira system gives ready passage to the Gulf of San Miguel and the Pacific Ocean (Sauer 1966: 254). Another Indian trail probably passed up the Río Tanela across the *serranía* to another tributary (Sauer suggests the Río Pucro) of the Río Tuira, thence to the Gulf of San Miguel (Sauer 1966: 252).

As to the sociopolitical organization of Darién, virtually no specific information is available. It seems justifiable to suggest, however, that the chief of Darién enjoyed the political advantages both of a bountiful food-producing area and of an advantageous exchange location.

Much more information is available concerning the important regional center Comogre and neighboring polities of Careta, Ponca, Pocorosa, Tubanama, and Tamao. The chiefdom of Careta adjoined Darién, its borders being placed at Cape Tiburón, where Darién is said to have ended, and Masargandi, where Comogre's territory began.[5] The *bohío* of Careta's chief was situated in the hills some twelve to fourteen miles inland and some twenty leagues from Darién town (Sauer 1966: 220; Romolí 1953: 93). Sauer notes that, like Darién, the territory of Careta extended from the Caribbean to the Serannía del Darién. These mountains were lower in altitude than those behind Darién, however, and several low saddles, or passes, gave ready access from Caretan territory to the Río Subcuti and the upper reaches of the Chucunaque river system. From here a trail led west to the upper Chucunaque and southeast across the low divides between the tributaries of the Chucunaque to the main river at Yaviza (see Fig. 5) (Romolí 1953: 318, and 1960: 22).

The territory of Careta included at least one very good sea port (renamed Acla by the Spaniards) at rich turtling grounds and possibly a second, in addition to two rivers of "good" water (Sauer 1966: 259–260; Romolí 1953: 94, 282, and 1960: 22). Careta's rugged coast is also reported to have been the sole source of the brightly colored and well-carved sea shells popular throughout Panama for penis sheaths (Andagoya 1865: 9; Oviedo 1959: 32).

The chief of Careta, who was said to command some two thousand warriors (Oviedo 1853: bk. 29, chap. 3, p. 9), wished to ally himself with Balboa in hopes of gaining Balboa's support in ongoing wars with the neighboring chiefdom of Ponca. He agreed, therefore, to assist the Spanish settlement at Darién with food, and he presented Balboa with a daughter as consort (see Romolí 1953: 94, 95). This incident provides a rare insight into chiefly motives for establishing alliances and tactics for cementing them. We glimpse another facet of chiefly competition and politics in the notation that the chief's brother was *saco* of the principal port (Romolí 1953: 282) and that there once had been a serious battle between these brothers at Acla because "one of them desir[ed] to possess all" (Andagoya 1865: 9).

Careta, then, had one or two good ports, ready access to low mountain passes leading to the important Río Chucunaque system (and to Comogre), and at least one popular exchange item (shells). All this suggests potential for long-distance exchange activities.

The chiefdom of Ponca was situated in the Serranía del Darién on the interior, or southern, slopes of the mountains, very likely in foothills drained by headwater tributaries of the Río Chucunaque (see Fig. 5). The *bohío* of the *cacique* was probably located on the Río Arquití (Romolí 1960: 23). The documents indicate that Ponca was at war with several neighboring chiefdoms, including Careta and Quareca (Torecha) (Oviedo 1853: bk. 29, chap. 3, p. 10; Sauer 1966: 220). Conceivably, Ponca's difficulties reflected an interior, landlocked disadvantage. According to approximate map locations, Ponca was barred from direct access to a Caribbean port by Careta. Similarly, Quareca, in Sauer's opinion located across the Río Chucunaque from Ponca in territory adjacent to the upper reaches of the Río Sabana (1966: 231–232), may have blocked access to the Gulf of San Miguel. Indeed, Balboa's party found the Chucunaque lowland basin between Quareca and Ponca difficult to cross because of flood and the lack of beaten trails due to infrequent communications (Oviedo 1853: bk. 29, chap. 3, p. 10; Anghera 1912: I, 283–284; Romolí 1960: 24). Thus, Ponca may have been cut off from direct connections with important travel routes leading in several directions, although Romolí cites the *cacique*'s elite center as a way station on the trail along the Chucunaque (1960: 23)—a trail, however, which Careta also directed (ibid., p. 22). The chief Ponca is also said to have told Balboa that the gold in his possession was left him by his forefathers (Anderson 1914: 177), which may indicate that Ponca had less access to immediate exchange activities. Similar remarks are on record for the chief of Tubanama and may be applicable to Pacra, too (see below). These two chiefdoms, like Ponca, also may have been restricted somewhat from access to important isthmian exchange routes.

Ponca's powerful neighbor, Comogre, appears as *queví* of the wealthiest, most powerful, and perhaps the largest chiefdom in eastern Panama. The territory of Comogre was centered in the upper tributaries of the Río Bayano with the *bohío* of its chief situated on a fork of the Río Bayano known as the Río Matumaganti at a place where forested hills gave way to a relatively thickly populated central valley and fertile, cultivated savannah (Anghera 1912: I, 218).[6] One hundred fifty years later Wafer encountered the powerful chief Lacenta in approximately the same general area.[7] Comogrean territory included the narrow divide between the Río Bayano and the Río

Chucunaque and then extended by an apparently broad and well-traveled route (Sauer 1966: 253) across the low *serranía* to the Caribbean Sea, where Comogre controlled one or two ports, including the principal fishing station probably located at the mouth of the Río Ailigandi (Sauer 1966: 253; Romolí 1953: 97). At the present time the trails used by the San Blas Cuna to travel between their coastal ports and interior settlements on the headwaters of the Chucunaque-Bayano require approximately one-half to one day's travel time (Holloman 1969: 87, 73; Howe, personal communication), and it is likely that a day's travel connected Comogre's ports with its highland capital.

We have already glimpsed the wealth and high status of the chief of Comogre in the Spaniard's description of the great house of the *quevi*, wherein were stored quantities of food and where the dessicated bodies of the ancestors hung from the rafters, each dressed according to rank and wearing golden masks (Anghera 1912: I, 219; see also Anderson 1914: 61–62; Sauer 1966: 221–222, 240; Romolí 1953: 98). When the Spaniards arrived, worked gold objects and war captive-slaves were diplomatically offered to them as goodwill gifts (Anghera 1912: I, 220, 222; Romolí 1953: 100). For situations when diplomacy failed, Comogre could amass some three thousand warriors from the numerous lords subject to him and from a population of ten thousand persons (Oviedo 1853: bk. 10, chap. 3, p. 9; see also Anderson 1914: 161; Romolí 1953: 97–99).

It is a thesis of this study that Comogre owed much of his importance to the strategic location of his domain with respect to regional and long-distance exchange. Balboa noted that natives traveled to Comogre by canoe from the south bringing pearls and gold from the Pacific coast (Andagoya 1865: xii; Sauer 1966: 229). Topographically, river routes between Comogre and Pacific regions would be available by way of the Río Bayano, the Río Sabana (via headwaters of the Río Cañazas), and the Río Chucunaque. According to Sauer, the Chucunaque was the river indicated in Balboa's account (1966: 230). By this route pearls (presumably from the Pearl Islands) were carried to the *quevi* Comogre, and access was had to gold-bearing regions in southeastern Panama. By way of the Río Cañazas, tributary of the Río Bayano, there was also exchange with hill chiefs who were said to exploit gold mines and gold-rich rivers of the Sierra de Cañazas (Andagoya 1865: xii; Sauer 1966: 229; Romolí 1953: 102).

According to Balboa, gold grains and pearls brought to Comogre were exchanged for cotton cloth and "good-looking Indian men and women," probably war captive-slaves (Andagoya 1865: xii). Although Balboa says that the gold grains were brought to Comogre to be melted (ibid.), there is, in fact, no specific mention in the Spanish documents of metallurgical works at Comogre. This omission seems rather significant in light of the Spaniards' frequent visits to Comogre, the conquistadors' virtual obsession with finding gold, and the frequent mention of gold in other contexts, such as, for example, the existence of gold-rich streams and the ownership of fabricated pieces by natives. Thus, it is postulated that gold grains and perhaps some pearls obtained by Comogre in exchange for textiles (locally produced?) and war captives were further exchanged by him with still other peoples, perhaps in return for fabricated (hammered) goldwork obtained from hill groups of the northern Sierra de Cañazas (see below), perhaps for craft items (such as cast gold pieces) from distant Colombia, which could have been readily contacted via Comogre's Caribbean ports and the Río Atrato. This postulated exchange would have made the well-situated chiefdom a hub of high-level politico-economic activity in eastern Panama and would have generated increased sociopolitical prestige and power for its ruler. Chief Comogre is also cited for his many wives and "numerous progeny" (Anderson 1914: 162). These marriages may also attest to his high power and prestige.

Very little is known concerning Pocorosa, Comogre's western neighbor (see Sauer 1966: 239–240; Romolí 1953: 171; Andagoya 1865: xi). The chiefdom appears to have been of modest size. Its territory included an interior basin on the Río Bayano, where the chief's *bohío* was located approximately at the juncture of the Río Diablo and the Río Bayano from the north (see Romolí 1953: 171), and extended across the *serranía* (crossed by a low pass) to Caribbean fishing grounds "seven leagues beyond the port of Comogre" (Anghera 1912: I, 350–351; Colón 1959: 263), that is, in the vicinity of Playón Grande. Pocorosa lay in the path of access to gold-bearing streams of the *serranía* (Andagoya 1865: xi), and perhaps Pocorosa's reputed enmity with Comogre reflected competition over these gold sources (ibid., p. xi; Anghera 1912: I, 222).

Very little is known, too, concerning Pocorosa's hostile neighbor, Tubanama, also located in the interior basin of the upper Río Bayano where the chief's *bohío* was situated in foothills of the *serranía*, perhaps some sixteen or seventeen miles west of Pocorosa (Espinosa 1864: 477–479; see also Sauer 1966: 235; Romolí 1953: 172). It is not clear if Tubanama territory also extended across the *serranía* onto the Caribbean coast; according to Peter Martyr it did not (Anghera 1912: I, 308). The *queví* of Tubanama and his subjects owned considerable fabricated gold reported, like that of Ponca, to have been inherited from ancestors, and the Spaniards found some indication of placer gold in rivers and arroyos but none of the gold mines that were reputed to be there (Anghera 1912: I, 310–312; Oviedo 1853: bk. 29, chap. 5, p. 19).

Even less is known of Tamao, which bordered Tubanama on the west in the Río Bayano lowlands (Sauer 1966: 253) and apparently was without a Caribbean outlet. This region and that of immediately adjacent areas is very poorly documented (see Espinosa 1864: 477–479).

A few additional words should be said concerning references to "hill peoples" inhabiting an interior area, possibly the north slopes of the Serranía de Cañazas. It is reported that inland beyond Comogre the land was well inhabited, but the chiefs "were of small account, being from a league to two leagues apart from each other" (Andagoya 1865: 11). These may have been the hill people said to have worked *serranía* gold mines and to have traded pottery, necklaces of gold worked (hammered?) into leaves, and other articles with Comogre via the Río Cañazas in exchange for agricultural produce, general supplies, and prisoners of war (Anghera 1912: I, 221; Andagoya 1865: xi–xii; Romolí 1953: 102). The description suggests small mountain tribes rather than chiefdoms, and Sauer suggests that the Serranía de Cañazas was a partial exception to the general existence of "cacicazgo" in eastern Panama (1966: 284). Judging from this limited information and from map location, these hill people appear as mountain dwellers living in one of the more isolated regions of eastern Panama, perhaps restricted to an inhospitable locale by more successful chiefdoms, who specialized in crafting mountain resources to exchange for agricultural produce and other goods from the established chiefdoms with greater access to cultivated areas and exchange routes.

Let us now consider Chape, possibly another focal chiefdom of eastern Panama, and the neighboring societies of Quareca (Torecha), Porque, Cuquera, Tumaco, Thevaca, and Pacra. The Gulf of San Miguel—which receives from the east the waters of the Río Tuira and Río Chucunaque; from the north, the Río Sabana; and from the southeast, the Río Sambú (see Fig. 2)—was undoubtedly an important focus for travel and exchange. The chiefdom of Chape, strategically located on the north shore of the gulf with access to the traffic of the

Río Tuira (tributaries of which linked eastern Panama with the Atrato system in Colombia), the Río Chucunaque (and thus Comogre), and the Río Sabana (which led toward the Río Cañazas and again Comogre and effected a short route with the Caribbean), must have been very favorably situated from the perspective of regional and long-distance exchange, perhaps in a manner comparable to Darién town's focus near trails and rivers converging on the Gulf of Urabá. Chape may have served as a point of collection and dispersal for various goods, including pearls and fabricated gold, which the Spaniards obtained there (Sauer 1966: 233; Wafer 1934: 14 n. 1). Unfortunately, we know very little about the chiefdom itself (see Oviedo 1853: bk. 29, chap. 3, p. 14). The *bohío* of the *queví* was located half a league from the bay of the Gulf of San Miguel on the bank of the Río Congo (Romolí 1960: 26), and the chiefdom appears to have been primarily a coastal province, possibly including the territory from the Río Iglesias to the Río Congo or beyond (see Fig. 5).[8] Although there is no direct mention of enmity between Chape and its immediate neighbors, Martyr notes that the *cacique* of Chape established friendship with Balboa in hopes that the alliance would be politically advantageous, for "all the naked savages cherish an inveterate hatred of each other, and are consumed with ambition" (Anghera 1912: I, 292).

The chiefdoms of Porque and Cuquera, which may have been adjacent to Chape, were situated farther inland in hill country toward the slopes of the Cerro Maje (Fig. 5). Porque is placed by Sauer on the western side of the Río Sabana estuary where an upland ridge extends (1966: 232–233); on the map this territory could also include headwater reaches of the Río Cucunati. Cuquera, according to Romolí (1953: 166), was located in the hills north of Chape and probably was reached via one of the main courses of the Río Congo. We are told that the *bohío* of the *cacique* of Cuquera lay some three leagues (eight or nine miles) beyond the head of canoe navigation, which would indicate the southern slopes of the Serranía de Cañazas (Oviedo 1853: bk. 29, chap. 4, p. 15; Anghera 1912: I, 289; Romolí 1953: 166). In terms of local resources, these locations would complement Chape's proposed coastal domain; they suggest a mutually beneficial exchange with the latter in which it may be postulated that Chape's coastal and agricultural produce as well as any high-status goods obtained by Chape's suggested long-distance contacts could have been exchanged with Cuquera and Porque for resources of the hills and mountains (see Anghera 1912: I, 289).

Another little-known interior chiefdom, Quareca, apparently was situated across the Chucunaque basin some ten leagues southeast from Ponca in the sierras directly across from the Río Morti and Río Subcuti near headwaters of the Río Sabana (Romolí 1960: 24). This river, in turn, leads to the Gulf of San Miguel and Chape (Sauer 1966: 232). Quareca was considered by the Spaniards as a rather poor land, being cold in temperature by their standards and lacking both gold mines and fertile soil, although some gold, presumably worked pieces, and pearls were obtained (Anghera 1912: I, 285; Sauer 1966: 232). However, Quareca was not very far from Comogre and may have enjoyed certain advantages of being located along a route connecting the Río Sabana and Chape with the Río Cañazas and Comogren territory.

To the northwest of Chape, along the coast of the Gulf of Panama, Balboa's party records the territory of an unnamed and "unimportant" *cacique* (Anghera 1912: I, 291) followed by the chiefdom of Tumaco. The *bohío* of Tumaco's chief, "whose authority extended along the Gulf coast" (ibid.), was located on the inner shore of the small bay behind Punta Brujas (Romolí 1953: 167). The chiefdom was of particular interest to Balboa because of its proximity to the Pearl Islands, some twenty miles offshore. This stretch of coast also yielded quantities of oysters, useful for food and for pearls which were gathered by skilled divers trained from infancy for this task.

Tumaco's domain may have included the region from Punta San Lorenzo (or the lands west of Río Congo), or perhaps from Punta Gorda to the mouth of the Río Mahagual or the promontory just beyond, and may have extended inland into the drainage between the Río Santa Bárbara and the Río Mahagual (Oviedo 1953: bk. 29, chap. 4, pp. 15, 16–17; Anghera 1912: I, 295; Romolí 1953: 168).

Both Tumaco and Chape were confronted by the militant *queví* of the Pearl Islands, who "whenever the sea was calm . . . attacked their territories with an imposing fleet of canoes and carried off everything he found" (Anghera 1912: I, 292, 394–395). With control of rich pearl beds, and thus of a valuable exchange item, this *queví*, whose *bohío* was situated on the largest island, Isla del Rey, might well have been a chief of considerable station.[9] We have no direct clues why hostilities occurred between this chief and mainland chiefdoms. Access to fabricated gold pieces and other high-status goods is one possibility, for the Pearl Islands could offer but little gold to the Spaniards although pearls were abundant (Anghera 1912: I, 395, 396). It is possible, too, that the Pearl Islands did not produce the diversity of local subsistence goods available to mainland groups.[10]

Returning to the mainland, the *bohío* of the *cacique* of Thevaca, *queví* of the chiefdom adjacent to Tumaco, may have been located a short distance inland on the Río Mahagual (Romolí 1953: 169) or at the site of the modern town of Chimán at the mouth of the Río Baca Bien (Sauer 1966: 235). Thevaca, perhaps a predominantly coastal chiefdom, yielded fabricated gold, pearls, and war captive-slaves for Balboa, indicating warfare and apparently some access to exchange centers (Oviedo 1853: bk. 29, chap. 5, p. 17).

The chiefdom of Pacra was located somewhere north or northwest of Thevaca, one day's travel from the latter, in mountainous territory on the Pacific slopes of the Serranía de Cañazas (Sauer 1953: 235). Pacra's domain thus appears as an interior chiefdom similar to Porque or Cuquera or the hill groups of the northern slopes of the Sierra de Cañazas. Like them, it also may have lacked lowland-highland resource diversity and may have been distant from ready access to exchange activities. The *queví*'s reputation for belligerency (among other things) may have reflected attempts to remedy these suggested deficiencies. In addition, although the territory was reported to contain gold mines, it did not produce any sources of raw metal; Pacra claimed that those who had mined gold in the mountains in his time or in the time of his parents were dead (Anghera 1912: I, 302). The *caciques* of the region, however, brought gifts of (presumably) fabricated gold to Balboa (Oviedo 1853: bk. 29, chap. 5, p. 18).[11]

Generally speaking, the western and southwestern slopes of the Sierra de Cañazas and the coastal territory between Chape and Chepo (see below) may have been somewhat marginal to major travel and exchange activities. This supposition rests in large part on the evidence suggesting separate coastal and interior hill chiefdoms in this region rather than the coalescence of interior and coastal land into single sociopolitical entities, such as in Careta or Pocorosa or Comogre. If, in fact, the political advantages derivable from participation in long-distance exchange were more limited here, then chiefly competitions by which territories might become united if a clear winner emerged, though perhaps aggravated by relative isolation, could remain inconclusive if no *queví* had significantly greater exchange advantages or other political leverage than his neighbors.

Western Panama

The major travel route in western Panama was a land trail which extended along the coastal lowlands on the west side of the Gulf of Panama. Its path is marked today by the Inter-American Highway and by towns still bearing the names of pre-Columbian chiefs and chiefdoms (Sauer 1966: 270). This trail passed through a series of polities from Chepo in the east, located at the mouth of the Río Bayano, to Escoria toward the southwest, situated near the Gulf of Parita. As Figure 6 indicates, at Chepo the land trail apparently met the Río Bayano, a gateway into eastern Panama (see Espinosa 1864: 179), and also would have conjoined with several short transisthmian routes leading to the Gulf of San Blas or, via the Río Chagres, to the Caribbean and, ultimately, northern South America. West of Escoria, at the other end of the land trail, our information becomes scant, although this major land route undoubtedly extended still farther west toward adjacent regions of Costa Rica.

The dwelling compounds of the *quevís* of the coastal societies through which this land trail passed were situated along the route at rather constant intervals, approximately six to eight leagues (about sixteen to twenty-two miles) apart, while one or two other major villages or border points were spaced approximately four leagues (about eleven miles) one from the other (Andagoya 1865: 5, 28–29; Sauer 1966: 260–261; Trimborn 1952: 256). The regularity of this spacing of chiefly *bohíos* or major settlements is intriguing, especially since these same figures appear when records of distance are given in the Spanish documents relating to eastern Panama. Thus, seven leagues was the distance separating the town of Darién from neighboring Abraime; it was also the distance between the Caribbean fishing port belonging to Comogre and that of neighboring Pocorosa. Similarly, the *bohío* of Tubanama was approximately six leagues from Chepo and five or more from Pocorosa (Espinosa 1864: 477–479).[12] There is one additional hint in the literature that may cast light on the significance of these distances: Andagoya mentions "a day's journey of three or four leagues" in a context implying that this was a somewhat slow rate of passage for the Spaniards, who at the time were burdened by a great number of captives (Andagoya 1865: 31). Quite possibly, then, these distances of three to four leagues and six to eight leagues represented the distances that could be covered in one or two days (respectively) of slow travel or one-half and one day (respectively) of ordinary travel. Oviedo tells us that chiefs traveling in litters carried by runners, who were replaced by fresh bearers when they tired without stopping the journey, could travel fifteen or twenty leagues per day over level terrain. This distance would presumably

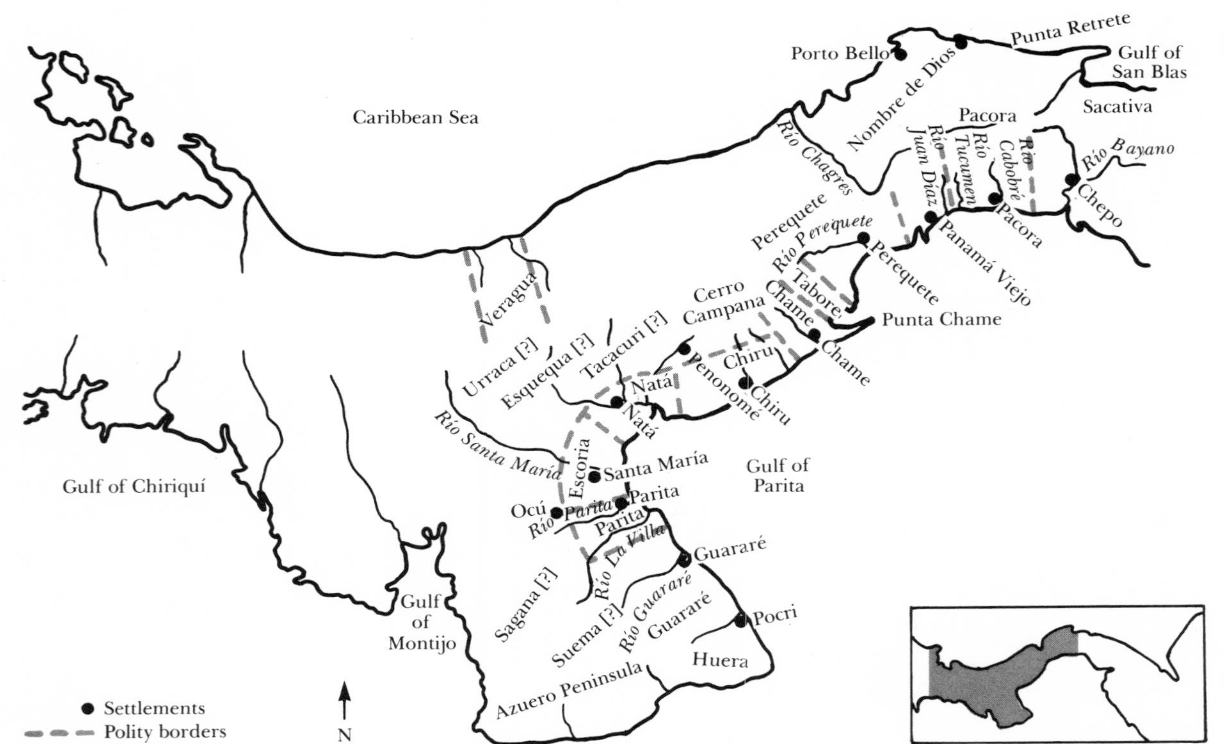

Western Panamanian chiefdoms: proposed locations ca. A.D. 1500.

be the maximum extent of a day's travel (1853: bk. 29, chap. 26, p. 126).

Since chiefly *bohíos* were situated six to eight leagues apart, these distances may also be interpreted tentatively as defining the extent of a chief's domain as that territory which could be covered in one day's ordinary travel. The three-to-four-league distances would readily fit into this scheme as border locations between chiefly domains.[13] Figure 7 schematically summarizes this line of thought, while Figure 6 illustrates the scheme as reflected in the location of settlements and *bohíos* along the western Panamanian land trail where these distances are most clearly evidenced. It is also appropriate in this context to recall that in eastern Panama the distance between Caribbean coastal ports and the mountain centers (such as Comogre) from which these ports were controlled was probably equal to approximately one-half to one day's travel. A comment by Young regarding the *krun* competitions of the Quaymí is of interest here, too, since he states that the *krun* sponsor goes to meet his honored guest (*edabáli*) when the guest's party is within a day's travel of the *krun* site (1976: 44). (Mixtec kingdoms of southern Mexico also were confined to an area that could be traversed in one day; see Spores 1974: 302.)

Let us turn now to the various chiefdoms located along or proximate to the coastal land route of western Panama, beginning with Chepo. The modern town of Chepo is situated slightly west of a northern tributary (Río Mamoni?) of the lower Río Bayano at about the same site as the pre-Columbian settlement of that name (Sauer 1966: 260).[14] According to Sauer (ibid., p. 264), at this point the lower Bayano is made convenient to the Gulf of San Blas by one of the lowest passes of the continental divide at the shortest crossing of the isthmus. According to the map, the Bayano tributary adjacent to the town of Chepo leads north, possibly close to this pass, and another river leading to the Gulf of San Blas can be met across the divide. Although there is no direct information indicating that such a route was used in pre-Columbian times, it is not unlikely that it was.

A convenient crossing connecting the Gulf of Panama and the Gulf of San Blas could also have been a significant factor behind the reported wealth of the chiefdom of Sacativa situated on the Gulf of San Blas. It is regrettable that we have no more information than this concerning Sacativa, for a Sacativa-Chepo connection appears reasonable and Sacativa's reputed affluence (Casas 1927: bk. 3, chap. 62, p. 594) may have reflected an advantageous exchange position,

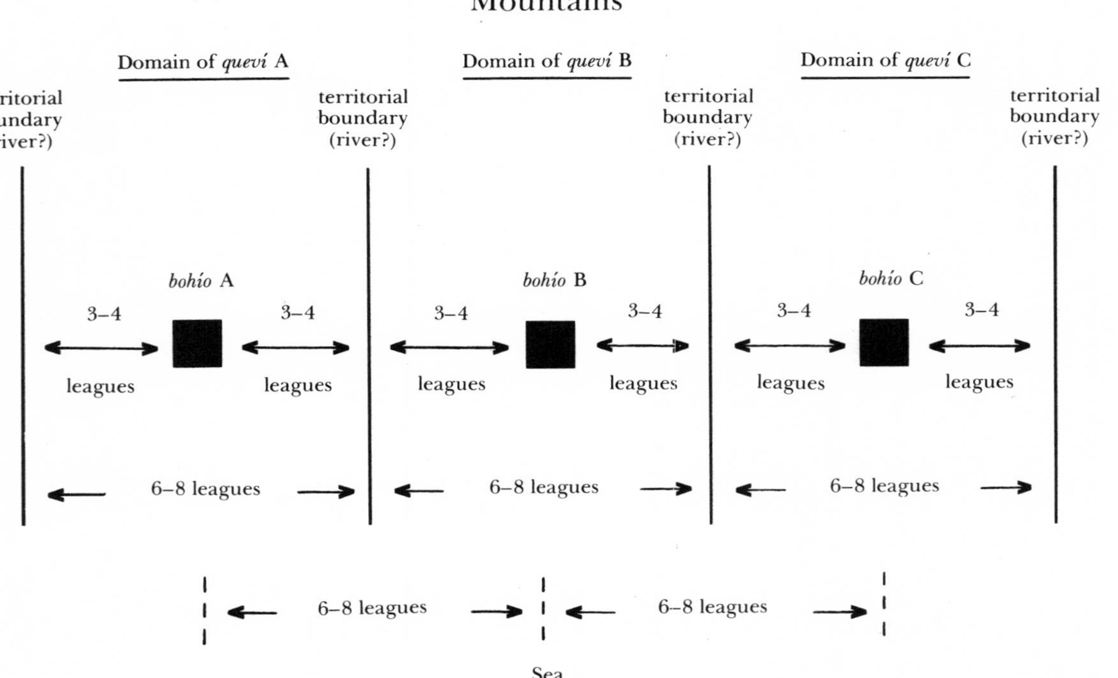

Fig. 7. Schematic diagram of proposed geographical extent of *quevis'* domains ca. A.D. 1500.

perhaps as a Caribbean outlet for goods moving to and from the western Panamanian land route.

Seven leagues west of Chepo, between that town and the village of Panamá Viejo, was Pacora (Espinosa 1864: 479–480). As with Chepo, the modern community that still bears this name appears to stand in approximately the same location as the Indian settlement found by the Spaniards (Sauer 1966: 260), that is, near the Río Cabobré midway between Chepo and the site of Panamá Viejo. Presumably, the territory of these chiefdoms reached north into the *serranía,* but no specific information is available on this point.

The town of Panamá, fabled to be rich beyond belief in gold and pearls, turned out to be a lowly fishing settlement (Casas 1927: bk. 3, chap. 68, p. 23; see also Sauer 1966: 256, 260, 276), probably located near the Río Juan Díaz west of the Río Tocumen. This fishing village does not appear to have contained a chiefly *bohío* and may well have been a local port exploiting sea resources for a *queví* located elsewhere, perhaps inland near the Río Chagres. Yet the village's location, some three to six leagues from Pacora to the east and seven or eight leagues from Perequete to the west, suggests that it served as a way station on the western land route (Espinosa 1864: 481–482). Panamá may also have stood at a junction with another transisthmian route, for Oviedo notes that from Panamá to the Río Chagres it was only four leagues by a very good road (1853: bk. 29, chap. 30, p. 148, and 1959: 119).

The Chagres River itself flowed fast and deep into the North (Caribbean) Sea some five or six leagues below Nombre de Dios. This transisthmian route and that suggested between Chepo-Sacativa also may have served as drawing points for the small settlement of Mesoamericans, possibly Maya traders, located at Nombre de Dios (see Sauer 1966: 239). It is on record, too, that a quantity of gold and pearls was acquired by the conquistador Rodrigo de Bastidas at nearby Punta Retrete (Anghera 1912: I, 404; Casas 1927: bk. 2, chap. 2, pp. 135–136). Columbus likewise reported gold in the territory of the bay he named Porto Bello, whose *cacique* and retinue wore gold leaves as nose ornaments (Anghera 1912: I, 325). It is indeed unfortunate that our data regarding this region are so limited.

Of Perequete, Tabore, and Chame, the chiefdoms immediately to the west of the village of Panamá, there is little direct information other than notations concerning the location of chiefly *bohíos* (see Enciso 1932: 179). That of Perequete was located seven or eight leagues from Panamá, probably at the river of that name (Espinosa

1864: 481–482; Sauer 1966: 260, 270). Seven leagues farther lay the town of Chame (Sauer 1966: 261), while in between was Tabore (Lothrop 1937: 4; Trimborn 1952: 256), cited for excellent fishing and situated possibly in the area of the bay behind Punta Chame (or perhaps more toward the interior) and possibly belonging to Chame (Espinosa 1864: 482–483, 519). The map suggests that Perequete and Chame may have included territory extending from the coast into the mountains (Cerro Campana) that rise a short distance inland. The *bohío* of Chame was seven or eight leagues from that of Chiru, whose domain included excellent saltworks. The country also yielded many gold ornaments to the Spaniards (Las Casas 1927: bk. 3, chap. 69, p. 27; Espinosa 1864: 483–484, 519; Anghera 1912: I, 406; Andagoya 1865: 25; see Lothrop 1937: 4 n. 1, regarding the confusions in the Spanish reports of this entire region).

Penonomé and Tacacuri were brothers and chiefs, reportedly rich in gold, of two interior polities located north of Chiru and its coastal neighbor, Natá (Anghera 1912: I, 406; Las Casas 1927: bk. 3, chap. 69, p. 27). The contemporary city of Penonomé may mark the dwelling place of the pre-Columbian chief of that name, while Tacacuri's *bohío* may have been situated somewhat to the west of Penonomé (Lothrop 1937: 4). A third interior chiefdom, Esquegua, whose *queví* had many subject lords and much gold, was located west of Tacacuri (Espinosa 1873: 37–38; Lothrop 1937: 6 n. 1). According to Oviedo, from the mountains of Esquegua it was possible to see both the North Sea and the South Sea, indicating that this and perhaps other interior chiefdoms (see Urraca) ran high into the western sierras, perhaps to the continental divide (1959: 118, and 1853: bk. 29, chap. 30, p. 147; Espinosa 1873: 35–37). Presumably, these interior chiefdoms were associated in some manner with coastal chiefdoms, such as Chiru and Natá. We can speculate that interior groups exchanged mountain resources, including raw gold from mountain streams (there is no mention of gold crafting), for salt, sea foods, perhaps for agricultural produce, and for long-distance exchange items obtainable from the coastal polities.

The chiefdom of Escoria and the neighboring polities of Parita and Natá appear as the most powerful rank societies on the west side of the Gulf of Panama, perhaps because of the fuller data available concerning them. The chiefdom of Natá, whose *queví*'s *bohío* was located four leagues from the domain of Chiru at the site of the present town of Natá, is described as small in territory but well populated and rich in food resources (Espinosa 1873: 42–43, and 1864:

487–488, 512). Natá's shoreline, some four leagues in extent, also produced excellent salt useful in preserving meat and fish. In addition, Natá may have been a center for the manufacture of ceramics; "an industry in cotton cloth" was noted, too (Anghera 1912: I, 406; Andagoya 1865: 25; Espinosa 1873: 42–43, and 1864: 519; Lothrop 1937: 4, 6, 11, 15; Sauer 1966: 261, 273–274, 282).

Eleven subchiefs are listed by Lothrop as subordinate to the *queví* of Natá, an important and powerful personage who had challenged and conquered neighboring chiefs, and more than a dozen local chiefs are reported to have submitted to the Spaniards through a summons issued via the Natá ruler (Lothrop 1937: 8, 11; see also Espinosa 1873: 83–119). Since we do not have listings of *sacos* or allied *quevís* for other chiefdoms, with the exception of Parita and the Río Sambu (Chochama; see below), it could be potentially misleading to consider the chief of Natá more powerful than some of the others we have considered, for all chiefs presumably had *sacos* and *çabras* of lesser rank under them and held alliances (if they were not at war) with neighboring *quevís*. Nonetheless, Natá's following seems considerable and his position impressive. It is also interesting to note that the territory that may have composed the domain of Natá included approximately eleven rivers and tributaries, according to reference maps. If, for the sake of argument, we assume a general rule of one subchief per river, the number corresponds nicely with the figures in the literature. (This speculation of a pre-Columbian *queví* as ruler over a river system that correlated with his political sphere has analogies with the political metaphors regarding chiefs, polities, and rivers used by the twentieth-century San Blas Cuna; see note 1 above.)

We can only surmise that the *sacos* and *quevís* allied with Natá benefited from their association in terms of access to local resource diversity, craft specializations, and long-distance exchange goods. Concerning the latter, the map indicates that Natá would have been excellently positioned to receive travelers from east and west. Contacts across the *serranía* with the Caribbean chiefdom of Veragua (see below) are noted from 1556 and likely are indicative of pre-Columbian connections between the north coast and the south side of western Panama (Anderson 1914: 270). The ceramics, salt, and textiles produced in Natá and the quantity of gold noted by the Spaniards further imply active exchange.

The ethnohistoric literature indicates hostilities between Natá and the neighboring polity of Escoria. The *bohío* of the *queví* of Escoria was situated six leagues beyond Natá and six leagues from the sea

(Espinosa 1864: 494). This site, Sauer notes, is near the present town of Santa María (1966: 261) on a small stream south of the river of that name (Lothrop 1937: 6, 10). As at Careta, the coastal lands of Escoria probably were under the control of a subchief of the *quevi* (Lothrop 1937: 8). The chiefdom of Escoria is cited in the Spanish documents particularly for the fighting capability of its valiant warriors and for the expertise of its craftsmen in fashioning fine weapons that were widely used in other areas, so that the chiefdom was noted for its arms "in the manner of Milan" (Espinosa 1864: 508; Andagoya 1865: 25; Sauer 1966: 271, 276).

Escoria's military prowess may have been correlated with its strategic location. As the map indicates, the chiefdom was situated on the east side of a low saddle that allowed ready access across the Azuero Peninsula from the Gulf of Parita to the Gulf of Montijo and to the lands beyond (Sauer 1966: 262). The documents also indicate a trail across the western *serranía* via the headwaters of the Río Santa María, a trip of six or seven days, which would have linked Escoria with important chiefdoms of the Caribbean coast (see Romolí 1953: 313; Anderson 1914: 270). Escoria is specifically reported to have warred with Natá to the north and with the polity of Parita to the south (Andagoya 1865: 25, 30; Lothrop 1937: 4). Following a defeat of Parita, the *quevi* of Escoria married a sister or cousin of his foe (Oviedo 1853: bk. 29, chap. 10, pp. 47, 48; cf. Lothrop 1937: 11).

Before further consideration of Parita, a few words should be said concerning the chiefdom of Urraca, although the ethnohistoric literature tells of little more than the great hostility of its *quevi* toward the Spaniards (Las Casas 1927: bk. 3, chap. 162; Lothrop 1937: 8–9). We do know that Urraca was an interior chiefdom located in the mountainous territory north of the Azuero Peninsula and probably west of Esquegua (see Fig. 6), possibly somewhere in the upper reaches of the Río Santa María. Oviedo says that, as in Esquegua, it was possible to view both the Caribbean and Pacific oceans from heights in Urracan territory and the chief of Urraca was able to obtain warriors for his forays against the Spaniards from both Caribbean and Pacific territory (Oviedo 1853: bk. 29, chap. 30, p. 147, and 1959: 118; Lothrop 1937: 9). The chiefdom, whose ruler is said to have had much gold (Las Casas 1927: bk. 3, chap. 162, p. 372), also may have been a way station on a travel route between the Caribbean coast of western Panama and the Azuero saddle route, but this possibility remains purely conjectural.

Parita and the Azuero Peninsula

The domain controlled by the *quevi* Parita seems to have included territory south of the Río Escoria (Río Santa María) to Pecora (Pocri) (Sauer 1966: 261, 270, 281; see Fig. 6). This region included fertile lands along the Río Parita and Río La Villa, rich hunting and fowling resources, and access to fish, shellfish, and salt works (in the vicinity of Guararé), though the salt produced is said to have been of only moderate quality (Espinosa 1873: 31–33; Lothrop 1937: 16). Parita's *bohío* lay some six leagues beyond that of Escoria in the area known as Parita today (Espinosa 1864: 495; Sauer 1966: 261; Lothrop 1937: 6, 10). The existence of a "Río Parita" (now the Río Asiento Viejo, the name the Spaniards gave to Parita's settlement) indicates this may have been the core land of the chiefdom.

From here the *quevi* Parita expanded his control to the south by conquering at least four major *caciques*: Suema (Quema), who was resisting the alliance, Chicacotra, Sangana, (Usagana), and Guararé (Andagoya 1865: 30; Espinosa 1873: 25, 32–33, 60; Lothrop 1937: 10). Eight additional chiefs are also listed as subject to Parita (Lothrop 1937: 10 n. 2). The location of the conquered chiefdoms can only be approximated. Sangana (Usagana) apparently lay to the west of Parita's settlement, perhaps in the interior of the Río Parita and/or to the north in the region of Ocú, a territory with good provisions (Espinosa 1864: 499; Lothrop 1937: 6). Suema (Quema), two days' journey from Parita, is also placed somewhere in the interior rim of the region over which Parita held control (Espinosa 1864: 507; Sauer 1966: 261). Guararé seems to have been a chiefdom to the southeast, probably based on the Río Guararé where the town of Guararé continues the name today. Of Chicacotra, four days' travel from Parita, the records remain silent.[15] It may also have been an interior polity (Espinosa 1864: 504, 507).

Parita's motives for southern expansion may be implied in ethnohistoric documents and physiographic data. The map (see Figs. 2 and 6) indicates that by his expansionary efforts the *quevi* had obtained dominance over the lowland basin and adjacent interior hill country lying north and east of the mountains that rise in the southernmost reaches of the Azuero Peninsula. The literature also suggests that both Parita and his allies derived potential benefits from the military manpower of this larger territory. Andagoya notes that in a lengthy series of battles with Escoria the warriors under Parita's control, being more numerous and in their home territory, were able to rest more often and could be replaced with fresh fighters. Conversely, Escoria's men, fewer in number, had to fight continuously (1865: 30). (Nonetheless, in this instance Escoria won; see Lothrop 1937: 10.)

In order to field these warriors, however, Parita must have had the support of the other Azuero lords. I suggest that Parita, being situated close to the major travel route that passed through his enemy Escoria's territory, served these notables as a valuable collection and redistribution point for high-status goods. The chiefs of the Azuero Peninsula, whose domains were farther from major isthmian exchange routes, remained within Parita's "field of influence" because it provided access to chiefly valuables. Two incidents mentioned by the Spaniards are of interest here. In the first, distribution of sumptuary goods was used to attract allies, for when Parita held council to decide whether to fight or to negotiate with the Spaniards, one of his brothers "strongly urged that gold be used to gain the support of allies and that they attack" (Lothrop 1937: 6; Espinosa 1864: 495, 496).[16] In the second incident, the lord of Parita requested help from the Spaniards to subdue his purported ally, Suema (Quema), who was resisting his alliance with the Parita chief, wishing to have gold without having to obey the regional lord (Espinosa 1873: 60).

Concerning the pre-Columbian chiefdoms lying to the west of Escoria and the Azuero Peninsula, virtually nothing can be said. The sparse documentation indicates only that the offshore islands of the Gulf of Chiriquí and the adjacent mainland were occupied by a number of polities (see Espinosa 1864: 513–518; Linares 1968: 75–77). The most interesting information for this study derives from a brief account by Andre de Cerezada (Fernández 1889: 32–33), who notes the several mainland coastal chiefdoms that probably were situated more or less along the route of the present Inter-American Highway from the present town of Chiriquí to the Burica Peninsula (see Fig. 6). Once again the chiefly *bohíos* of these polities are separated from each other by the regular distances noted before. Thus, Chiriquí is said to lie six leagues from Copesiri, which is three leagues from Charirabra, which is ten leagues (that is, seven plus three) from Burica.[17] At least one route also crossed the mountains to the North Sea and Veragua, a three-day trip (Espinosa 1864: 517).

Veragua

The Caribbean territory of northwestern Panama from Almirante

Bay to about Nombre de Dios was visited by Columbus on his fourth and final voyage to the New World (see Fig. 8). He found a rugged and cliffed coast with a forested shoreline broken by numerous rivers that flowed north from the *serranía* across a narrow range of foothills and littoral to the sea. The region was well supplied with natural resources. Mention is made particularly of fields of maize, of palms and fruits useful for "wines," and of an abundance of anadromous fish that were moving upstream to spawning grounds at the time of Columbus' visit (Colón 1959: 250, 253–254; Sauer 1966: 132–133; Wafer 1934: 74). The numerous streams also produced gold, which was further obtained in modest amounts from interior mines—shallow pits about three feet deep located high in the mountains where mining was conducted with ceremony at certain times of year (Colón 1959: 250, 251–252; see also Sauer 1966: 133–134; Anghera 1912: I, 329; Anderson 1914: 99).

We know very little about the peoples of this region other than that they valued gold ornaments and wore earrings, neck plates or mirrors, and necklaces crafted of *tumbaga* (gold-copper alloy) and of pure gold in the form of eagles, frogs, jaguars ("lions" and "tigers"), and similar animals (Anghera 1912: I, 323; Colón 1959: 241–242, 244, 250; see also Anderson 1914: 93–95, 103; Sauer 1966: 133–134). Of the polities mentioned in the literature—Catebra, Zobraba, Urira, Cubiga, Veragua—only a few can be even tentatively located (see Fig. 8). Veragua was apparently centered on the Veragua River with the *bohío* of the *quevi* a league and a half from the sea. Cubiga extended at least as far as Punta Rincón and the Río Palmilla, where the gold-bearing lands probably ended (Sauer 1966: 126), while Urira was located on a river of that name seven leagues west of Río Belén (Río Yabra). Interior chiefdoms, which would have been located in higher mountainous regions, are noted in the documents, too, but there is no information concerning them other than that they contained gold and warriors (Colón 1959: 253).

The most powerful of these polities appears to have been the chiefdom of Veragua.[18] We have no direct information concerning the nature or extent of the *quevi* Veragua's influence, but the sources suggest that his chiefdom served as a focal point for regional exchange. Although Columbus notes that the entire coast from Almirante Bay to Cubiga was an area of exchange, sometimes prefaced with initial hostility (see Colón 1959: 242; Anghera 1912: I, 323; Anderson 1914: 93–95), he observed particularly that between Zobraba and Cubiga, that is, in the domain of Veragua as determined by map

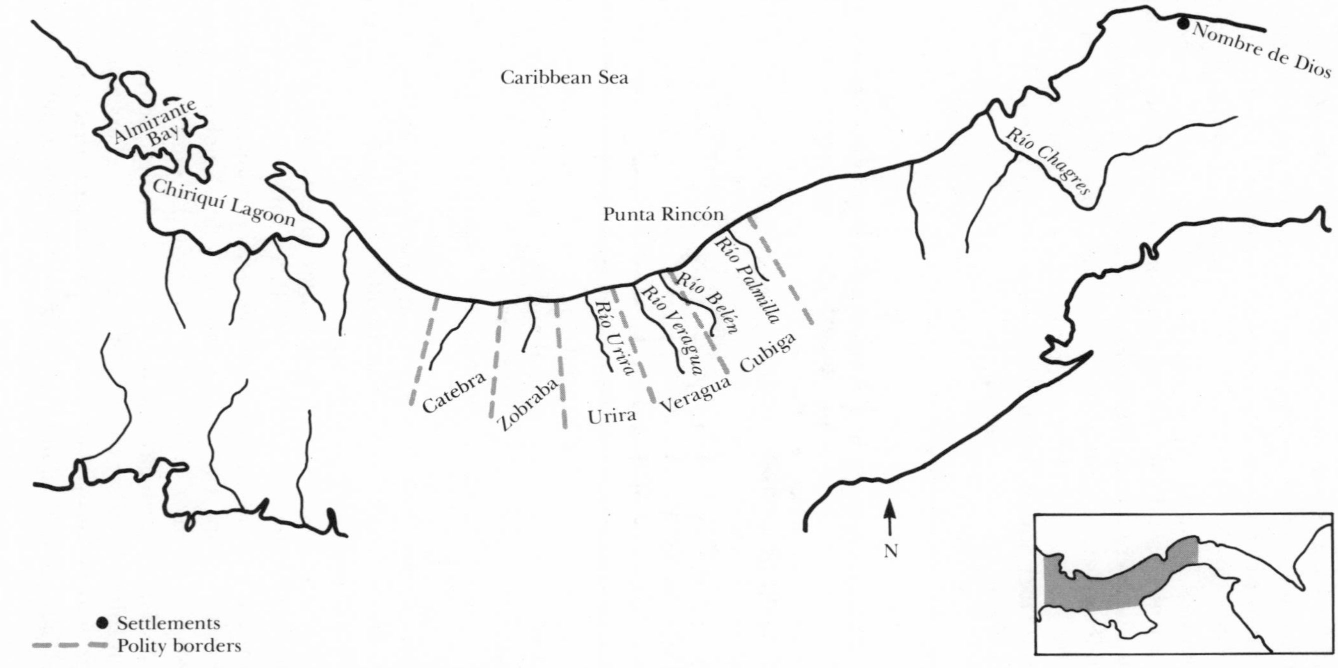

Fig. 8. Chiefdoms of Veragua: proposed locations ca. A.D. 1500.

placement, were "five towns of active trade," including the town of Veragua, that is, the chiefly *bohío* settlement (Colón 1959: 243). Here gold was collected and gold neck plates were made for distribution about the coast (Colón 1959: 243; see also Anderson 1914: 94–95). The documents also indicate a land route across the western sierras between Veragua and the wealthy, densely populated Pacific coast of western Panama (Anderson 1914: 270), although the term "Veragua" in this context may refer to the general region, also called Veragua by the Spaniards, rather than to the specific chiefdom of that name. It is possible, too, that much of Veragua's contact came by sea.[19]

Southeastern Panama and the Río Tuira

Included in this region of the isthmus are societies of the Sambú River system of southeastern Panama, with Chochama as possible central focus, and chiefdoms to the north of Chochama along the coast of the Gulf of San Miguel and on the south side of the Tuira estuary. There is no primary evidence indicating in this region a chiefdom comparable in scope or influence to Comogre or Escoria or Parita, or even Veragua or Chape. Instead, the territory south of the lower Río Tuira is interpreted as marginal to the major exchange routes postulated for eastern and western Panama. It must be emphasized, however, that data regarding this region are meagre and very likely present a false impression of marginality.

The chiefdom of Toto was probably located on the south side of the Tuira estuary across from Chape (Oviedo 1853: bk. 29, chap. 10, p. 45; Sauer 1966: 255), somewhere in territory from the Río Marea (at the mouth of the Tuira) to Punta Alegre on the Gulf of San Miguel (see Fig. 9). There is no additional information concerning Toto in the Spanish sources except for a comment noting an exchange of maize "bread" from Toto for fish from Perequete (Anghera 1912: I, 405–406).

The Río Taimatí, south of Toto, may have been the location of the chiefdom of Tumeto (Oviedo 1853: bk. 29, chap. 10, p. 45; Romolí 1953: 252), while south of Tumeto was situated the polity of Chochama. The *cacique* of Chochama is credited with control of the lower Río Sambú and the lower reaches of tributaries flowing north from the Serranía del Sapo (Romolí 1953: 252). Farther east, in hill country containing headwaters of the Sambú, two "interior" societies, Topogre and Chuchara, were located (Oviedo 1853: bk. 29, chap. 10, p. 45). Another hill chiefdom, Garachiné, was situated just inside the

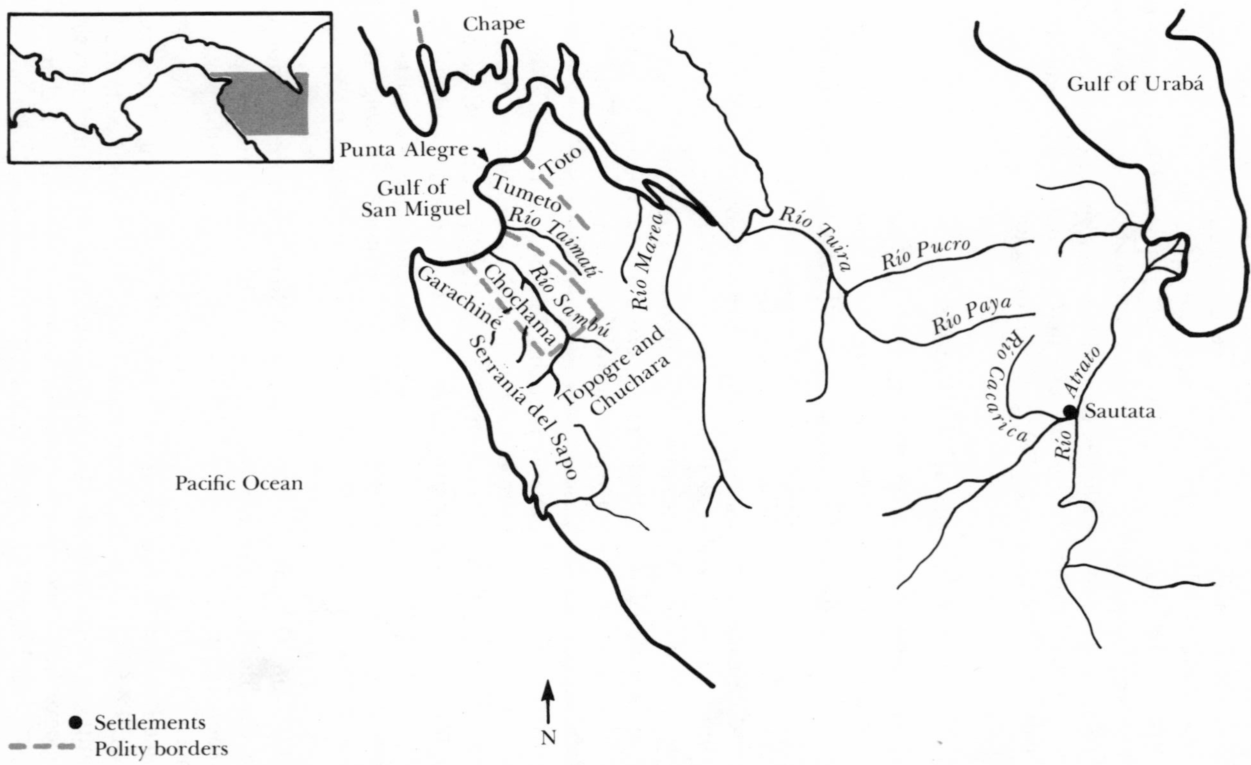

Fig. 9. Southeastern Panamanian chiefdoms: proposed locations ca. A.D. 1500.

barrier promontory between the Gulf of San Miguel and the Pacific (Oviedo 1853: bk. 29, chap. 10, p. 45; Romolí 1953: 255), that is, south of Chochama but including upper reaches of some Río Sambú tributaries.

By their geographical location on the Sambú river system, Chochama, Topogre, Chuchara, and Garachiné may have composed a field of influence centering on Chochama on the lower river. We know that when Gaspar de Morales traveled through this area ("the province of Chochama") and, through a captured *cacique* identified as Chiruca, ordered all the chiefs of the region to appear, eighteen did so (Romolí 1953: 272). The Río Sambú system contains at least nine rivers directly tributary to the main stream. If control of each tributary river system were divided between an average of two chiefs, one located toward the headwaters and one farther down, eighteen local rulers can readily be accounted for (see note 1 above and compare the situation suggested for Natá; see also Oviedo 1853: bk. 29, chap. 10, p. 44, regarding the association of rivers with *caciques*).

It is particularly unfortunate that so little specific information is available concerning the Tuira river system, the last region to be considered. The Río Tuira likely formed a major transportation route between Panama and Colombia since its upper tributaries, particularly the Río Paya and Río Pucro, were linked by land trails that crossed the *serranía* to waterways leading to the Atrato river system. The conquistador Francisco Beçerra visited fifteen chiefs between the "Trepadera" (the pass over the mountains connecting the Río Tuira system and the Río Atrato) and the Gulf of San Miguel, some of whom were said to have been powerful rulers with subjects numbering in the thousands (see Romolí 1953: 252).

We can hypothesize that such powerful lords may also have served as focal points for regional fields of influence. Consulting the map (Fig. 9), one sees that powerful chiefs might be expected on the lower Río Pucro, especially since the trail across the *serranía* to Sautata via the Río Paya meets the lower Río Pucra close to its confluence with the Río Tuira. One or more of the chiefs of the Río Paya may also have enjoyed superior sociopolitical positions, again because of travel and exchange advantages.[20] Regrettably, further details are lost. We do know that the rivers of the Tuira system yielded a great quantity of gold (Wafer 1934: 3 n. 5, 14–15 n. 2), and mention was made previously concerning the movement of gold from this area to Comogre. Very likely, then, raw gold was one of the resources that strategically located rulers could inject into the wider exchange network.

Levels of Exchange

I have argued in this chapter that in the early sixteenth century the Isthmus of Panama was comprised of a number of regional networks or "fields of influence" each of which centered on a chiefdom of major power and prestige. It is hypothesized that each focal polity was surrounded by "hinterland" chiefdoms of no greater and perhaps somewhat lesser strength whose rulers were frequently allied with the major *queví* by conquest, economic-political pacts, and/or affinal ties. I suggest further that the *quevís* of these leading chiefdoms based their influential position in considerable measure on their privileged access to long-distance exchange networks and travel routes that linked the regionally influential *quevís* with each other and with lands beyond Panama (cf. Price's "cluster model," Price 1977).

In addition to regional and long-distance exchange networks, there surely was also a measure of exchange at what can be termed the "local level" between chiefdoms situated in immediately adjacent but contrasting ecological zones, particularly between coastal or lowland peoples and interior mountain groups in situations where coast and interior were not united politically. Perhaps the greatest diversity of resources moved within this local exchange network. Here lowland and coastal subsistence products, such as salt, fish, game, and general agricultural produce, including maize and cotton goods, were exchanged for mountain resources, including gold grains and, in some instances, ceramics. Valuable local products, such as raw gold, pearls, shells, or salt, would also link the elite of local groups with a regional field of influence.

Within the regional exchange network both utilitarian-subsistence goods and sumptuary items indicative of elite rank and power may have moved, but with emphasis now on the latter. Salt, cotton hammocks and textiles, war captive-slaves, pearls, perhaps high-quality ceramics, and raw and fabricated gold were among the items exchanged among the greater and lesser chiefs within a regional field of influence (see Oviedo 1853: bk. 29, chap. 28, p. 140). Within the widest exchange networks—those long-distance ties postulated to have linked the focal *quevís* of Panama with each other and with lands beyond the isthmus—only the "scarcest" and therefore most prestigeful items moved, generally sumptuary goods indicative of rank and power. These materials may have included elaborate gold pieces, fine weaponry, the most precious textiles, the highest quality ceramics, and like goods.[21]

Goldman, speaking of Polynesia, describes a comparable situation in somewhat different terms, focusing on the relative rank of the elites active in the various exchange spheres within a single polity. "In aristocracies the roles of giver and receiver depend upon rank, which governs the scope of giving and the patterns of reciprocity. The highest ranks are givers to the widest networks, the lowest rank to the narrowest" (1970: 19). A comparable association between the extent of chiefly control and the scope of exchange activities is postulated for ancient Panama with reference not to a single polity (although it undoubtedly would apply there, too) but to the elites of the isthmus as a whole. The highest ranked and presumably most powerful Panamanian chiefs were those engaged in the widest long-distance exchange networks, while those of lesser rank or influence were restricted to regional and local networks in their exchange contacts and activities.

Circulation and Display

Except, perhaps, for the most localized highland-lowland exchanges in which basic utilitarian and subsistence goods probably were prominent and in which strictly economic imbalances may have had to be rectified, the basic rationale underlying Panamanian exchange systems may be best expressed not in economic terms per se but with reference to the elite sector's constant concern with power. Anthropologists have long recognized to some extent that the *activities* surrounding the movement of goods may signify chiefly well-being and ability as much as they reflect need for the items themselves. This point is basic, for example, to discussions of the political importance of "grandiose gestures of generosity" by the chief toward the populace (see Sahlins 1972: 139–148). Similarly, I shall argue that the simple movement of goods in reciprocity or redistribution by elites is a politically significant activity in its own right regardless (for the moment) of the ultimate end to which the goods themselves may be put.

This position follows Goldman's interpretation of status systems in Polynesia, where, he argues, the high honor, authority, and potential power inherent in chiefly status are celebrated in a more honorable and efficacious manner by activity than by inertia. "In status, as in mechanics, the measure of force is the energy of motion. Mass must be moved. It must be assembled and circulated and moved outward into wider orbits. That which is inert is low in vitality and hence in standing" (1970: 498). The political value inherent in such activity is also understandable in Balandier's terms, discussed above in the context of warfare, of making the political life of the elite overtly visible. Circulation or exchange of goods, can, like warfare, become a strictly "political occasion" or activity when the dynamics of political life are made clear and the persons revealed as "men of power." All of this is to say, as Adams also remarks (1975: 36–37), that power is not a static thing but a dynamic process, not something that is "held" or "obtained" but an active exercise. The San Blas Cuna would agree. Speaking of the constant criticism and scrutiny to which chiefly activities are subjected today, McKim states that "the Cuna respects merit. Respect is the greatest homage he pays; but *merit must be demonstrated*" (1947: 63, my emphasis).

The implication of these remarks for ancient Panamanian society can be expressed by the hypothesis that the *quevi* who engaged most enthusiastically in exchange and circulation of goods stood higher in chiefly prestige, honor, authority, and power than the *quevi* who merely "owned" or displayed fine products, apparel, and ornaments but did not (perhaps could not) engage in their exchange as actively.[22]

This distinction may also have bearing on the patterns of chiefdom size, location, and political significance suggested in the previous pages. Keeping in mind once more the very fragmentary and inconclusive nature of the ethnohistoric data, let us consider the few scattered statements concerning inheritance of chiefly wealth, specifically gold pieces. Such references are found for the *quevis* of Ponca (Anderson 1914: 177), Tubanama (Anghera 1912: I, 310), and Pacra (Anghera 1912: I, 301–302), none of whom was considered the major *cacique* of a regional field of influence. Rather, I suggested that these chiefs may have been located in hinterlands distant from major travel routes (Pacra), removed geographically from the exchange center of the region (Tubanama), or blocked from access to exchange routes by neighboring peoples (Ponca). Yet surely it was incumbent on these chiefs, as on all *quevis*, to evidence the symbolic aspects of their status and office by maintaining a chiefly *bohío* and affecting proper dress and chiefly ornamentation. If sumptuary goods were more difficult to obtain through exchange, then such chiefs as Ponca, Pacra, and Tubanama might have been forced to rely more heavily on gold pieces and other wealth inherited from predecessors to maintain the requisite chiefly display.

Acquisition of wealth by inheritance, however, does not involve the chief in dynamic exchange activities. On the contrary, inheritance is a very static political situation, one which provides sumptuary display without any activity on the part of the inheritor. Thus, if we follow Goldman's and Balandier's arguments, inheritance would not convey the same degree of honor, prestige, and political visibility as accrues to chiefs playing more active roles in exchange networks. It is conceivable that the Spaniards specifically noted inheritance of gold pieces for certain chiefs because this fact was regarded by their native informants as a significant commentary on the character and prestige of a given ruler.

3

Symbolism and Power

The Sanctity of Power

The successful operation of rank societies depends heavily on the ability of the elite, and especially chiefs, to generate and sustain the belief that they can control all facets of life, including people, natural resources, and the supernatural. Bolstered by this ideology they then, in fact, attempt to effect a measure of secular control over these same resources. In preceding pages early sixteenth-century Panamanian chiefs were associated with various modes of seemingly "secular" performances and controls as in warfare, the staging of *krun,* procedures for successful succession to chiefly office, and participation in regional fields of influence and long-distance exchange networks. Indeed, the proposed correlation of Panamanian chiefdoms with Goldman's Open society would necessitate that we particularly stress pragmatic avenues of elite performance.

In ancient Panama, however, as in other rank societies, "secular" expressions of high status and of the dynamics of chiefship are possible only so long as popular credibility in the basic propriety of the system is maintained, that is, so long as the population believes that status differentials, or distinctions between commoners and chiefs, and the concentration of controls with high status are "normal" or "proper" characteristics of "human nature" and of their mode of social living. Therefore, in addition to pragmatic, or secular, evidence of ruling capability, ancient Panamanian leadership also rested upon, gave expression to, and reinforced certain symbolic and ideological conceptions regarding the "basic nature" of man and society (Swartz, Turner, and Tuden 1966: 10–11; Cohen 1969: 221). In other words, the ancient Panamanian political order was closely linked with sacred as well as secular expressions of power.[1]

Once again the Polynesian sources provide helpful insights into the particular philosophical systems associated with the sociopolitical structures of rank societies and suggest features that we may consider as more or less characteristic of the belief systems common to chiefdoms in general. It is apt to begin with a quotation from Goldman's study concerning the concept of aristocracy that specifically stresses belief in the sacredness of the elite as fundamental to chiefly authority and legitimacy (see also Adams 1975: 232–243; Balandier 1970: 99–122): "Aristocracy is commonly considered a political system—as 'rule by the best,' or by an hereditary elite. Aristocratic rule, however, is not to be interpreted narrowly as technical administration, but broadly as the imposition of a commanding and 'natural' authority over the entire cultural domain. The Polynesian conception of chiefs as the *sources of divine authority and power* established them as the overseers of standards and of custom" (1970: 4, my emphasis).

The Polynesian chief's sacred power and authority—indeed, whatever "inherent" power or force or ability *any man* possessed—were expressed in the concept of *mana*.[2] *Mana* has been described as a form of all-pervasive supernatural (as distinct from strictly physical) force or power or influence that was expressed in any kind of ability, skill, or excellence an individual possessed. *Mana* could be acquired to some extent but was also regarded as an inherited quality, and as such it became a basic aspect or foundation of social rank and status.

Status and *mana* were inherited together in Polynesia. He who stood in line of succession to a high office inherited great *mana* along with the right to office, and he who stood in a lower rank possessed correspondingly less *mana*. The elite stood separate from the common man by virtue of their greater *mana*—and thus their greater sanctity. He who became high chief inherited the greatest *mana* and thus the greatest sanctity of all. Since *mana* was essentially a religious expression of efficacy (see Balandier 1970: 108), it was also by virtue of his *mana* that a chief exercised his chiefly powers and abilities. More specifically, "all conspicuous success is a proof that a man has *mana*; his influence depends on the impression made on the peoples' mind that he has it; he becomes a chief by virtue of it. Hence a man's power, though political or social in its character, is his *mana*" (Codrington, quoted in Goldman 1970: 10; see also Firth 1940).

Conversely, to the extent that *mana* was an acquired quality it also could be lost, but "to lose *mana* is to lose vitality and, therefore, all genuine significance as a person. To lack *mana* is to lack significance—to exist in a lower sphere" (Goldman 1970: 12). Consequently, great effort had to be expended to guard against such loss and to prove through exercise of powers and capabilities that one's *mana* was still as strong as it should be. The chief in particular was quick to react against any indication or suggestion, however slight, that his powers were declining, and he strove continuously to give proof through sumptuary display and the active exercise of the prerogatives of his office that his *mana* and sanctity, and thus his power, were undiminished.

Returning to the Panamanian materials, we find no direct mention in the ethnohistoric documents of the sixteenth century of any single "sacred" political-ideological concept comparable to *mana,* although there are a few statements linking leadership with sacred realms or with a wider "universal" or "cosmic" power, which will be considered in later pages. Yet there is reason to think that an ideological system embodying comparable politicoreligious concepts existed. Indeed, what may be elements of such a belief system are currently expressed by indigenous peoples of Panama, particularly the San Blas Cuna.

Although the structure and activities of the rulership or "elite" sector of contemporary Cuna society are in all likelihood greatly reduced from that of their pre-Columbian antecedents, the Cuna still see chiefly leadership as a "natural" aspect of all life. The necessity and ubiquity of leaders and followers are taken for granted. "The Cuna believe that God created the world in an orderly way, and they feel very strongly that everything has its proper place in the world. Within the village men have their places, some of them as leaders" (Howe 1974: 139–140). In the words of a Cuna text, "God put us into this world having leaders . . . If there is no leader, the village cannot be maintained . . . The place would be full of fights, everything would be wrong, if there were no chief, the maintainer of the place. All the animals have leaders, and we that much more . . . In the morning when the sun has risen, the minnows will come around here . . . The minnows come in one big group. They have a leader it's said. Their leader carries all his followers . . . at sunset, the minnows will go out of our waters and back into their whirlpools. Not one minnow will stay behind. They'll go back in following their leader's word. *That's the way the world is*" (text quoted in Howe 1977: 139–140, my emphasis).

This belief in leadership carries with it recognition of the separateness and distinctiveness of chiefs, at least when in their chiefly roles (see Howe 1977: 157). It considers the chief as "head" of the body politic, suggesting, in this metaphysical use, "intelligence, direction, primarity, and uniqueness" (ibid., pp. 138, 153). "Chiefliness" is manifested in varying ways, some of which will be elaborated upon in later pages. Basic to the distinction, however, is the belief that religion and politics are closely interrelated, that ritual and political statuses are largely equivalent, and that chiefs and other leaders are more closely associated with "sacred" aspects of life in that, as "men of intelligence," they are privy to forms of esoteric knowledge "hidden" from ordinary people. It is by virtue of this understanding that chiefs are considered "men of importance" or "men with names" and are held responsible for directing and maintaining the ritual and moral (social) order of the families and communities under their charge. There is also in Cuna political thought an often stated metaphorical association of chiefship with mythical culture heroes and celestial figures (see Howe 1974, 1977, 1975; Chapin 1970; Nordenskiöld 1938).

The Cuna further subscribe to a series of principles or concepts comparable in their totality to the Polynesian *mana*, which also can be associated with individual role or status inequalities in some contexts. One such concept, termed *purba* (*purpa*), refers in part to an individual's immortal, invisible, nonmaterial self or selves and, more broadly, to the sense of covertness and incorporealness in plants, animals, and inanimate objects. The invisible or "hidden" essence, or *purba*, can be concretely evidenced, however, as, for example, in shadows, in the heat of the sun or fire, in the gurgling of the brook, in the growl of an animal, in the hum of a motorboat (Nordenskiöld 1938: 334–356; Stout 1947: 42–43). *Purba* is also contained in the songs or chants performed by chiefs and ritual curers using special euphemisms and metaphors that are unintelligible to the common population: "The *purpa* of a medicine chant is its secret key meaning or essence, and perhaps the best gloss of *purpale* [modifier form derived from *purpa*] in the context of chiefly metaphors is 'in the hidden essence of things' " (Howe 1977: 137). *Purba* in this chiefly context is particularly significant for this study in that, as I shall discuss at some length below, one of the major attributes of Cuna politico-religious leadership concerns the chiefs' (or other specialists') mastery of "hidden things," that is, of esoteric knowledge.

The Cuna also give credence to a power called *niga*, "with which all are born and which grows as the individual grows and which can also be developed or decreased with medicines. It manifests itself in bravery and in industriousness but is not these things themselves" (Stout 1947: 43). According to Nordenskiöld, *niga* is a kind of aura held by men and animals alike that may be supplemented by certain means, for example, by the wearing of a jaguar's teeth under certain circumstances (1938: 361–362).

Stout also discusses a third power or facility called *kurgin* (*kurkin*), which "can be translated as predilection, predisposition, faculty, ability, or talent . . . not only is there a *kurgin* for every activity, as, for instance, hunting, but also for every kind of learning . . . In addition to being able to increase, decrease, or even completely vitiate *kurgins* with medicines it is also believed that different persons are born with different *kurgins* and that each sex has special *kurgins* for the occupations proper to them . . . It is also believed that greater or smaller amounts of *kurgin* run in families" (1947: 43). Nordenskiöld defines *kurgin* in similar terms as a special capacity for a skill or as intelligence in the sense of ability (1938: 363).

If these contemporary Cuna concepts are extrapolated to the pre-Columbian rank societies of Panama (whence they may well have derived) and are correlated with the system of status and rank differentials that then existed, it can be suggested that in sixteenth-century Panama gradations in status were believed associated with differences in inherent capacities for *niga* and *kurgin* and that recognition was given to invisible or hidden "essences" of things and beings (*purba*). Stated differently, varying degrees of sacred *mana*-like characteristics, some inherited and some achieved, accrued to both individuals and the various family lines or descent groups inheriting these statuses.[3]

We have possible ethnohistoric evidence of these concepts in Oviedo's passage regarding the differential treatment of the dead (1853: bk. 29, chap. 31, pp. 154, 156). Oviedo claims that those of high status were accorded elaborate burial or preservation after death while commoners received shorter shrift. This contrast could well reflect beliefs in the high degree of *kurgin* and *niga*, that is, of sacred value or "worth," accruing to elites in contrast with the much lesser degree of general sacredness or "worth" associated with ordinary persons, who, because of their smaller amount of "inherent value," were indeed little different from the birds and beasts of the forest, as Oviedo expressed it.

Sanctity and Scarcity

The exchange systems of the pre-Columbian Panamanian elite can also be considered within this context of belief in supernatural qualities or powers expressing inherent personal worth that are overtly evidenced in talents, abilities, and actions (see Goldman 1970: chap. 22). In this perspective the circulation of gold pieces, fine cotton goods, pearls, war captives, and the like along regional and long-distance networks becomes a signification not only of pragmatic chiefly abilities and rivalries but also of the nature and quantities of the sacredness that are inherent in high status and that underlie ("legitimize"), and are expressed in, chiefly efficacy (ibid., p. 479). In performing this function, the pearls, gold, and other valuables acquired and displayed by the elite also received "inherent" sacred value themselves. This sacrality can be expressed in several ways. First, the items used in sumptuary display and as items for circulation via chiefly exchanges would be scarce items. Second, the items so used might be carved or painted or otherwise crafted to illustrate symbolic representations or metaphors of sacredness and power. Let us consider each of these points.

The significance of scarcity is discussed by Goldman. Chiefs are required by the nature of the philosophical system that underwrites their position to be expansive, extravagant, and generous in the exchange and distribution of status goods. However, "these honorific criteria . . . have significance only against the constant of scarcity" (1970: 480). Consequently, the goods used in chiefly exchanges, distributions, and displays must be scarce commodities (as high status itself is a scarce commodity); as such, chiefly exchange and display items are frequently nonutilitarian exotic goods. Resources become recognized as exotic if they are not required for basic subsistence or household needs and if they are not everywhere available in great quantity, if they are received from geographically distant sources, and/or if they require exceptional craft skills to produce.

A number of measures could be employed not only to create or maintain a general condition of scarcity in chiefly exotic goods but also to assure a sufficient supply of scarce resources for the requisite circulation and generous distribution that, from the view of a *quevi,* constantly "consumed" his supply of scarce goods. In Goldman's opinion, the nature of these measures can be an important factor determining the nature or character of a particular rank society. He suggests various methods by which scarcity can be handled, including changes in productivity and/or consumption, raiding or conquest of enemy tribes to acquire their resources, chiefly competition for scarce supplies, and reduction of the scale of status spending (1970: 480).

With respect to Panamanian cultural systems, absence of data precludes the question of changes in local productivity and consumption patterns. Chiefly competitions (such as *krun*) are suggested, however, and warfare with neighboring groups is amply attested to in the historical literature, although the role of scarce goods in these activities is not clear. Alternatively, efforts could be made to extend exchange systems and other, related forms of chiefly contact into more distant territories whose remoteness, and thus relative infrequency of contact, would both restrict the amount of goods that could be exchanged and create an aura of esoterica for those acquired (cf. Flannery 1968).

This last approach to the problem of scarcity of chiefly goods may have been highly significant in determining the "character" of early sixteenth-century isthmian society. In ancient Panama the success of chiefly efforts to deal with the problem of scarcity of high-status goods undoubtedly varied among individual rulers. It can be hypothesized that those chiefs with direct access to major exchange routes also had the best personal opportunities to maximize this outreach and to contact distant peoples and places in northern South America (Colombia) and, probably, Mesoamerica.[4] Those chiefs farther removed geographically from long-distance routes fell behind their more strategically placed colleagues not only in terms of the reduced quantities of scarce resources that could be obtained (and the limitations placed thereby on status display and distribution) but also in the restrictions on opportunities to evidence personal capabilities by establishing distant contacts and participating actively in the exchange that followed. It was previously argued that only a few regionally outstanding Panamanian chiefs were likely to be in direct contact with territories beyond the isthmus, and it is suggested now that the fruits of these associations rebounded to their even greater personal control, prestige, influence, and power at home.

Regrettably, we remain ignorant of what wider effects the *quevi*'s expanding personal power and influence could have generated in the home society. Further expansion or, perhaps better said, further control of his regional "field of influence" is one likely consequence, for it was by means of alliance with such strategically located chiefs that Panamanian rulers farther away in the exchange hinterland could hope to acquire greater quantities of scarce goods, though at the price (presumably) of a somewhat subordinate political position vis-à-vis the central lord. By the same token, we can suggest that hinterland chiefdoms grew more slowly and fell increasingly behind the regional centers in size, productivity, and political clout to the extent that their rulers failed to attain positions of personal power and influence comparable to those of the major *quevís,* who had means to decide which hinterland elites to support and which to deny. As a corollary of this hypothesis, it can also be postulated that hinterland chiefdoms may have endured relatively more successful political coups and challenges for the chiefly office to the extent that rulers were unable to evidence their personal abilities as fully or to reward followers as satisfactorily. Competition for high office within more powerful chiefdoms (that is, those regional centers advantageously located with respect to long-distance contacts and exchange networks) may have been more successfully countered, though by no means eliminated. Indeed, given the greater wealth and personal opportunities to be gained, status rivalry may well have been more intensively pursued (even if more successfully restrained) within the major chiefdoms.

Universal Energy and Its Control

The high chiefly sacredness, or *mana,* reflected by sumptuary items may be expressed not only by their scarcity but also by crafting the goods into certain shapes and forms that illustrate symbolic representations or metaphors of this sacred power. The Panamanian prestige items which can be most readily discussed in this context include fabricated gold pieces and the polychrome ceramic wares for which ancient Panama is also justly famous. According to Oviedo, wood was also crafted in comparable style (1959: 37, and 1853: bk. 29, chap. 31, p. 155), and archaeological materials reveal that stone and bone were similarly carved. Cotton textiles may have been woven with symbolic designs in pre-Columbian Panama, too (see Lothrop 1937: 46; cf. Sawyer 1972), but no examples of such textiles remain. Similarly, the painted designs on the floors of *bohíos* are now lost.

Let us consider goldwork, the ornamentation that the native peoples of pre-Columbian Panama "esteem[ed] and prize[d] above all

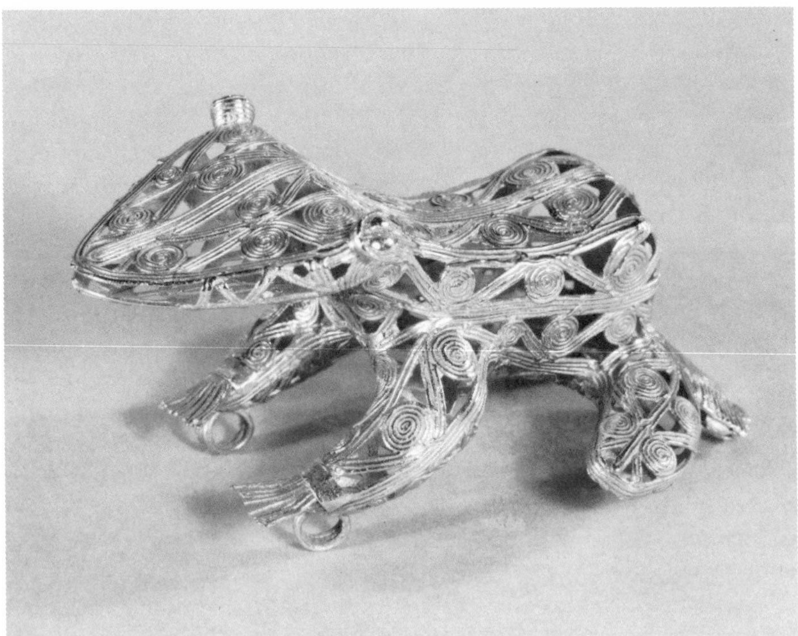

Fig. 10. Two gold pendants from Venado Beach, one in the shape of four double-headed ducks, 3¼″ long, and the other a filigree frog, also 3¼″ long. (Collection of The Art Institute of Chicago; courtesy of The Art Institute of Chicago)

others" (Oviedo 1959: 107). Most metallurgical pieces were displayed as headbands or helmets, armbands, chest plates, pendants and necklaces, nose pieces, earrings, breast supports, penis sheaths, leg bands, and disks sewn on cotton cloaks (Anderson 1914: 93, 95, 320; Oviedo 1959: 32, 44; Anghera 1912: I, 202; Sauer 166: 131–133 passim, 270, 271; Lothrop 1937). Some of these ornaments were relatively simple in shape and design. Necklaces made of beads or of leaf-shaped pieces are noted in the literature or in archaeological finds (Lothrop 1937: 156–159), while nose rings and earrings and earplugs were frequently in the form of plain rings, rods, disks, or crescent-shaped plates (Lothrop 1937: 141–152, 156–159; Anghera 1912: I, 221; Wafer 1934: 85–86). However, many pieces of gold or *tumbaga* (gold-copper alloy), particularly pendants and nose clips, were cast into elaborate zoomorphic or anthropomorphic shapes, and zoomorphic-anthropomorphic motifs were embossed on flat hammered pieces, such as chest plates, armbands, greaves, and helmets (see Lothrop 1937: 115–129, 141–152, 159–162, 133–139, 162–191). The many forms of fauna represented are generally identified in the anthropological and museological literature as eagles, frogs or toads, felines (jaguars), snakes and other reptiles, owls, parrots, bats, and monkeys (see Lothrop 1937; Anderson 1914: 93).

We also know that to the ancient Panamanians the value of these gold pieces lay not so much in the metal itself, though the medium of gold probably held some "inherent" significance to them (see below), as in the fact that it was crafted. This point is evidenced in the reprimand reportedly given the Spaniards by the son of the *queví* Comogre, who, perplexed by the conquistadors' melting of artistic pieces into ingots, is said to have pointed out that rough gold had no more value than a lump of clay before it was transformed into a useful or pleasing container (Anghera 1912: I, 221; Anderson 1914: 177).

What, then, did the art of the goldsmith signify? The cultural significance of symbols, particularly sacred symbols, has been succinctly discussed by, among others, Clifford Geertz (1966, 1957). Symbols, which can be any objects, acts, events, or relations that convey a concept or meaning, "are tangible formulations of notions, abstractions from experience fixed in perceptible forms, concrete embodiments of ideas, attitudes, judgments, longings, or beliefs" (1966: 5). Furthermore, these notions, ideas, and attitudes that are concretized in symbolic forms are socially or publically significant and observable. As such, symbols serve as *models of* the pre-established world and of man's place therein and as *models for* ongoing social behavior and individual activity within the world (1966: 7–9).

Returning to ancient Panama, the significance of gold pieces as *models of* the world and *models for* behavior may be considered from three perspectives, recognizing, of course, that in reality these three aspects were intertwined into a whole and that a given gold piece could carry several of the connotations. Gold pieces may be considered, first, as metaphors for the belief (common in native cosmologies) in a distinctive cultured, or "civilized," socially ordered, or "moral," state of human society that separates man from the natural (animal) world and that in rank societies further elevates some men (the elite) above their brethren as superior representatives of this human uniqueness. Second, gold pieces may stand as indicators of social rank and status. Third, they may also be regarded as symbolic of the elite's "activated status," or sacred-secular economic-political power.

Since all members of human society are part of the cultured and socially ordered (moral) rather than the natural domain, the wearing of gold pieces to express belief in a generalized human condition would be expected to be society-wide. Conversely, since within the particular Panamanian "cultured world" social status and rank were unequally distributed, the use of gold ornaments as indicators of social standing would be expected to vary among members of the population according to rank. Since "activated status," or sociopolitical power, was an elite prerogative, those gold pieces symbolic of power would be expected to be restricted to elite persons, particularly to those in positions of actual sacred-secular authority.

Ethnohistoric data evidence the use of gold as a status indicator and power manifestation in pre-Columbian isthmian society, and

myths of the contemporary San Blas Cuna strongly suggest the use of gold as symbolic of cultured society and of elite power and uniqueness. Let us begin with ethnohistory. The literature indicates that nose pieces and perhaps ear pieces were worn by the entire, general populace, but in such a way as to also indicate status (Anderson 1914: 95). Wafer says that large nose plates, which covered the mouth from corner to corner and extended "so low as to lie upon the Under-lip with its lowest side," were worn by men on special official occasions, as at a feast or when in council, "but that which they wear abroad upon a long March, Hunting, or at ordinary times, is . . . much smaller, and does not cover their Lips." Also, on formal occasions "the King or Chief, and some few of the great ones . . .

wear in each Ear, fastened to a Ring there, two large Gold Plates, one hanging before to the Breast, and the other behind on the Shoulder." Among women a nose ring rather than a plate was worn, the size "also differing according to their Rank, and the Occasion" (1934: 85–86).

In addition, it is likely that these ear and nose pieces carried connotations of social morality, or "humanness." This hypothesis stems in large part from the work of Seeger (1975) and Turner (1969), who have discussed the meaning of body ornaments among the Suya and the Tchikrin and related groups of central Brazil. Their researches show that ear disks, lip plugs, penis sheaths, and the like serve as obvious and tangible statements of the symbolic significance accorded various parts of the body as metaphor for social (moral) living. Thus, for example, among the Suya, ears and ear ornaments associate with the concept of "hearing," not only in the sense of physically sensing sound but also in the sense of "understanding" the proper customs and forms of social etiquette. When a person behaves according to social norms, he is said to "hear," or "understand," well; when he fails to observe these regulations, he is said to "hear" poorly (Seeger 1975: 214). Similarly, lips, and thus speech and singing, carry social meaning in the form of public oratory and singing by men, especially village leaders, who, in their public addresses, admonish the population (apparently meaning particularly women and children) to follow cooperative and peaceful social conduct. Eyes and nose, that is, vision and smell, also carry symbolic meanings, although among the Suya vision and smell are associated with nonsocial and "animal" realms. Thus, the Suya wear lip disks and ear disks, which celebrate and overtly emphasize the "social" faculties but do not ornament the "antisocial" nose or eyes. Furthermore, Suya body ornaments serve as indicators of social status, for as children grow to adulthood their progress through the social life cycle is marked by ear piercings and lip piercings (for example, at puberty and when boys enter the men's house as young husbands). Finally, Seeger notes that the Suya (and, one suspects, other groups, too) "define themselves as a tribe, different from other groups, by their use of lip discs, ear discs, and a particular singing style. They claim that no other group has those three attributes, and thus no other group is . . . fully human" (1975: 212–213).

Although the primary data are virtually silent on the matter, I suggest that the ear pieces and nose rings and plates worn by the ancient Panamanians carried socially significant meanings perhaps

Fig. 11. The *queví* Lacenta with family and attendants en route to a feast or a visit. Note examples of nose rings in lower left and lower right foreground. (From Lionel Wafer, *A New Voyage and Description of the Isthmus of America,* 1934 ed., p. 140)

comparable to those connoted by Suya body ornaments. Possibly, too, the combination of body ornaments also served to tangibly identify the people of Panama in their own eyes as a distinctive "human" group, different from all others, as in contemporary Cuna thought "the Golden People" see themselves as the "best" people in the world, distinguished from all others, past and present (Howe 1974: 117). Cuna women, it is interesting to note, still wear golden nose rings and earrings as well as large golden chest ornaments and many golden finger rings, although men have not affected such ornamentation since the mid- or late nineteenth century (Stout 1947: 68; Nordenskiöld 1938: 57; Howe 1974: 264; Wassén 1949: 26). In addition, it is reported that when a Cuna girl reaches puberty the nose ring first given to her as a small child is replaced by a new one as part of the puberty ceremony, which sees her socially "reborn" as a woman (see Marshall 1950: 237, 239).

That these golden rings carry a connotation of proper social, or "human," living is also indicated in several Cuna myths concerning the creation of the world and of human society in which the culture hero Ibeorgun not only established such basic elements of social living as the kinship system, girls' puberty rites, and proper domestic life but also instructed the populace how to manufacture nose rings of gold, particularly for their women (Nordenskiöld 1938: 267–268). Given these various bits of data, it can be suggested that the golden rings and plates worn in ears and nose by ancient Panamanians stood as metaphors for proper human, that is, social, ordered, or moral, behavior and identified the individual wearer as a participant in this ordered social life.[5]

Although it is likely that the elaborate size of the chiefly ear plates and nose plates described by Wafer also connoted the superior power of these men of rank, the distribution of ornamental gold pieces specifically symbolic of sacred-secular power cannot be clearly ascertained by the data at hand. It is to be expected, however, that members of the elite would display many more power indicators than would commoners and that high chiefs would display more power indicators than lesser elites. Furthermore, such display probably would be greatest at times of public activities when rank and power were "officially" or "formally" demonstrated. The Spanish accounts do indicate some specific uses of gold in ancient Panamanian society that are in accord with these hypotheses. We know, for example, that gold pieces were exchanged as tokens of peaceful alliance and chiefly goodwill between *quevís* (or between a *queví* and the Spanish *entrada* leader) and were offered as ransom for a captured *queví*; that *quevís*, *sacos*, and warriors going into formal battle were proudly arrayed in fine gold pieces and feathers; that the remains of the recently deceased *queví* Parita were literally covered from head to foot with goldwork prior to burial (Oviedo 1853: bk. 29, chap. 3, pp. 10, 14, chap. 5, p. 19, chap. 10, pp. 47–49, chap. 23, p. 118, chap. 26, p. 130, chap. 28, p. 138, and 1959: 107; Espinosa 1873: 27–28, 51, 54, 62, and 1864: 496, 497; Sauer 1966: 220, 222, 235, 271; Lothrop 1937: 4, 6, 8, 22). The high-status burials excavated at the Sitio Conte, which compare with the Spaniards' description of Parita's funerary attire "item by item," have yielded a multitude of the fine objects of gold and other materials that formally accompanied a ruler to whatever afterlife was thought to await him (Lothrop 1937: 14; see also Oviedo 1853: bk. 29, chap. 31, p. 156). Such wealth did not accompany the commoner in death, although the secondary urn burial of commoners included at least a few gold pieces (Stout 1947: 98; see Lothrop 1937: 52–61, regarding differences in grave goods between large, intermediate, and small graves).

Analysis of the rich diversity of gold pieces recovered from the chiefly graves at the Sitio Conte and known from collections associated with other regions of Panama, particularly the provinces of Veraguas and Chiriquí (see Lothrop 1950; MacCurdy 1911; Holmes 1888), also suggests another approach to the problem of ascertaining what type of gold pieces may have stood specifically as symbols of elite power. One of the hypotheses underlying this analysis of ancient Panamanian political systems argues that a significant number of the cast and alloyed gold pieces usually attributed to Panamanian provenience (although not necessarily all of them—see Chapter 5) in fact were not manufactured in Panama but were acquired as finished objects from sources outside the isthmus. The ethnohistoric data do suggest, however, that hammering of gold and possibly, therefore, annealing and embossing were known and practiced by Panamanian craftsmen.[6] The gold pieces found at the Sitio Conte include a predominance of hammered pieces (some with elaborate iconography embossed upon the flattened metal surface), including headbands and helmets, beads and bead necklaces, nose and ear ornaments, armbands and greaves, large and small chest plates, and disks to be sewn onto clothing (see Holmes 1888: 49; MacCurdy 1911: 223–226). The Sitio Conte graves, however, have also yielded exquisite cast gold and *tumbaga* items, particularly the more elaborate nose rings

Fig. 12.a Gold pendant from Veraguas in the form of a standing male figure, 2¼″ high. (Collection of The Art Institute of Chicago; courtesy of The Art Institute of Chicago)

Fig. 12.b A cone-shaped nose ring from Venado Beach, 1″ in diameter. (Collection of The Art Institute of Chicago; courtesy of The Art Institute of Chicago)

and nose clips and a grand array of effigy pendants. This collection of cast gold or *tumbaga* pendants and nose ornaments includes most of the pieces that, in Lothrop's opinion, were "imported" from outside the isthmus (mainly from Colombia) or are "local copies" of foreign gold styles. I would suggest that the cast gold or *tumbaga* effigy pendants and nose clips showing "outside" characteristics (see Chapter 5) were the type of gold pieces most likely to be acquired through long-distance contacts and as such can be viewed as particularly designative of the active expression of chiefly power (see Sauer 1966: 133–134).

In addition, the diverse shapes and forms of these effigy pendants and nose ornaments, which are also carved from various fine stones and bone, and the use of gold as ornamentation for warriors in battle and as "golden clothing" (helmet, chest plate, greaves, etc.) for deceased *quevis* may have carried sacred or symbolic connotations that went beyond mere display. In several myths from the San Blas Cuna that recount the brave exploits of the mythological celestial being and culture hero-chief Tad Ibe (Tat Ipe), we find the hero-chief engaged in various trials of strength and intellectual cunning with rival, sometimes evil, supernatural chiefs who are eventually defeated by Tad Ibe's greater bravery (*niga*) and intellectual ability (*kurgin*) and are transformed into animals (Chapin 1970).[7] In the myths detailing these encounters we sometimes find Tad Ibe and his chiefly opponents described as wearing "golden clothing" (ibid., p. 24).[8] When the myths are thematically and structurally analyzed, the "golden clothing" appears to be correlated with, or symbolic of, the celestial realm, particularly the sun (Helms 1977: 77, 116–118). The solar-celestial realm, in turn, is source of the vital energy which suffuses the world with life and energy (see Reichel-Dolmatoff 1971). Thus, when Tad Ibe defeats his opponents and condemns them to a strictly terrestrial existence as animals, they are stripped of their celestially associated golden attire.

It is tempting to interpret the gold-bedecked warriors and gold-covered chiefs of pre-Columbian Panama as literally clad in analogous "golden clothing" that dramatically symbolized their association with the same celestial-solar strength. Just as Tad Ibe, clothed in gold and emboldened by mystical *niga,* fought his rivals, so the golden warriors of ancient Panama bravely ventured into battle against a foe; as Tad Ibe in his golden attire was a mythological embodiment and earthly representative of celestial energy engaged in eliminating evil from the world by virtue of his superior intelligence and ability, so the deceased chief Parita was dressed in the shining metal garb that bespoke his role as earthly representative of celestial heroes and symbolized the *queví*'s beneficial, suprahuman, celestially associated strength and intelligence. In short, just as we may interpret the wearing of golden earrings and nose pieces as indicative of the relative social status of an individual and as symbolically expressive of his membership in "ordered" human society, so we can consider the more elaborate gold pieces worn by the elite both as signifiers of political power and as symbols of the supernatural realms from which this power was thought to derive. Conceivably, this was the thought expressed by the *queví* of Darién when he insisted to the Spaniards that his golden ornaments came from the sky ("del cielo") until the conquistadors forced him to identify a more earthly source (see Casas 1927: bk. 2, chap. 63, p. 351).

Let us consider the nature of this supernatural realm more carefully. Symbols in general, and sacred symbols in particular, represent concepts identifying a people's "general orientation in nature, on the earth, in society, and in what [they] are doing" (Langer, quoted in Geertz 1966: 14). Symbols make the world comprehensible; they provide order and meaning for those who live within it (see ibid., pp. 14–17). The order and meaning expressed in ancient Panamanian sacred symbols are very poorly indicated in the ethnohistoric literature. To the best of my knowledge, the only statement bearing on the matter is by Oviedo, who simply says that the images fashioned in gold or sculpted in wood depicted *Tuira*, a major deity accorded great wisdom ("the devil" in Spanish interpretation), who, by implication, may have had celestial associations (1853: bk. 29, chap. 31, p. 155, chap. 26, pp. 125, 127). Some additional insights can be obtained, however, by broadening our scope of inquiry to review briefly some of the principles of cosmology and ideology characteristic of contemporary twentieth-century peoples in adjacent culture areas of Middle America and northern South America—beliefs that also seem to underlie the cosmology of the Cuna of Panama. (A systematic study of Cuna symbolism and ideology has yet to be made and, though pertinent to this analysis, lies beyond the scope of this work.)

Although specific details vary from group to group, a number of scholars, including Furst (1968, 1974), Reichel-Dolmatoff (1971, 1972*c*, 1975), Lévi-Strauss (1969, 1973), and others (see, e.g., Lathrap 1973*a*; Benson 1972; Gossen 1974; Turner 1969), have shown that native belief systems are generally concerned with what Walter Ong has termed "the world as event" (1969). This concept emphasizes the interrelatedness of all living things as manifestations of and participants in the dynamic creative forces or energy of the cosmos or universe at large. It also recognizes the need to control the potent forces of natural energy, more specifically, to utilize this energy for man's good in diverse cultural and social ways. Evidence of the meaning of living things and of the nature of the cosmic life-giving forces is sought in the world of nature. Naturally occurring phenomena—including geographical features, flora and fauna, meteorological phenomena, sounds, and colors—are examined, analyzed, ordered, and classified by native peoples, who thereby achieve a system of thought that identifies and organizes "reality" and clarifies the place of man in the wider world of nature and life. An understanding or interpretation of the origins and characteristics of the biosphere and the universe also provides a store of sacred-secular knowledge useful for controlling the forces and energy of the cosmos and turning them to human benefit. This esoteric knowledge, in turn, creates power for those best able to understand the intricacies and secrets of the natural-supernatural and capable of establishing contact with representatives of the supernatural forces of life (see Whitten 1976: chap. 2; Reichel-Dolmatoff 1972*a*: 102, 1975, 1971; Lévi-Strauss 1969).

In the mythologies and tales that embody these concepts, at least three fundamental sources of life-giving energy are usually identified:[9] celestial power, with the sun as maintainer of life through its light, warmth, and protection; the earth, that is, the land and its waters, sources of useful plants, game animals, and fish, which support human life with nourishment; and woman as potential child bearer. These universal "energy sources" are often translated into a male-female duality (though with many nuances) in which celestial-solar phenomena are associated with maleness and earth-vegetation-fish are correlated with femaleness.[10]

Native cosmologies and mythologies, however, not only consider the creative aspects of cosmic energy but also recognize with equal emphasis its negative or destructive potentialities that cause storms to rage, fire to burn out of control, vegetation to grow wild and rank, incest and adultery to rend the social fabric, and illness to threaten the lives of individuals who are, in any event, doomed eventually to die in the final triumph of negative forces. Fortunately, the destructive propensities of universal energy can be guarded and controlled. This is a major undertaking that requires those charged with the task not only to contain exceptional personal strengths and energies commensurate with the work but also to be able to contact the proper sources and supernatural representatives of universal energy. In the egalitarian societies of the tropical lowlands of South America, from which many of our ethnographic data on these topics are obtained, these awesome responsibilities usually fall to the adult men of the society who work to acquire the necessary supernatural contacts and to build personal strength and bravery.

This responsibility, however, is particularly laid upon shamans, who are most closely allied with the mystical representations of the energy sources of the universe. By virtue of this unique personal contact, the shaman acquires supernatural energy in his own right, which gives him the power to influence the weather, to watch over the production of crops, to guard the social life of the community, and to cure illness. Although shamans still function in chiefdoms, within rank societies the duty and obligation of establishing contact with supernatural sources so as to control and direct the affairs of human society devolve mainly upon the high elite, particularly the priests or priest-chiefs, men of highest social status who also serve as society's highest religicopolitical practitioners. The sanctity of great *mana*, or *mana*-like forces, that these men carry by virtue of their high social status (and that can be re-interpreted now as a personalized expression of universal energy or life force) authorizes them to seek supernatural associations. It is by virtue of their mediation with the mystical representatives of supernatural energy that priests and priest-chiefs obtain the necessary sacred authority to guide and direct human affairs.

Chiefdoms no longer exist in native tropical America, but such personages as the *kumú* of the Tukano-speaking Desana of the Vaupés region of Colombia still exemplify to some degree the sacred role of chiefs. The *kumú* holds very high social status and is considered to be the direct representative of celestial powers, particularly the sun. His function essentially is to "perpetuate moral teachings in the highest ethical sense" (Reichel-Dolmatoff 1971: 129, 135, 128). Therefore, the *kumú* must show exceptional ability to give constructive advice and to settle interpersonal conflicts, but his main public function involves ceremonial distribution of quantities of smoked fish and wild fruits contributed by the population for multiday feasts during which the sun is asked to foster growth and abundance (ibid., pp. 136–137).

As Reichel-Dolmatoff briefly notes, the ceremonial activities of the *kumú* in Desana society point toward the "priest-temple-idol complex" of the pre-Columbian sub-Andes (1971: 139 n. 6). The *kumú*'s responsibilities in conflict resolution and public food distribution are also fundamental activities for priest-chiefs of rank societies. Thus, I would extend Reichel-Dolmatoff's comparison to suggest that the *kumú* is a contemporary (and somewhat simplified or deculturated) version of pre-Columbian, generally celestially associated, priest-chiefs who directed the sacred-secular life of numerous chiefdoms of the Intermediate Area, including Panama, prior to European contact.

The ethnographic record pertaining to the political life of the twentieth-century Cuna reveals a clear association still pertaining between leadership and celestial phenomena. In mythologies we encounter culture-heroes and celestial beings who may be associated with the sun and who are sometimes said to have descended to earth from heaven on plates of gold. These heroes (such as Tad Ibe, solar-associated "Grandfather-Lord" and "Grandfather-Bright" or Ibelele, another name for Tad Ibe, and Ibeorgun, "Lord-Gold") [11] instructed the mythological Cuna, or "Golden People," in the appropriate forms of ritual and social behavior, that is, in the proper expression of kinship, marriage, and puberty rites, in ritual paraphernalia and its uses, in sacred medicines, and in various arts and crafts. In comparable fashion contemporary chiefs may be compared with solar phenomena, as these words from a speech made at the installation ceremony for a new chief indicate. In this excerpt, reported by Howe, the speaker compares a chief with the sun, saying that both must be active and work hard, that both must serve Great Father (God), and that the chief, like the sun, should not shirk his duty:

> [All the people sit watching you, everyone sees you.] Amidst the members your name as chief is made. It is said moreover that this happens so you can work for Father [that is, God] . . . We live in the name of Great Father alone, and if I should go to another village, I'm working for Great Father. I'm not working for anyone else. . . . You see, *Tat Ipe* [Tad Ibe, the sun] is there. Every day *Tat Ipe* circles around us, and he's working for Great Father. He's not working for anyone else. . . . Father admonished him, "Every day you will pass above my children, the Golden People, every single day you will work above the Golden People." Father gave him the way, so he works according to Father's word. He can't refuse to work on even a single day. . . . And in just that way we too are workers for Father. (Howe 1975: 6)

Some Cuna tales and cosmological beliefs have a considerable antiquity. We find ancient versions of some contemporary myths recorded in seventeenth-century sources (see Wassén 1949: 125, 131). Even earlier Andagoya and Oviedo wrote that the natives of Panama believed in a god in the sky who created everything and who was the sun (Oviedo 1853: bk. 29, chap. 5, p. 20, chap. 26, p. 125; Andagoya 1865: 14). The Spanish writers, however, do not associate *quevís* or other pre-Columbian rulers with the sun or other celestial phenomena, but I propose that there probably was a complex of metaphors associating chiefship with the solar-celestial realm, with brightness, and with gold. I have argued that the metaphorical "golden clothing" worn by Tad Ibe in his mythical combats was evidenced literally in the golden plates and helmets, greaves, and anklets worn by pre-Columbian Panamanian warriors and rulers in life and in death, and that this attire connoted solar-associated strengths and ability. Indeed, gold appears frequently in Cuna tales and traditions today and carries a wealth of metaphorical significance that has yet to be adequately investigated by scholars. It is likely that the significance of gold as a medium with which to portray celestial-solar association is not accidental in contemporary Cuna myths and was not accidental in ancient times. Conceivably, in Cuna thought gold represents tangible manifestation of the *purba*, or invisible essence, of the sun as revealed in its golden light and heat (see Nordenskiöld

1938: 345, 354). Quite possibly, comparable symbolism was attributed to gold by pre-Columbian peoples of the isthmus.[12]

If gold was considered expressive of solar *purba* or other aspects of universal energy in ancient Panama, then the importance of the golden "ornaments" for those who wore them presumably lay largely in the supernatural associations they conferred upon the wearer. The yellow of the golden nose rings and earrings worn by all members of ancient Panamanian society and interpreted above as indicators of civilized, "human" identity could convey a concomitant concept of joint participation in the basic circuit of life-giving energy, particularly as expressed in ordered ("good") social living (see discussion of color symbolism below). Supernatural association would be significant particularly for priest-chiefs, for such celestial ties underwrote the legitimacy of their more pragmatic activities as political leaders. The chiefly obligation to exercise authority by resolving disputes, waging war, conducting resource redistributions, sponsoring competitive exercises (*krun*), and controlling and directing supernatural forces toward human benefit could be elegantly abbreviated and succinctly stated in the form of a golden chest plate or helmet or other piece of golden attire. Even more, by virtue of the very great quantity or efficacy of life force (*niga, kurgin*) available to those of the high elite, the priest or chief in his golden ornamentation could become himself a solar-celestial figure!

The same supernatural energy and sacred chiefly authority could also be expressed with other media and colors (see note 12 above). Let us consider Lionel Wafer's account of the headgear of the seventeenth-century *queví* Lacenta and his attendants:

> I once saw *Lacenta,* in a great Council, wear a Diadem of Gold-plate, like a Band about his Head, eight or nine Inches broad, jagged at top like the Teeth of a Saw, and lined on the inside with a Net-work of small Canes. And all the armed Men, who then attended him in Council, wore on their Heads such a Band, but like a Basket of Canes, and so jagged, wrought fine, and painted very handsomely, for the most part red; but not cover'd over with a Gold-plate as *Lacenta*'s was. The top of these was set round with long Feathers, of several of the most beautiful Birds, stuck upright in a Ring or Crown. But *Lacenta* had no Feathers on his Diadem. (1934: 86–87)

Now compare Wafer's description and the headdress illustrated in Figure 13 with the description by Reichel-Dolmatoff for the Desana where "the feather headdress symbolizes the Sun with its rays" (1971:

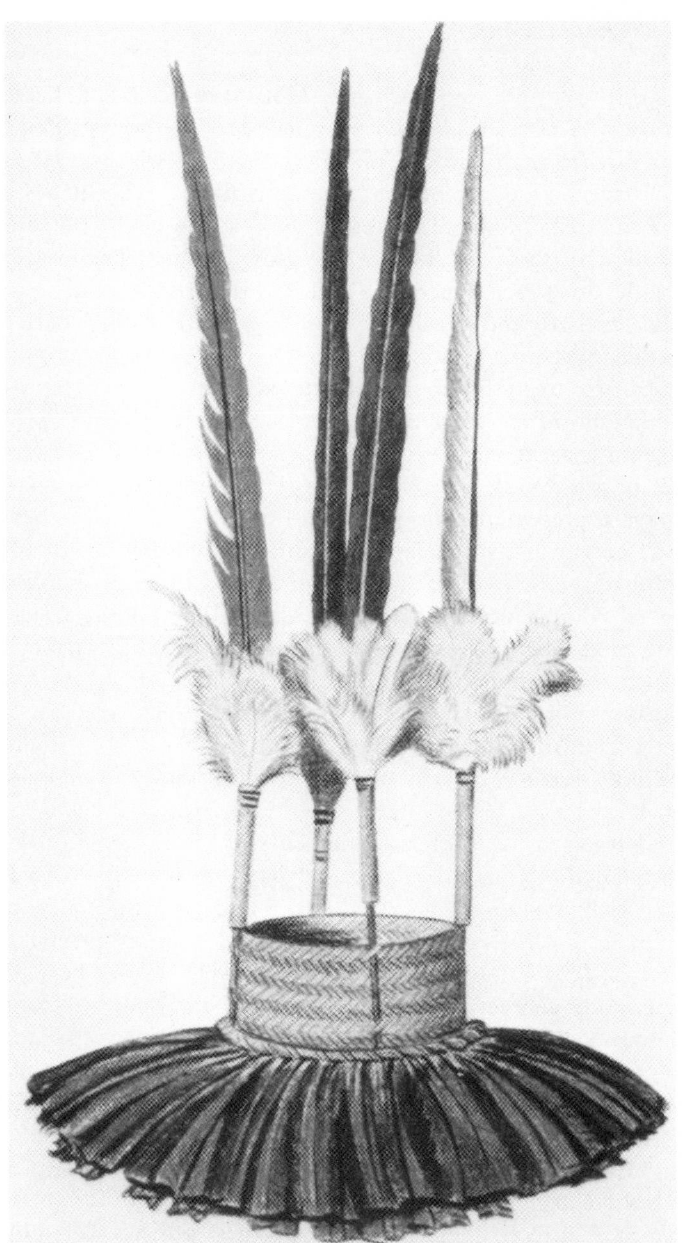

Fig. 13. Cuna *kantule*'s headdress. Tall feathers are red (*left*), blue (*center*), and yellow (*right*). (From S. Henry Wassén, "Original Documents from the Cuna Indians of San Blas Panama," *Etnologiska Studier*, no. 6, 1938, plate I; by permission of the Göteborgs Etnografiska Museum)

98; see also Whitten 1976: 96, 98). More specifically: "The feather crown consists of a ring-shaped, woven base of thin reeds and fibers, decorated with small feathers placed vertically, with a series of long, radial feathers added, somewhat spread apart. . . . the little feathers at the base are yellow and represent the fertility of the Sun . . . the large radial feathers are blue and signify contact, communication. . . . the Kumu wears a special crown . . . that consists only of yellow and red feathers and does not have large tail feathers" (Reichel-Dolmatoff 1971: 116).

In addition to the symbolism of the sun and its rays, represented by the small yellow feathers of the Desana crowns and, probably, by Lacenta's jagged-edged gold band, the red paint of the cane band composing the lower section of Lacenta's councilmen's crowns may well have represented concepts of the fertility of the earth and of woman; such, at least, is the significance of red among the Desana. The blue of the large radial feathers of Desana headdresses represents themes of communication between solar yellow and terrestrial red and the need for human beings of the earth to establish contact with the supernatural and extraterrestrial forces of energy as well as with each other in human society (Reichel-Dolmatoff 1971: 24, 47–48, 122–123; see also Whitten 1976; chap. 3).[13]

The use of color to symbolize ideological concepts is evidenced also in body paint. Oviedo notes that the natives of Panama painted their bodies with red (*bija,* or annatto) and black (*jagua,* or genipa) coloring (1959: 33, and 1853: bk. 29, chap. 28, p. 138). According to Wafer, the Panamanians painted their bodies and especially the face with figures of birds, beasts, men, and trees, using primarily red, yellow, and blue colors, "very bright and lovely" (1934: 82–83). Warriors painted their faces red and the rest of the body in large spots of black and yellow and other colors (ibid., see also pp. 22 n. 1, 79). In twentieth-century ethnography Alphonse mentions that in preparation for *krun* festivities Guaymí men paint their faces red, blue, black, or yellow (1956: 123). Young indicates red, black, and white. Young also notes that men wore hats decorated with bright-colored bird feathers at *krun* festivals (see 1971: 207). Both the participants and various objects used in the Cuna girls' puberty ceremony are painted red or black (Stout 1947: 35–36; see also Wassén 1949: 47).

Judging from the colors employed, the body paint used by both ancient and contemporary natives of the isthmus very likely expressed aspects of the general world view that has been explored above. There are only hints of color symbolism in the Cuna ethnographic record, but Nordenskiöld felt it "strongly probable" that color had a "magic significance" for the Cuna (1929: 153 and 1930: 676). He notes particularly red, yellow, and blue colors but says little concerning what these colors may signify. In his opinion, however, yellow correlates with the sun and with "good" (1929: 154, 155), while gold (as in various golden items) "is the metal of the righteous" (1930: 675–676) and is associated with that which is "God-given" (Howe 1974: 117). Red and also black are said simply to associate with "evil" (Nordenskiöld 1929: 150).

It is interesting that the color black, which Oviedo cites as body paint in conjunction with red among sixteenth-century Panamanians, was used mainly by those Panamanian warriors who had killed an enemy, according to Wafer (1934: 79). Both death and the concept of enemy can be interpreted as involving negative, destructive, "evil" aspects of cosmic energy, which, as we have seen, contains a fundamental creative-destructive duality and ambiguity. Conceivably, too, the ancient Panamanian use of red and black coloration for body paint, as well as the red and black paint used in contemporary Cuna girls' puberty rites, expressed not simply "evil" but this dualism and ambiguity in life processes. Among the Desana red and black colors are taken to represent the dynamics of life and particularly the theme of fertility, sexuality, and regeneration (Reichel-Dolmatoff 1971: 144, 163). The Tchikrin of central Brazil employ red and black body paint to express health, vitality, and sensitivity (red), on the one hand, and, on the other, the need to "socialize" or control this essential life energy so that it does not erupt in undirected chaos (black) (Turner 1969: 70).

The use of red with black as a decorative-symbolic motif by ancient Panamanians is also known to us from the polychrome ceramics for which the isthmus is famous. Panamanian polychromes as known, for example, from the Sitio Conte (Lothrop 1942*a*), Chiriquí (Holmes 1888; MacCurdy 1911), and related areas (Ladd 1964; Lothrop 1950; Baudez 1963: 47, 48) show great diversity of form and decorative motifs (see Linares 1977*b*), but these are predominantly painted in red and black, applied as black-on-red, red-on-black, red and black on light or dark buff or cream backgrounds, or black on buff with red interior, sometimes with purple as an auxiliary color (Mahler 1961; Ladd 1964; Lothrop 1942*a*: 13; Haberland 1957). Almost surely this pairing of red and black was not accidental but was meaning-

Fig. 14. Polychrome ceramics from the Sitio Conte. (From S. K. Lothrop, *Pre-Columbian Designs from Panama: 591 Illustrations of Coclé Pottery*, Dover Publications, 1976, p. 51)

ful within a symbolic context. In light of the foregoing discussion, the combination may be tentatively interpreted as symbolic of the dynamics and renewal of life.

Crocodilians and Iguanas

In another attempt to delve into the significance of ancient Panamanian sacred prestige symbols, I should like to briefly consider the so-called alligator or crocodile god, sometimes also known as the crested crocodile or crested dragon, one of the most commonly portrayed iconographic motifs found on Panamanian goldwork and polychrome ceramics. This creature was first identified as a crocodilian by Holmes (1888). His interpretation was refined somewhat by MacCurdy (1908, 1911) and then elaborated upon by Lothrop (1937: 115, 174, and 1942*a*: 17–18), whose excavations at the Sitio Conte yielded numerous polychrome ceramics and richly embossed gold pieces bearing images of the reptile in question.

The so-called crocodile god or crested crocodile is one of a number of zoological forms which appear on ancient Panamanian gold pieces and ceramics. If ethnographic analogy be taken once again as guide, it can be assumed that these forms carried significant symbolic meaning within the mythological and cosmological systems to which the pre-Columbian Panamanians subscribed. In another essay (Helms 1977), I have analyzed at length the so-called crocodile god and crested crocodile motifs in light of ethnographic, mythological, and zoological evidence that suggests they do not depict crocodilians but lizards, specifically iguanas. I also have argued for an association between iguanas, solar forms of "cosmic energy," and chiefship. The general thrust of my argument is briefly summarized here.

The mythology of native peoples of tropical America generally portrays the lizard, or iguana, in a variety of roles, but frequently in association with culture heroes, often as a food for the hero (see Lévi-Strauss 1969: 36, 200). Iguana is also specifically associated with the celestial realm, particularly the sun (cf. Thompson 1970: chap. 7). Sometimes, for example, the sun's rays, that is, its active energy, are derived from iguana attributes, especially its "beard" or dewlap and tongue (see Stone 1962: 66). Iguana may also be associated with themes concerning the need to control the energies and strengths of the "natural" world (as expressed symbolically in food and sex) lest they become disruptive to ordered social or "human" life (see Lévi-Strauss 1973: 139–145 and 1969: 124). This symbolism stands in marked contrast with that accorded the "crocodile," more accurately the caiman, which is associated with terrestrial waters and the underworld. It is also interesting to find that the caiman sometimes appears as an aquatic guise of the lizard (see Lévi-Strauss 1969: 200).

Given this general background, let us briefly consider three myths of the San Blas Cuna in which iguanas and crocodilians feature prominently. These tales, in addition, cast new light upon the qualities and activities expected of elite leaders. The three myths—the Origins of Fire myth, the tale of Evil Ibelele, and the tale of the Iguana-Chief—are recorded in their entirety in Chapin's excellent compendium (1970). A brief paraphrase of these tales is presented in the Appendix, and select points relevant to iconographic interpretations are discussed here.

The Origins of Fire tale (Chapin 1970: 32; Wassén 1937: 27–29) recounts how, long ago, before animals and humans were differentiated, a small iguana, or a *borriguero* in Panamanian Spanish idiom (see Alonso 1958: 752; Robe 1960: 32, 93), was ordered by Tad Ibe, the sun-related culture hero, to steal fire from Jaguar, a strong animal-man who was greatly feared by other animal humans and who lived on the other side of the river. One rainy night Iguana, who was able to cross the storm-swollen river, went to Jaguar's camp and by trickery and deception succeeded in stealing coals from Jaguar's fire while Jaguar slept. Hiding the vital coals in the crest on the back of his neck, Iguana carried them safely across the raging river, which Jaguar, who couldn't swim, was not able to cross. Iguana gave the precious coals to Tad Ibe, who then distributed fire to the people.

In Lévi-Straussian metaphorical terms the iguana's crest, in which fire could be carried, and his water-crossing ability, which conveyed fire from Jaguar to Man, appear as major characteristics of this lizard and signify the mythological origins of cultured, ordered, "human," or "civilized," life, which is also identified by cooking fire (see Lévi-Strauss 1969). I further suggest that the iguana's river-crossing ability may also associate this reptile with chiefship, for one of the several metaphors used by the Cuna to express the role and significance of the chief compares chiefship with rivers, specifically (as in the myth) with stormy swollen rivers.[14]

In zoological terms the reptile's crest and his water-crossing ability readily describe iguanas of the genus *Basiliscus*, which range in Central America and northern South America. The adult males of the five species of *Basiliscus* are characterized by conspicuous crests on the head and, in some cases, on the back and tail. These small (10–

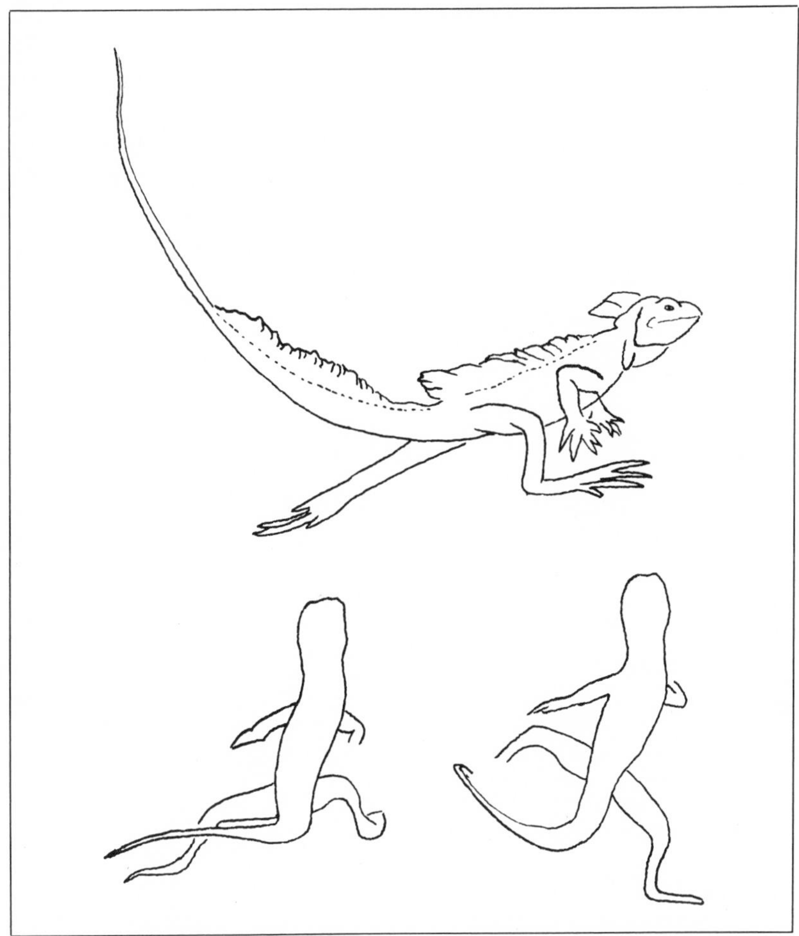

Fig. 15. Bipedal running in basilisk iguanas. (After fig. 20 in *The Life of Reptiles*, vol. 1, by Angus Bellairs, Universe Books, New York, and George Weidenfeld & Nicolson Ltd, London, 1970; by permission of Universe Books and George Weidenfeld & Nicolson Ltd)

20 cm), dark lizards are associated with human life in that they find shelter and food as a "commensal animal" (along with rats, roaches, other lizards, flies, and the like) in Cuna homes on the mainland (Bennett 1962: 37), although they more properly frequent the forest edge near streams and rivers or may be observed on the seashore. *Basiliscus* lizards are also able to rise to a semierect bipedal posture,

Fig. 16. "Crested Dragon" motif as depicted on an embossed gold plaque from the Sitio Conte. (After S. K. Lothrop, ed., *Essays in Pre-Columbian Art and Archaeology*, 1961, p. 261; by permission of Harvard University Press; copyright © 1961 by the President and Fellows of Harvard College)

and several species have been observed to run with a fast, waddling bipedal gait across the surface of water for distances of a few yards (Fig. 15) (Maturana 1962: 16–18, 22; Bellairs 1970: 73–74; Schmidt and Inger 1957: 76, 113; Mac Chapin confirms by personal communication that a *borriguero* is in fact a basilisk iguana). In addition, I believe it possible that the lively creature shown in Figure 16, which derives from a pre-Columbian gold plaque, also denotes a *Basiliscus*, as evidenced by the bipedal posture and conspicuous head crest, among other identifying characteristics.

Before assessing Figure 16 in detail, however, let us briefly consider the major points of the Evil Ibelele tale and the tale of the Iguana-Chief (Chapin 1970: 23–28). In both stories Tad Ibe faces a powerful opponent whom he eventually defeats just as in the Origins of Fire tale Iguana faced powerful Jaguar and broke Jaguar's power by stealing his fire. In the Evil Ibelele tale, Evil Ibelele, the chief of evil spirits (apparently a negative version of Tad Ibe, who is sometimes also called Ibelele but who is a power for good), is approached by Tad Ibe in the manner of a potential son-in-law offering his services to his father-in-law in return for a wife. Evil Ibelele (acting as would any potential Cuna father-in-law) then challenges Tad Ibe to show his capabilities as a cultivator and as a hunter and in the process attempts to destroy Tad Ibe. By virtue of his great mystical power acquired by powerful plant medicines, the celestial hero is able to escape unharmed and instead destroys his evil opponent. Evil Ibelele's remains are then thrown into the river, where he is transformed into a caiman (*taim*) that will carry evil spirits, that is, illness, from the underworld to plague man. Evil Ibelele's wife and daughters are also destroyed and transformed into smaller varieties of caimans.

When, in the tale of the Iguana-Chief, Tad Ibe faces another powerful opponent, the circumstances are somewhat different. Tad Ibe approaches Iguana-Chief, not as a potential son-in-law, but with pomp and ceremony as a chiefly rival. The two then engage in a series of challenges to see who can swim farthest underwater, who can survive a jump from a high cliff, who can withstand the most physical pain, and who has the "longest" nose, that is, who is most moral (see Holloman 1969: 92). In these contests Iguana-Chief clearly exhibits the greater physical strength, while Tad Ibe can hold his position only with the aid of various forms of trickery and deceit. For example, after his swim, Tad Ibe runs along the bank a bit farther to seemingly increase the distance he swam; when cliff jumping he arranges to have his fall broken by a soft cushion of cotton; and when testing pain endurance he cheats so that he feels nothing. Finally, Tad Ibe kills Iguana-Chief (during the morality test), again by means of a deception, and transforms him into an edible iguana (*ari*) that henceforth will serve as food for man. Iguana-Chief's sons are similarly transformed into small lizards.

The Evil Ibelele tale clearly associates the aquatic *caiman* with *evil* forces and with *female* themes (wife and daughters; father-in-law and son-in-law), while the Iguana-Chief tale associates the edible land *iguana* with *physical strength* and with *male* themes (sons; chiefly competition). These two tales also identify "evil," such as illness (personified by Evil Ibelele), and sheer physical strength (personified by Iguana-Chief) as potentially dangerous natural elements or energies that must be controlled ("defeated") by a beneficial force (solar-related Tad Ibe) for human good. This vital control, in turn, is effected by *mystical strength and power*, as developed by herbal "medicines," which defeats immaterial evils, particularly illness, and by *the use of the intellect,* or "out-thinking," shown in the tales as deception and trickery, as a foil to sheer physical strength or energies. These two capabilities—to establish mystical or supernatural powers and to develop the powers of the intellect—can be identified further as those qualities peculiar to man as a controlling element and as those qualities that (like cooking fire) set man apart from the natural, or uncontrolled, world and give him the means to live a more controlled, that is, ordered or moral, life.

In the Cuna myths, as Table 3 summarizes, these unique abilities are held either by the celestially related hero Tad Ibe (in the Iguana-Chief and Evil Ibelele tales) or by the *borriguero,* or basilisk iguana (in the Origins of Fire tale), who tricked ("out-thought") Jaguar out of fire. In Cuna society intellect and mystical strength, identified by the concepts of *kurgin* and *purba,* are thought to obtain most strongly among the highest chiefs and highest religious leaders, or *neles* (sometimes spelled *leles,* that is, "those who know"; note the etymology of Ibe/lele, another name for Tad Ibe), and among the shaman-curers. In the next chapter I shall argue that the sacred-secular leadership of ancient Panamanian chiefdoms, which included priest-chiefs and shaman-curers, probably also emphasized the development of knowledge and wisdom and the use of the supernatural (curative) powers of various floral "medicines" as the hallmarks of their respective roles.

Returning to iconography, I have suggested on the basis of these mythological and zoological grounds, which are considered in much more detail elsewhere (Helms 1977), that the so-called crested crocodile or crested dragon, which is very commonly portrayed in various stylistic forms in ancient Panamanian art (see Fig. 16), may represent the basilisk iguana, who in Cuna mythology obtained the all-important cooking fire, which transformed the mythological ancestors of the Cuna from "natural" beings to "civilized" members of human society. This same iguana image, I propose, also symbolized the chiefly leaders of ancient Panama who, like the mythical Tad Ibe and like Cuna leaders today, were responsible for maintaining or controlling the "civilized," "moral," ordered life style of their followers. Consequently, I propose that iguanas are portrayed on at least some of the golden helmets, chest plates, greaves, and other golden ornaments worn by ancient leaders in life and in death.

A common mode of iconographic depiction shows an anthropomorphic being with two animals hanging from his waist, as shown in Figure 17. Lothrop has described the central figure of this image

Table 3. Structural Comparison of Three Cuna Myths

Origins of Fire Tale	*Evil Ibelele Tale*	*Iguana-Chief Tale*
Jaguar (physical strength of nature)	Evil Ibelele (evil spirits)	Iguana-Chief (physical strength of nature)
Defeated by (loses fire to)	Defeated by	Defeated by
Tricky basilisk Iguana	Mystically powerful sun hero (Tad Ibe) (as potential son-in-law)	Tricky sun hero (Tad Ibe) (as chiefly rival)
Who brings cultured life (cooking fire) to man	Who brings powerful medicine to control illness to man	Who brings intellect to man to control brute force
And leaves Jaguar in natural state	And changes Evil Ibelele into caiman (wife and daughters changed into caimans, too)	And changes Iguana-Chief into edible iguana (sons changed into small lizards)

Fig. 17. Motif depicted on embossed gold plaque from the Sitio Conte. (After S. K. Lothrop, *Treasures of Ancient America*, Skira, 1964, p. 143; from the Collections of the University Museum, Philadelphia)

as an anthropomorphized crocodile god and considers the waist- (or belt-) dependent animals to be smaller repetitions of the crocodile motif (1937: 125, 142). I suggest instead that we may see here a celestial figure, such as Tad Ibe, with edible iguanas (that is, conquered transformations of Iguana-Chief) hanging from his waist—a depiction indicating basically the manly triumph of intellect and morality over the physical, or natural, world.[15] Such golden imagery adorning the head or chest of a *queví* readily identified the ruler as the source of great knowledge and wisdom (*kurgin*), as the guardian of ordered, or moral, human social life, and as the embodiment of the powerful (wise, moral) celestial being himself (cf. Eliáde 1959: 157).

To be sure, since Tad Ibe also triumphed over caiman (Evil Ibelele) and since control of evil (which caiman connotes in this context) is a major task of human society, it could be argued that Lothrop's crocodile identification is equally valid, at least in terms of mythic evidence. However, I think there are at least two lines of argument that make this unlikely. First, the Cuna myths make clear that caimans and "evil" also carry female associations, while a distinct (although not unrelated) realm of physical strength and rivalry is associated with maleness and with the iguana.[16] I am further assuming that male-related symbols would be most likely to appear on the attire of the (male) rulership. Second, zoological features consistent with an identification of iguanids rather than crocodilians can be seen in the iconography.

The most significant zoological trait is found in the dentition of the belt-dependent animals as portrayed in Figure 17.[17] Dentition is not casually portrayed in the iconography of native America, as the persistent use of overlapping canines to depict feline themes, the appearance of curved fangs to represent the serpent, and the uniquely visible upper tooth row of the caiman indicate (see Coe 1965: 757; Rowe 1967; Clewlow 1974: 13, 95; Reichel-Dolmatoff 1972*b*: 52; Kan 1972: 70–73, 84; Lathrap 1973*a*: 95; Caso 1961: 169). With respect to Figure 17, Lothrop considers the rectangular tooth pattern depicted on the central image as evidence of the anthropomorphic quality of this personage. Similarly, the distinctive multicusped side teeth and peglike front teeth of the belt-dependent creatures in Figure 17 may be strong clues to the animals' identity. This tooth pattern is not at all characteristic of crocodilians, whose dentition is entirely conical or peglike. It is distinctive of certain New World lizard families, including the Iguanidae, which have conical anterior teeth but whose

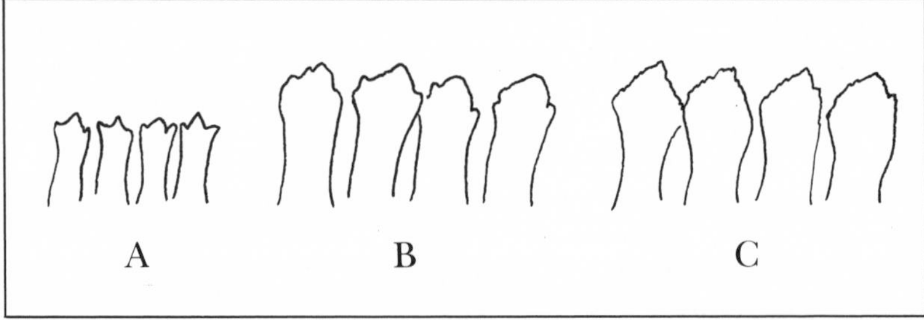

Fig. 18. Comparative dentition in three iguanid lizards: *A – Basiliscus; B – Ctenosaura; C – Iguana.* (After R. R. Montanucci, "Comparative Dentition in Four Iguanid Lizards," *Herpetologica*, vol. 24, 1968, fig. 2.)

maxillary teeth show varying degrees of cuspidation, depending on the species (see Montanucci 1968; Schmidt and Inger 1957: 96, 137; Bellairs 1970: 172, 173). Figure 18 from Montanucci illustrates this dental pattern in four genera of iguanids, three of which (*Iguana iguana, Ctenosaura,* and *Basiliscus*) occur in Panama. (The fourth occurs in Michoacán.) Although it may be fortuitous, the cusp pattern evidenced in the belt-dependent creatures in Figure 17 corresponds most closely with that of *Basiliscus.*

Another iguanid characteristic seen on the belt lizards in Figure 17 is the thick, rounded, protruding tongue. It may be quite significant in this context that, according to Lévi-Strauss (1973: 228), native people of Amazonia believe that the caiman does not have a tongue (see also Ruiz Blanco 1892: 19). Natives of Yucatán apparently held a similar opinion (Tozzer 1941: 192 n. 1017). In fact, in several myths from tropical America, including one from the Talamancan groups of Costa Rica, we learn how the crocodilian lost his tongue (Lévi-Strauss 1973: 228–229; Stone 1962: 66). Following the gist of the discussion by Seeger (1975) concerning the symbolic significance of parts of the body, the portrayal of tongued as opposed to tongueless creatures in iconography might be construed as indicative of those who orate or "speak for the public benefit" as opposed to those who do not, that is, as indicative of social leaders (men; elite chiefs) as opposed to those who follow (women and children; commoners). Although in zoological reality crocodilians do have tongues, given the mythic context in which crocodilians appear in Cuna tales and in other tales of tropical America, I would not expect crocodilians to appear iconographically with tongues, for

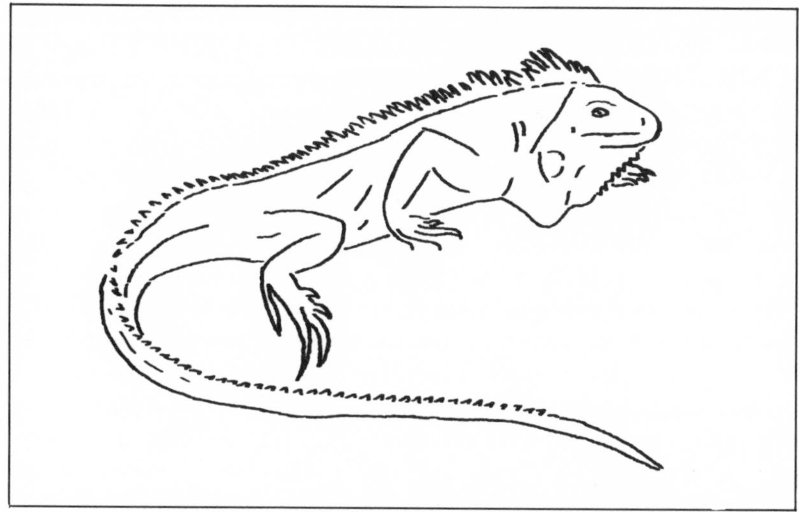

Fig. 19. *Iguana iguana.* (From *The Life of Vertebrates,* 2d. ed., 1962, fig. 233, by J. Z. Young, published by Oxford University Press; by permission of Oxford University Press)

these reptiles generally correlate either with female themes or with antisocial themes. Conversely, animals associated with chiefship could readily be expected to be iconographically depicted as tongued (or, if the form is human, with "speech scrolls").[18]

In addition to dental pattern and tongue, the long, tapering tail, used very conspicuously in iguanid locomotion and defense, may be a relevant iguana "marker" in Figure 17 (Schmidt and Inger 1957: 113). So, too, may be the row of protruding spines shown on the tail on the belt lizards in this figure (in some depictions also on the back). Lothrop considered these spines to be crocodile scales, but they could also signify the row of back and tail spines characteristic of *Iguana iguana* (see Fig. 19). The small head crest that appears on the belt lizards of Figure 7 is also another possible iguana characteristic relating to the proposed "crested iguana" shown in Figure 16.

These arguments present some of the data that lead me to suggest that one of the most significant symbols, and a very frequently depicted iconographic motif, of the elite of ancient Panama was the "Iguana," perhaps a compound figure identifiable zoologically with both the genus *Basiliscus* and the edible *Iguana iguana.* If the Cuna myths be taken as a guide, Iguana in this context was metaphor for the mythological celestial culture hero in his competition with, and conquest of, the physical, or natural, world by means of knowledge and the intellect.[19] Iguana thus also served as "model for" symbolically comparable chiefly activities, including admonishing oratory and competitive rivalries between *quevís* who sought to defeat each other in physical battle or *krun*-like displays.

I also propose that pre-Columbian chiefs competed in terms of intellect and knowledge itself, particularly knowledge of distant peoples, places, and things; but before moving into this topic, one additional point should be made regarding the iguana as a chiefly symbol. So far as I am aware, ethnographic materials relating to the contemporary San Blas Cuna do not give clear evidence outside of myth of either the recognition of the iguana as a sacred symbol or the use of species of iguana in public ceremonies, although the iguana is a basic subsistence item (Bennett 1962: 42, 47; Bell 1910: 629). Since much of the Cuna elite subculture pattern has been either lost or greatly attenuated in the centuries following European contact, the recognition and utilization of the iguana as elite symbol or metaphor might be expected to decline or even totally disappear. Such, for example, seems to have been the fate of Itzam Na, the all-pervasive Iguana deity that, if Thompson's argument is correct, was the ultimate symbol of supremacy among the elite of the Classic Maya but is absent from the folk beliefs of the Maya peasantry today (see Thompson 1970: chap. 7).

It is interesting to note in this respect, however, that various crocodilians, particularly large and small varieties of caiman, are amply attested to in contemporary Cuna thought, not only in myth but also in curing chants. I would suggest that, while the iguana was part of the "Great Tradition" of the ancient rulership, crocodilians were—and still are—more broadly regarded within the commoners' "Little Tradition."[20] It is as part of this belief sphere and particularly within the context of illness and of female themes, including childbirth (see Helms 1977 for details), that crocodilians have survived in Cuna traditions while the iguana may have suffered the same decline as the traditional elite it symbolized.

4

Ideology and Exchange

Ritual, Tobacco, and Trance

One of the major tenets of this analysis of ancient Panamanian political life holds that attempts by the high elite to ritually contact the distant supernatural were activities of essentially the same magnitude and significance as long-distance exchange. A second hypothesis states that both areas of chiefly activity were pursued to effect the same goals: that is, to demonstrate chiefly efficacy in the *pursuit of esoteric knowledge* so as to extend the range of the chiefly sphere of influence, out-maneuver elite rivals, and maintain the volunteered support of the populace at large.

In Chapter 2 some of the regional fields of influence that may have emerged in Panama as a result of long-distance exchange contacts were identified, and the significance of scarce goods and the importance of the active circulation of such goods were considered. In Chapter 3 some of the symbolic content of chiefly sumptuary items and of the ornamentation worn by the populace were discussed. It was also argued that some of these goods, such as elaborate gold pieces, were acquired by means of regional and long-distance exchange contacts. This chapter considers the nature of long-distance contacts that the elite sought to establish, not with geographically distant places but with supernaturally distant realms. In later pages I shall argue that, in fact, the geographically distant and the supernaturally distant were closely related, and that this association was succinctly stated by the acquisition from distant geographical regions of elite prestige items with sacred significance. First, however, let us establish as best we can the nature of the supernatural realm and consider the means by which ancient Panamanian elite rulers may have contacted this sphere.

Brief statements relating directly to religious ritual and to religious functionaries are found in Andagoya's *Narrative* (1865) and in Oviedo's *Natural History* (1959) and *Historia general* (1853). These accounts identify special, chosen men, greatly feared and respected, called *tecuria* or *tequina* (a word meaning "master"), who were in charge of "communications and intelligence with the devil," a being called Tuira. The religious functionary entered a small doorless hut or enclosure open to the sky, called a *surba* (*surpa*) by Cuna today, to speak with the deity. He received information from the supernatural contact regarding the proper course of events and predictions for the future, which he revealed to the *quevi* and to the people. The *tequina*'s powers also included control of the weather and of food productivity (Oviedo 1959: 33–34, and 1853: bk. 29, chap. 26, pp. 125–126, 127; Andagoya 1865: 14; see also Salcedo 1908: 88; Cooper 1949: 594).[1]

A century or so after initial Spanish contact, a native prognostication session was held to assist Lionel Wafer and his companions during their sojourn in Darién. Concerned with rescue, Wafer's party wished to know when ships might be expected. The Indians

> told us they knew not, but would enquire; and therefore they sent for one of their Conjurers, who immediately went to work to raise the Devil, to enquire of him at what time a Ship would arrive here; for they are very expert and skilful in their sort of Diabolical Conjurations. We were in the House with them, and they first began to work with making a Partition with Hammocks, that the *Pawawers*, for so they call these Conjurers, might be by themselves. They continued some time at their Exercise, and we could hear them make most hideous Yellings and Shrieks; imitating the Voices of all their kind of Birds and Beasts. With their own Noise, they join'd that of several Stones struck together, and of Conch-shells, and of a sorry sort of Drums made of hollow Bamboes, which they beat upon; making a jarring Noise also with Strings fasten'd to the larger Bones of Beasts: And every now and then they would make a dreadful Exclamation, and clattering all of a sudden, would as suddenly make a Pause

> and a profound Silence. But finding that after a considerable Time no Answer was made them, they concluded that 'twas because we were in the House, and so turn'd us out, and went to Work again. . . . after a little time, they came out with their Answer. (Wafer 1903: 60–62)[2]

Oviedo also states that "in certain places"[3] sacrifices were made of blood and human lives or, elsewhere, of aromatic smoke. He further indicates that when the supernatural "devil" appeared to and spoke with the *tequina* he assumed a variety of forms and colors, which were depicted in figures of gold relief and were carved on wood (Oviedo 1853: bk. 29, chap. 31, p. 155, and 1959: 37; see also Salcedo 1908: 90).[4]

The wording of the Hispanic accounts suggests that the *tequina,* or *tecuria,* was distinct from the *queví.*[5] However, an observer of Wafer's day refers to a native chief or "clan leader" who was also an "Indian clergyman" (Wafer 1934: lvii n. 2). In Alphonse's twentieth-century account of the Guaymí, the *sukya* or "medicine person is always the first born of his family. He is supposed to be endowed with special spiritual favor and the power to heal" (1956: 122). Sherzer notes that sacred-secular leaders of the contemporary Cuna may fill several roles as chief and as one or more chanters of sacred texts, but that these roles are always kept separate and do not coalesce into a single multifaceted position. They do add to the prestige of the individual, however, and may be an important factor in status competition (1974: 280–281, 464, n. 29).

Andagoya further indicates, and Oviedo implies, that a second category of religious curers was recognized in ancient Panama. Shaman-curers were men with great knowledge of herbs appropriate for various illnesses who also utilized contacts with the "devil" to aid in effecting cures (Andagoya 1865: 14; Oviedo 1853: bk. 29, chap. 26, pp. 125–126; see also Salcedo 1908: 90, 134–135; Stout 1947: 101). Regrettably, nothing more has been recorded concerning the activities of these persons.

It is particularly unfortunate that we lack primary data concerning how *tequinas* and shaman-curers contacted the supernatural powers with whom they "spoke." However, several possibilities can be suggested via ethnographic analogy. Among the indigenous societies of tropical America, contact between man and the supernatural is frequently effected by way of trance produced with the aid of various narcotic or hallucinogenic agents, including (among others) mushrooms, morning glories, coca, tobacco snuff or juice, *Banisteriopsis,*

Anadenanthera, and *Datura* (see Reichel-Dolmatoff 1971 and 1975; Harner 1973; Furst 1968, 1972, 1974, and 1976; Whitten 1976; Benson 1972: Wassén and Holmstedt 1963: Cooper 1949). Conceivably, the same held true for ancient Panama, although no hallucinogenic agent is clearly designated in the sixteenth-century literature. Ancient Panamanians, however, did utilize chicha and also tobacco.

Tobacco may have been the unidentified herb chewed mixed with lime or ashes, although coca may have been the herb in question (see Colón 1959: 252–253; Lothrop 1950: 51 and 1973: 17; Thompson 1970: 110–112; Furst 1976: 29). Tobacco was definitely smoked. Wafer recounts how, at large gatherings of as many as two or three hundred persons, the lighted end of a very long (two or three feet), very thick ("as big as ones Wrist") cigar was placed into the mouth of a boy, who then puffed the smoke through the length of the tobacco roll into the faces of those assembled, who funneled their hands around mouth and nose to receive the smoke (1934: 63; see Fig. 20). Smoke probably served as a means of contacting the supernatural, for the use of tobacco smoke in a magico-religious context was a widespread and probably very ancient practice in Middle and South America (Cooper 1949: 27, 535; Lévi-Strauss 1973: 368, 260, 65, 43; Wilbert 1975; Mendoza 1956; Furst 1976: 23–32). According to Fray Adrian's seventeenth-century account of isthmian conditions, the supernatural forces enjoyed the smell of tobacco smoke and were thereby coaxed into benevolence (Salcedo 1908: 130). The contemporary Cuna clarify this statement by saying that smoke is the "chicha" of the spirits, and that it is by "intoxicating" them with smoke that they may be controlled (Howe 1976: 73–74; cf. Wilbert 1972).

The "intoxicating" properties of tobacco smoke raise the question of whether tobacco was used as a trance-inducing agent by sacred specialists in the privacy of the *surbas* where they "spoke with the devil." Although tobacco is not, strictly speaking, a hallucinogen, trance and visions can be achieved by swallowing the smoke; by intensive, rapid, and long-continued smoking; by swallowing the juice; by snuffing; and by drinking tobacco water (Cooper 1949: 534; see also Wassén and Holmstedt 1963). Native peoples of the Americas have utilized tobacco widely in this context, and it is clear that tobacco is a vehicle for shamanic ecstasy (see Janiger and Dobkin de Rios 1973; Wilbert 1972 and 1975; LaBarre 1972: 275–276; Furst 1976: 23–32; Wagley 1943; Weiss 1973: 43; Harner 1968: 25; Dole in Bourguignon 1974: 9).

Fig. 20. Cuna men smoking tobacco in council. (From Lionel Wafer, *A New Voyage and Description of the Isthmus of America,* 1934 ed., p. 102)

In some cases the narcotic state achieved via tobacco is a preliminary or preconditioning stage for further shamanistic activities that entail use of other hallucinogenic agents, such as *Banisteriopsis* (see Weiss 1973: 43; Harner 1968: 5; Dobkin de Rios 1973). Conceivably, additional narcotic or hallucinogenic agents were similarly employed by ancient Panamanian *tequinas, quevís,* and shaman-curers after preliminary preparation with tobacco. Indeed, since there is evidence for the use of various hallucinogens in neighboring pre-Columbian Colombia and Costa Rica, it is quite possible that trance-producing substances other than tobacco smoke were utilized by the high priests and chiefs of ancient Panama (Reichel-Dolmatoff 1972*c*: 107; Cooper 1949: 536, 555; Furst 1974: 63, 75, 77; Cieza de León 1864: 39–40, 71–72; Stone 1958: 16, 25, and 1977: 158–159; Furst 1968: 345–346; Wassén and Holmstedt 1963: 17, 23–24; Duque Gómez 1965: 396).

Ethnographic data concerning contemporary natives of Panama may help to clarify this question. There is no record of the use of narcotics or hallucinogens among twentieth-century Guaymí or Cuna. During some Cuna curing ceremonies and at Cuna girls' puberty rites, however, tobacco is smoked in pipes or as long cigars, and cacao beans and hot peppers may be burned in braziers to produce smoke reported to be protective and beneficial to those involved in the ceremony (Stout 1947: 35–36, 45–46, 93). More specifically, the smoke is said to facilitate the conquest of evil spirits either by soothing them (cacao smoke) or by irritating them (pepper smoke) so as to drive them away (Howe 1976; Holloman 1969: 100; see also Holmer 1951: 21; Bell 1910: 628; Chapin 1970: 13).[6] Moreover, speaking of a group ritual known as the Nek apsoket, which rids communities of oppressive spirits by ritually "intoxicating" the spirits with smoke (the spirits' "chicha") and which requires heavy smoking of tobacco by the participants under ritual conditions for eight consecutive evenings, Howe says, "It appears very likely . . . that the great amount of smoking involved results in altered physiological and psychological states which contribute to the work of the ritual. The Cuna in fact may be a little intoxicated while they are trying to get the spirits drunk" (1976: 9).

Intoxication by one means or another may indeed be a crucial element in the ritual. Among native peoples of Middle and South America in general, fermentation is considered a supernatural phenomenon and extensive group drinking bouts of a social-sacred nature are common (Cooper 1949: 544; McKim 1947: 87; Karsten

1926: 80; Lévi-Strauss 1973: 145–148, 150). During such sprees, which may last from several hours to several days, "the participants imbibe until they reach various stages of intoxication, from mild tipsiness to complete alcoholic coma" (Cooper 1949: 54). Lévi-Strauss, discussing a Cuna shaman's technique for assisting difficult childbirth in Panama, mentions that the officiating shaman calls upon "spirits of intoxicating drinks" for help (1967: 188). Chicha is also an important ritual product for the important girls' puberty rites (Kramer 1970: 85; Stout 1947: 93–95). Intoxication is also mentioned in ritual context by earlier observers of native Panama. Wafer, for example, vividly describes heavy ceremonial drinking where participating men imbibed to the point of unconsciousness (1934: 157, 159; see also Salcedo 1908: 130), and Oviedo mentions drinking and dancing sessions of social-ceremonial significance (1853: bk. 29, chap. 28, p. 137, and 1959: 38). Since both heavy ceremonial drinking and inhaling or ingesting of tobacco smoke are documented for ancient Panamanians, it is conceivable that this combination was the means by which communication with spiritual forces was achieved.[7]

Cuna myths are another source of evidence suggesting that trance was utilized by ancient Panamanian religious leaders. Tales and legends recorded by Wassén (1938: 74–75, 80–88, and 1952), Nordenskiöld (1938: 145, 157ff.), and Chapin (1970) refer frequently to journeys made by former religious seers to the heavens or to the underworld, sometimes in company with their wives or assistants. In contrast, the religious seers of the present, termed *neles* by the Cuna, are said to confine their clairvoyant powers to dreaming (Wassén 1938: 76; see also Kramer 1970: 78–80). Nordenskiöld states the matter in somewhat different terms (1931: 466–467, and 1938: 84–89). *Neles,* he notes, pay visits to the extraordinary or nether world, which contains several levels or layers (see Fig. 21). It is believed that the *neles* of the present, however, cannot penetrate into as many levels or layers of the nether world as could the great religious specialists of the past (a past that, it must be noted, can be interpreted as mythological, or as historical, or as a combination of both). Similarly, Holmer records the Cuna belief that in "ancient" times the *neles* could "directly" visit the animal or spirit "owners" (*dueños*) who lived in certain spirit abodes (*kalus*) in the mountains where they directed the quantity of game animals that would be released from these spirit homes to the earthly world of the hunter (1951: 29). Now, the *nele* still visits the *kalu,* but in his dreams (see Reichel-Dolmatoff 1971: 80). Again in contrast with contemporary *neles,* the ancient *neles* could control the weather, could make their deer-bone-handled rattles vibrate by themselves, and could summon such wild animals as jaguars, caimans, and peccaries at will (cf. Wafer's account of a shamanic performance quoted above).

Wassén describes a demonstration by one of the last of the great *neles* of the past (1938: 76–77). Pertinent sections are quoted here (again cf. Wafer's seventeenth-century account).

> [The people] built a *surba* for [the *nele,* who] said . . . that no one should talk or disturb him while he sang, noisy people could absolutely not come into the hut, only serious people. During the incantation, people smoked. One held a roll of tobacco which was burning and another blew the smoke in his nose. All were supposed to smoke. They even smoked pipes and burned cocoa-beans. None of this was to be left out. *Without this smoking the demons would not be able to come.* . . . [The *nele*] had an *absogedi* (medicine man) with him in the *surba.* Suddenly the rattle began to sound. [The *nele*] had placed it in a clay dish and it began to rattle of itself. After a while the grunting of the peccaries could be heard and after this the roar of the jaguars, the sounds from many kinds of birds and finally the voices of the evil spirits, but one could not understand what they said *as they spoke a special language.* Suddenly there was heard a very powerful voice which said something like *ya-ye-ya* and the people began to laugh because it sounded like a deaf-mute who was trying to force out some sounds. But when the people laughed the rattle at once fell down and the great *nele* asked why they had laughed, as it was dangerous for him. *They had to begin again with the smoking before the voices of the demons could come again.* This *nele* demonstrated his powers only a single night for the Indians in Narganá. (Wassén 1938: 76–77; lengthy emphases mine)

Wassén's description indicates that inhalation of tobacco smoke, quite possibly to alter the senses, was a crucial preparatory step, at least for the "laymen" observing the demonstration. It does not relate what ensued in the *surba,* or enclosure, in which the *nele* and his assisting *apsogedi* (*apsoket*) were closeted.

A series of myths concerning the origins of useful plants, however, strongly suggest that the *nele* entered a trance. In these tales the paraphernalia required for a trance session are specified, although it is not clear which materials were used by the *nele* himself and which might have been used by onlookers in order to achieve altered states of awareness during which they heard and saw (or thought they did) supernaturally caused events. The myths relate that in preparation for journeys to places in the "other" world where various useful plants could be acquired for the benefit of their people the great *neles* and their assistants (*apsogedi* or *apsoket*) "chose a man to make [long tobacco], a hunter was chosen to kill the [deer] and finally an old woman to make a[n] . . . earthenware plate. When all this was ready they made a *surpa*, and the *nele* . . . went into the *surpa* with the *apsoket*." The *nele* began to sing, answered by the *apsoket*, who sang a lengthy song, the gourd rattle began to move and rattle by itself, and a wind arose from the rattle. "Now the soul of [the] *nele* and the *apsoket* went away" (Hayans 1952: 91, 92, 93). In preparing for another such journey, the people again built a *surba* with all the equipment to be used, including "long tobacco," "tobacco fire," a cacao brazier, the *nele*'s gourd, and "medicine stones" (ibid., pp. 90–96; see also Chapin 1970: 61–62).

The most interesting aspect of Hayans' account is the mention of "long tobacco" and "tobacco fire." "Long tobacco" (*warsuit*) probably was used for "smoking" *surba* observers in the manner discussed previously. Does "tobacco fire" (*walso* or *warso*), however, refer to another use of tobacco, perhaps as a hallucinatory juice or snuff ingested by the *nele* and his assistant to effect direct contact with the supernatural? A tale collected by Chapin indirectly suggests that perhaps it does (1970: 13–14).[8] The hero in this myth, which concerns (among other things) the origins of tobacco, traveled to the home of the chief of evil spirits in the fourth level of the underworld. The evil chief gave him calabashes of hot-pepper juice to drink, which he consumed without any trouble, to the surprise of the evil spirit. In his turn, the hero took some of the newly grown tobacco leaves from his pocket, *squeezed them, put them in a calabash,* and gave the juice to the evil chief and his wife *to drink*. Both drank some but suffered a terrible nausea so that they could not empty the calabash. The hero then went to Tad Ibe and told him of the effects of tobacco on the chief of evil spirits, and in this way another "medicine" to combat evil was "discovered." According to Wilbert, ingestion of tobacco juice produces just the effect suffered by the chief of evil spirits and his wife. "Repeated drinking of large doses of tobacco juice or syrup eventually brings on extreme nausea, especially in women," and then produces a comatose state and intense visions (1975: 443–444). In yet another tale we find references to "red" and "white" tobacco as "medicines" for the *nele* (Chapin

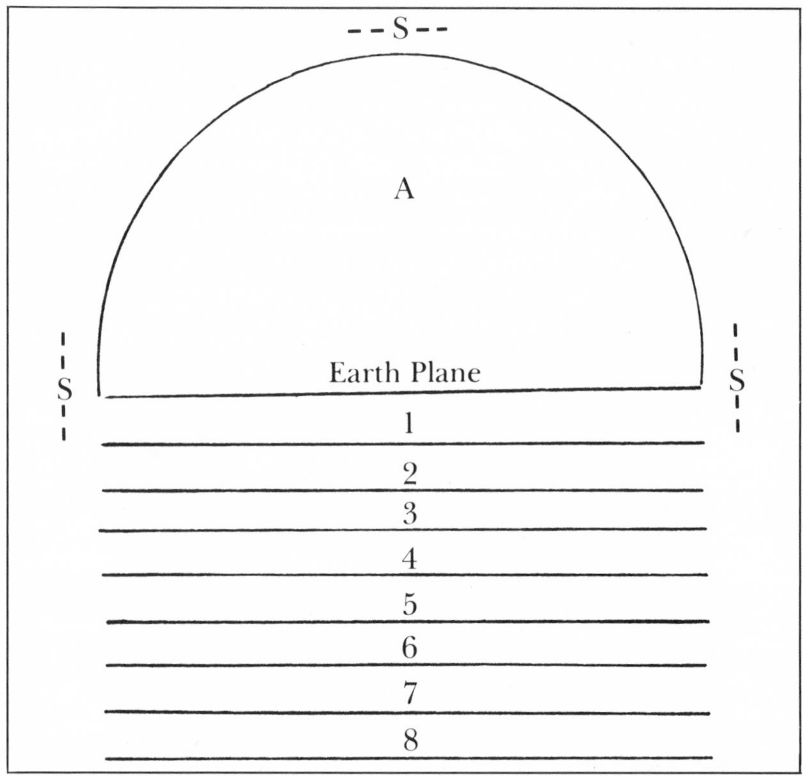

Fig. 21. Cuna concept of the construction of the world according to Pérez. Both heaven and earth are thought to be built up of eight layers. In this sketch the "heavens" (A) above the earth plane contain eight invisible layers. The sun moves around this heaven and goes down under the earth, where there are eight underworld layers. (After E. Nordenskiöld, *An Historical and Ethnological Survey of the Cuna Indians,* Comparative Ethnographical Studies, No. 10, 1938, fig. 22; by permission of the Göteborgs Etnografiska Museum)

1970: 61). This distinction possibly indicates two different varieties or types of tobacco (or of tobacco use), the "red" possibly referring to the tobacco "fire" (juice?) and the "white" to the smoke of the "long" tobacco (cigar) mentioned in Hayans' sources.

In sum, considering these diverse bits of information, it is possible, indeed probable that, in addition to the use of tobacco smoke (perhaps in conjunction with chicha) by peoples of pre-Columbian Panama as a means of achieving altered states of awareness by "intoxication," the sacred elite of these societies in the privacy of the *surba* also ingested another substance, possibly tobacco in the form of a potent juice or a concoction of cacao and chili pepper (see n. 6 above), in order to achieve a hallucinatory trance. By the agency of this trance these specialists in sacred phenomena then "journeyed" into the distant reaches of the underworld or the heavens to mediate on behalf of their human dependents with the good and evil spirits and powers of the universe.[9]

Esoteric Knowledge and the Elite

In considering the significance of gold pieces for pre-Columbian society, an initial distinction was made between the nose pieces and ear pieces worn by all persons, interpreted as indicators of common membership in ordered, human society, and other forms of elaborately crafted gold work, frequently bearing zoomorphic motifs, interpreted as symbolic of sacred-secular power and reserved for use by the elite. These more esoteric gold pieces were construed as ornaments that identified the wearer as one authorized to command, control, and lead the members of the polity because of his particularly close association with supernatural forces of the universe. If ethnographic analogy with Polynesia is considered, this relationship of the *quevís, tequinas,* and shaman-curers with the supernatural was, in turn, an inherent right or prerogative accorded those born to high status who also were thought to inherit great personal potential and mystical powers, that is, great *mana.* However, as with other aspects of the political role, this right or prerogative had to be activated in order to be politically effective.

Data concerning the nature of high political ritual in ancient Panamanian society are woefully insufficient. Yet it is certain that in some manner, probably involving altered states of awareness achieved by trance, ritual not only established contact and communication between supernatural powers of the wider universe and the sacred-secular ruling elite of human society, but also offered verification to the populace at large of the truth of their beliefs and of the legitimacy of their rulers' authority (see Adams 1975: 232–243). I suggest that the fundamental mode of verification evidenced by ritual emphasized the *high degree of esoteric knowledge* controlled by the rulership, that is, knowledge of the meaning of sacred symbols, insights into the "meaning" of life, and understanding of the mystical origins and operations of the cosmos whose creative-destructive energies could be controlled for human use by the application of uniquely human intellect. Whatever other activities were required of the political elite, essentially it was by developing and displaying a store of exceptional knowledge and understanding (that is, by evidencing exceptional intellect) that the *quevís, tequinas,* and shaman-curers of this nonliterate society were able to authenticate and legitimize their positions.

The political significance accorded esoteric knowledge was by no means unique to ancient Panama. Indeed, control in one form or another of "hidden things" is undoubtedly a fundamental criterion for leadership in virtually all societies.[10] In pre-Columbian Mesoamerica, for example, "an ancient Indian text . . . affirms that in Teotihuacan the domains were organized by conferring command upon learned aristocrats—'the wise men, those who know hidden things.' . . . Similarly, Tula and other Nahuatl domains used systems for selecting political leaders that allowed some men to achieve positions of power through demonstrations of their knowledge and ability. The prototype of this kind of leader was the famous Quetzalcoatl, One Reed, Our Prince" (León-Portilla 1960: 9).[11]

Wassén also states the point succinctly when he notes the fundamental importance the contemporary Cuna attribute to knowing things, particularly the origin of things, so as to acquire the use and control of things (1949: 124).[12] More specifically, Stout tells us that chiefs must be very learned in tribal tradition and must possess extensive knowledge of myths and legendary history (1947: 29, 30; see also Wassén 1938: 32–45). In like fashion, Sherzer records that village chiefs must be expert in Cuna political, religious, and historical traditions (1974), while Howe stresses the importance of "the acquisition of knowledge, particularly specialized and secret knowledge," for those who would be leaders (1974: 55).

Exceptional knowledge is also required of Cuna *neles,* the seers or prognosticators who have the ability to look into the past and future and into the "hidden realms" of the present (Howe 1974: 225). *Neles* are men "born to wisdom" who "know things intuitively, and [have] insight into the minds of men" (McKim 1947: 59; see also Stout 1947: 46, 32; Nordenskiöld 1931). The various other types of Cuna shamans and ceremonial leaders who work with pharmaceutical medicine or know various ritual or curing chants (*ikars*) all possess "exceptional" knowledge obtained through lifetimes devoted to perfecting chants and learning about medicines (Stout 1947: 32, 33; see also Nordenskiöld 1938: 80–89).

As we have seen, the Spanish records identify at least two major categories or roles of "knowledgeable" leadership in pre-Columbian Panama: that of the *tequina,* who as a prophet and prognosticator was believed able to predict the course of future events and to control weather and the growth of crops (Oviedo 1959: 33–34), and that of the shaman-curers, who held special knowledge of herbal salves derived from the supernatural (Andagoya 1865: 14). Similarly, the myths of the contemporary Cuna speak of the abilities of the ancient heroes and *neles* (who for our purposes may be equated with *tequinas* when speaking of pre-Columbian Panamanian society) to control the weather, the availability of game, and the growth of crops, and of their knowledge of the properties of certain woods and vines useful for effecting cures and as ritual "medicines" to enhance the *neles'* (*tequinas'*) mystical strength and bravery in contacts with the supernatural (see Chapin 1970). As was argued in the preceding pages, it is quite conceivable that such knowledge included awareness of narcotic or hallucinogenic agents, the use of which would form part of the esoteric insights known to the sacred-secular leadership. *Quevís* of ancient Panama also are portrayed as particularly "knowledgeable," for we read that when Ponca first met Balboa the two spoke privately of many things, especially of "los secretos é riqueças de la tierra"; similar high-level discussion was held between the regent of Chape and Balboa (Oviedo 1853: bk. 29, chap. 3, pp. 10, 14).

These specific expressions or applications of esoteric, "elite" knowledge can be seen as manifestations of a broader intellectual exploration of the general meaning of life. However, members of Cuna society attempt such intellectual endeavors in varying degrees; that is, some seek knowledge more avidly than others. It is likely that a comparable variance in pursuit of esoteric knowledge characterized ancient Panamanian society, too. Reichel-Dolmatoff's analysis of the religious symbolism of the Desana of eastern Colombia is illustrative of the situation. In *Amazonian Cosmos* (1971) Reichel-Dolmatoff notes that members of the adult population in general are aware of principal characteristics of sacred personifications and know fundamental myths and the rules for group ceremonial activities. But some Desana know additional invocations, songs, dances, and myths, including specific myths referring to creation and to the genealogies of kinship groups. Some particularly knowledgeable persons are able to interpret ritual hallucinations in more detail, understand the details of the *kumú*'s role, and know the symbolism of animals. According to Reichel-Dolmatoff, only specialized religious practitioners, that is, *kumús, payés,* and a few other men, understand the full scope of the great force of energy that encompasses the biosphere, comprehend the full significance of the hallucinations, and fully experience the ultimate meaning of hallucinogenic revelations (1971: 250–252; cf. Griaule's work on the idea system of the Dogon of West Africa discussed in Redfield 1964).

The Cuna also recognize varying degrees of knowledgeability in "esoteric" matters. The vast majority of the population, including young people and women (who do not hold special community or supracommunity politico-religious positions), know the essential basics of Cuna world view and ceremonial behavior. A majority of the men, particularly older men, have acquired knowledge of various myths and chants or are expert in some aspect of medical lore (see Howe 1974: 245–248). The three or more village chiefs of each community and their "interpreters" (*arkars* or *arkalas*) command additional bodies of lore and have learned a distinctive ceremonial "chief's language" (Stout 1947: 29; Howe 1974: 149–160). In like fashion, the *neles* are exceptionally well versed in matters of lore and ritual, as are the few regional high chiefs or other ritual specialists, whose influence goes beyond the local community to include peoples of many islands (and who may be regarded as the contemporary correlate of the ancient regional *quevís*).[13] Nordenskiöld has succinctly summarized the situation, noting that knowledge is distributed differentially among individuals in the Cuna community, and in such a way that no one knows "everything" (1938: xvii–xx). More specifically, he claims that the "thinking elite" are particularly concerned with the processes or reasons behind phenomena.

In a related vein, Howe says that, from the viewpoint of the chiefs, "ordinary people handle matters [in the frequent village-wide meetings] in terms of the immediate issues at hand; they deal with them 'just superficially.' Chiefs, on the other hand, attack problems 'thoroughly, in depth,' by anticipating the future of an issue, pointing out parallels from past history, and drawing analogies from nature and non-political parts of the cultural world such as the family" (1977: 161; see also 1974: 115 n. 12).

Sherzer describes this distinction between those who "know in depth" and those who "know superficially" in slightly different terms. He discusses how, during chiefly chants of admonition, puberty-rite songs, or curing chants, the "addressee" to whom the chanter is directing his song is not necessarily the general populace assembled at the evening *congreso* or at the puberty rite or the ill person or his household. Rather, during village assemblies (*congresos*) the chief formally addresses other chiefs and village officials, speaking in intricate metaphors, which are elucidated for the villagers by the interpreter. When curing chants are needed, the chant "knower" visiting the invalid directs his song to the wooden figurines (*suar nuchus,* or "stick dolls") who are believed to be the actual source of curing power. The other individuals present generally continue about their household affairs, talking conversationally among themselves. Similarly, during a puberty rite the *kantules* (chanters) address their songs not to the persons assembled for the festivities but to flutes, which they also play. The general populace again "can be viewed as 'non-knowing auditors,' aware of the social and stylistic significance of the *kantule*'s ikar [song] but not its referential details" (Sherzer 1974: 276).

The content of elite knowledge and the procedures by which it is expressed contain some additional features that should be noted in more detail. For one thing, the esoteric knowledge controlled by Cuna sacred-secular leaders is frequently expressed in equally esoteric linguistic forms that evidence most clearly, both to those who speak them and to those who listen, the formal differences between "ordinary" and "extraordinary" thought and the sociopolitical distinctions between the persons employing them. During the *congresos,* or village "general assemblies," held on a daily or weekly basis in a large community house in the evening (see Chapter 1, note 10 above; Howe 1974: chap. 3, gives a general discussion of these meetings), a chief of the community chants in "euphemistic language allegories" based on myths and legends concerning the behavior of the villagers. His songs will be repeated by an "interpreter," or "spokesman" (*arkar*), using ordinary language for the benefit of the audience (see Stout 1947: 29; Nordenskiöld 1938: 45–49, 376–378; Sherzer 1974: 264–271). In Howe's words, "according to at least the formal logic of the gathering, the chief's audience cannot understand the underlying meaning of his singing until after he finishes. . . . Each time the chief sings, he sets out an opaque mystery, and then afterwards the interpreter renders the mystery into a transparent lesson for the assembled people. The two thus carry forward a process of continuing and repetitive revelation, *in which they make the hidden essence of things intelligible by unravelling secrets*" (1977: 163, and 1974: 105; my emphasis). A distinctive form of speech is used in comparable fashion by curers when discussing the qualities of healing plants among themselves and when presiding over cures and by *kantules* when conducting girls' puberty rites (Nordenskiöld 1938: 508–509, 515–516; Sherzer 1974).

Sherzer has investigated these esoteric language forms in some detail and notes distinctions not only between esoteric or ceremonial speech events and ordinary conversation but also among the various types of esoteric speech events themselves (1974). The curing chants and the songs of the girls' puberty rites must be learned and performed more or less as taught by older practitioners and teachers, for their efficacy lies in replication of the traditional verses. The speeches and chants of chiefs, in contrast, while requiring demonstration of the speaker's mastery of traditional religious-political history and customs, are expected to be more flexible and innovative.

The adherence to traditional format required of curing chanters and of puberty-rite singers (*kantules*) may be interpreted as "stabilizing" the ephemeralness or evanescent quality of the information presented by spoken words—the form in which knowledge and belief are materially and socially expressed in nonliterate societies (see Ong 1969: 638). It is also a reiteration of the probably ancient and very widespread native American belief in the need to continually control certain potentially disruptive dangers of the "natural" world, particularly illness and unregulated sexuality (which were first conquered or controlled long ago by mythical heroes, such as Tad Ibe), so that civilized "humanness" is preserved. Thus chants and ceremonies to combat illness and to emphasize the propriety of sex controlled by marriage adhere to traditional forms of presentation, "which have been passed down through generations," in effect preserving the ancient powers of control revealed by mythological heroes and making them available for contemporary need (Sherzer 1974: 282).

In contrast, the innovativeness and flexibility expected of chiefly speech forms emphasize the "energetics" in speech[14] as well as the need for adaptiveness within the formal sociopolitical structure if society is to continue to exist. Many of the chiefly speeches delivered at public gatherings, or *congresos*, are concerned with pronouncing admonishments and judgments on those whose activities have caused a breach in custom or have led to disputes. Chiefs also admonish the assembled villagers to adhere to proper social behavior as expressed in traditionally valued forms of "moral" conduct (Howe 1975 and 1974: 98). However, these chiefly pronouncements and judgmental decisions, though seeking support by reference to past history and tradition, are modified to take into account current life styles and contemporary situations. Chiefs, therefore, are admired not only for their grasp of traditional history but also for the creative and individual expression they bring to the traditional metaphors around which their speeches are shaped. Thus, contemporary Cuna chiefs, like the Desana *kumú*, whose role also focuses on the singing of sacred songs before assemblies, continue to honor the undoubtedly ancient elite responsibility to direct the social behavior, or "moral" life, of the society. This point is frequently expressed in the Cuna myths, too, for there are frequent references to the persistent teaching and behavioral admonishing expected of a good *nele*.[15] Moreover, the fact that the role of the Cuna chief requires individuals who are flexible and adept at maneuvering to meet new demands and situations is consistent with the hypothesis that successful chiefs of ancient Panama were also men of action and ability who could "outperform" others and successfully deal with challenging situations.[16]

The esoteric speech used by the Cuna leadership can itself be considered metaphor for the distinctly "human" or "controlled" or "cultural" state of existence achieved by mankind and guarded by the leadership (see Holloman 1969: 232). In this context the special language forms used by chiefs, curing chanters, and *kantules* become another type of "sacred symbol" signifying, like the golden ornaments of the ancient rulers, the sanctity of the message, the uniqueness of those who speak it, and their legitimate right to direct the sociopolitical environment of people and things. If esoteric language be considered another metaphor for cultured, ordered, social living and as a form of "elite" sacred symbol in native Panamanian society, then it would not be surprising to find evidence for the use of "poetic" or metaphorical languages in the pre-Columbian society of the isthmus. The data are scant, yet chiefly languages and interpreters are definitely recorded by Andagoya with reference to the polities of Escoria and Natá (1865: 31; see also Sauer 1966: 272). Use of a separate chief's language may also account in part or in full for the unusual degree of linguistic diversity recorded for western Panama—a diversity that Sauer has interpreted as indicating the presence of foreigners, perhaps Mesoamericans, but that may also be evidence of the distinct linguistic forms of the rulership (ibid.).

Acquisition of esoteric knowledge may have generated and expressed some of the chiefly competition and rivalry postulated for pre-Columbian Panamanian polities. Competition in degree of knowledge is clearly part of Cuna political activities today. Cuna ethnographers note that, since there is a "staggering abundance" of lore to be learned, even the most knowledgeable chiefs and the oldest shamans do not know all the historical stories and myths, medicines and chants (Howe 1974: 102; Stout 1947: 44; Nordenskiöld 1938: xvii). Furthermore, since there is great prestige in knowledge and since "the general populace accords status in ratio to one's command of esoteric knowledge" (Marshall 1950: 202), the chanters and shamans frequently dispute among themselves as to who is most learned either in overall quantity of knowledge or in the correctness of the version each knows. Howe, who discusses this topic at some length (1974: 252–260), notes that "assessments of learning, skill, and general prestige necessarily involves ambiguity, subjectivity, and disagreement," inevitably creating jealousy and rivalry concerning relative prestige. Rivalries and knowledge competitions are most likely to occur openly between those holding the same public position and on public occasions: "The Cuna talk a lot about jealousy and competition, and it is a constant theme in the mythology; they expect it most often between those who know the same things or occupy the same offices. Thus, for instance, in the puberty ceremonies, which provide the major occasion for men to sing and show off their ritual knowledge, *they fear status challenges in which one man casts doubt on another's knowledge*. . . . The admonishments urge that instead each man alternately sing and listen respectfully to what his neighbor is singing" (Howe 1977: 158; my emphasis). It is in this context that the Cuna emphasize secrets and "obscurities," such as chiefly languages and esoteric chants, for it is via "secrets" that the learned differentiate themselves from each other and from less skilled laymen (Howe 1974: 253–254).

These serious concerns with relative "learnedness" among contemporary Cuna leaders may provide additional insights into the world of the elites of pre-Columbian Panama. Then, as now, community *congresos* apparently were held where lords and *tequinas* presided, chants were sung, and community-wide decisions were made (Oviedo 1853: bk. 29, chap. 26, p. 130; see also chap. 28, p. 137). Then, as now, the chiefly "repertoire" of knowledge and performance may have included a command of "history-cum-mythology. . . . conventional wisdom and morality, [and] singing techniques" (Howe 1977: 133), for Oviedo tells us that the *congreso* chants embodied the learning and past history of native society ("Estos areytos . . . son sus letras y memoriales"; 1853: bk. 29, chap. 28, p. 137). Then, as now, sacred-secular leaders may have issued mutual status challenges in terms of their respective control over esoteric "secrets." Then, as now (see Howe 1977: 133), the degree to which a chief had mastered this material and the skill with which he used it may have determined as much as anything else his reputation among his peers and followers. In sum, the Cuna "knowledge" system, which reveals differential control over esoteric information by members of the populace and which identifies a competitive "knowledge elite" in terms of increased understanding of sacred-secular affairs, surely had its counterpart in pre-Columbian Panama.

In this ancient stratified society, degree of knowledge can be expected to have correlated with social position even more strongly than it does among the relatively more egalitarian Cuna of the twentieth century. Whereas commoners and perhaps lower elites (*çabras*) may have accepted "superficial fact" and were thought to understand only the most basic ideological concepts,[17] men of the high elite—the *quevís, tequinas,* and shaman-curers—undoubtedly were expected to pursue deep philosophical matters and to master exotic lore, to explore the deeper significance of beliefs and symbolisms, and to experience the more profound revelations of ultimate ideological reality. These highest members of the elite thus stood above and apart from the rest of society not only by virtue of high birth and great "*mana*" but also by their investigations into the most rarefied aspects of sacred-secular knowledge.[18]

The significance of such intellectual investigations for the elite of ancient Panama, as for Cuna *neles* and chiefs today, undoubtedly centered on the expression of political power through the diagnoses, prognostications, moral admonitions, and general aura of great insight and credibility generated by close study of and intimate association with the workings and processes of the universe (see Wassén 1949: 124). In other words, an understanding of the powers of nature and of the origins and history of human society and its relationship with the natural-supernatural realms legitimized chiefly rule. Even more, it is likely that elite power itself was thought to derive directly from the fundamental energies of nature, was but a manifestation of them, since the *tequinas* and *quevís,* like the Desana *kumú* and like Tad Ibe of the Cuna myths, were the highest points of mediation between the world of men and that of the supernatural (compare Elmendorf 1970, 1971, 1974). Indeed, it is not unlikely that the *quevís* and *tequinas* were regarded by the populace at large as more closely allied with supernatural realms than with the human world, that is, were considered more divine than human. If so, then the powers that the rulership employed for the direction of human society were considered simply as an extension or continuation of the powers of nature and of that universe whose deepest secrets were unveiled only to those of the elite who had achieved the highest level of wisdom or esoteric knowledge.

Scarce Knowledge and Scarce Goods

This broad association of esoteric knowledge with active chiefly powers can cast additional light on some of the themes of rulership we have considered before. For example, esoteric knowledge can be viewed as a "scarce good" exactly like gold ornaments or any other elite sumptuary item. As such it was more useful when actively expressed than when passively held. Chiefly jealousies and competitions in the sphere of knowledge encouraged both the acquisition and the "activation" of knowledge (as they facilitated the acquisition and circulation of other, more material, scarce goods) and thus further enhanced the sociopolitical prestige and effectiveness of those who emerged victorious in these rivalries. Those lords who fell behind in this competition were shown to hold less control over the powers of the universe and thus presumably enjoyed less sociopolitical prestige and influence over earthly people and resources.

If profound understanding of the cosmos, acquisition of supernatural power, and mediation with supernatural forces were the prerogatives of the elite, and particularly of the highest elite, then ritual means of contacting the supernatural would also be part of the rarefied realm of highest wisdom known only to a few. The ritual use, on formal occasions, of esoteric languages by the rulership and the purported ability of the sacred-secular leaders to understand the "special language" of the spirits conjured by them (see quote from Wassén earlier in this chapter) are cases in point. It is also possible that knowledge of a particular narcotic or hallucinogenic agent (other than the tobacco smoke and chicha used by the populace at large) by which a state of trance could be achieved in the privacy and sanctity of the *surba* was known only to the *tequinas* and *quevís* who closeted themselves in the enclosure in order to speak with the gods. If such was the case, if, in fact, knowledge of the means by which actual contact with the supernatural world was achieved was part of the highest level of secret understanding and thus was limited to those few high-status persons qualified to make such contacts, then the absence of clear documentary evidence for the use of trance, which in turn suggests the apparent attenuation of this mode of supernatural association after European discovery, would correlate with the gradual decline of traditional elite statuses in Panamanian society after the conquest (see Dobkin de Rios 1975: 410, for a general statement of this phenomenon; Roberts 1827: 49, records a type of "medicine" known to the nineteenth-century Cuna religious elite, knowledge of which, so far as I know, is no longer extant).

Indeed, much of the most esoteric lore of traditional Panamanian society may be irretrievably lost. This is to say that even though differential attainment of knowledge still exists in contemporary Cuna society, the highest degree of "elite" knowledge attainable today by Cuna intellectuals probably is not as deep or as profound as was the highest level of insights and understanding achieved by the elite of the pre-Columbian era.

Geographical Distance and Supernatural Distance

Achievement of wisdom requires long years of training in contemporary Cuna society, and it is probable that similar preparation was required of the high elite in ancient times. In fact, according to Romolí, the education of a potential *tequina* began in childhood and concluded with several years of isolation in the forest. During this time the trainee was taught the esoterics of his calling by an established "master" (see Romolí 1953: 110). Analogy with Cuna ethnography also suggests that, while any qualified intellectual or "master" may have attracted "students," special "schools" may have existed at select locations where those who aspired to learn received the necessary tutoring in lore and ritual from renowned thinkers and religious leaders (*tequinas* and *quevís*), who may have had numerous young men "in residence" for this purpose at any given time.

Among the twentieth-century Cuna, student-chanters and ambitious young *neles* frequently travel to traditional centers in the interior of the country where they may study for periods of several years to acquire a particularly good education. Wassén and Holloman have documented this procedure, describing in some detail (see below) the systematic travels of a young *nele* to places in northwestern Colombia and eastern Panama where various specialists in traditional medical, historical, linguistic, and political skills and lore could be consulted (see also Wassén 1949: 29; Hayans 1952: 97; and especially Howe 1974: 5, 160–165, 229–235). The villages of Caiman, east of the Gulf of Urabá, and Arquia (Arki), west of the delta of the Río Atrato between the river and the *cordillera,* are two of the places of learning in Colombia mentioned in this context (see Fig. 22). Nordenskiöld

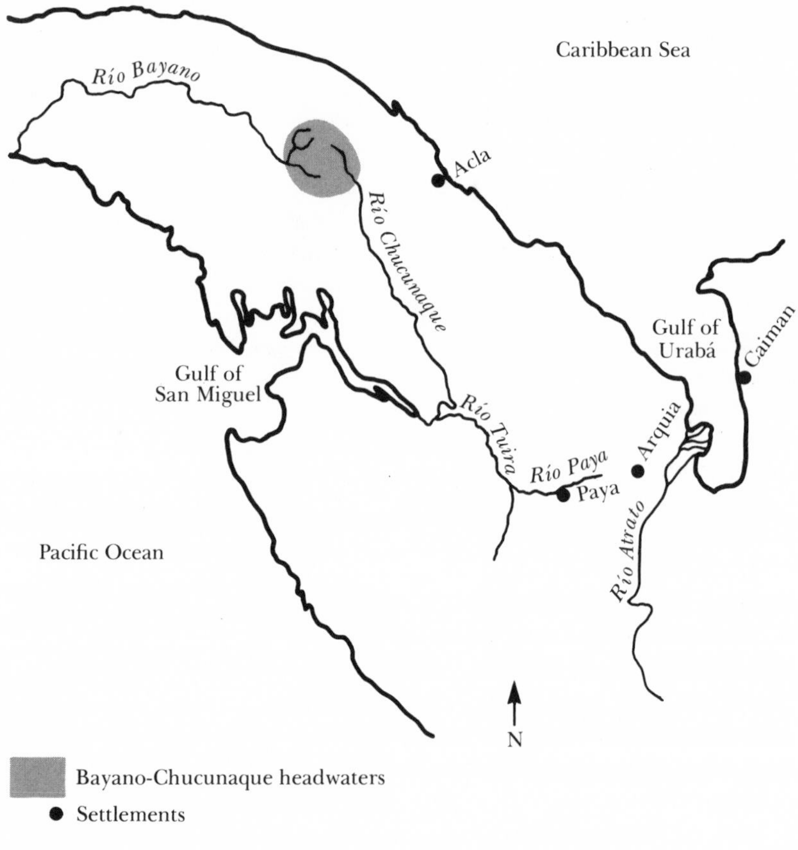

Fig. 22. Major Cuna study centers and places of origin.

noted that much of the old ideology of the Cuna had been preserved in Arquia (1938: 422), and Howe (1974: 100) cites it along with Paya in eastern Panama as a place where some Cuna chiefs of the late nineteenth and early twentieth centuries went to study with teachers. Paya, or Pae, near the Río Tuira in the Serranía del Darién, is one of two small villages still inhabited by the "Tuira Cuna" and is regarded as an ancient place, the source of the religious tradition dominant in San Blas today (Howe 1974: 5). Similarly, several communities in the Bayano-Chucunaque headwaters are centers for the learning of medicinal lore and curing chants (Howe, personal communication; see Hayans 1952: 97).[19]

Holloman gives a rather lengthy account of this educational system. She relates in part that, while any Cuna boy is allowed to undertake studies, the educational arrangement functions primarily for leadership training. As such, a young man with political ambitions may undertake fifteen to twenty years of formal study of religious and medical chants and legends, of the lives of famous chiefs of the past, and of the history of Cuna dealings with non-Cuna peoples. This education is obtained by a series of associations, which could last for years, with distinguished teachers. Since each student arranges to study under the mentors of his own choice, however, no two men receive identical instruction. Each teacher transmits to his pupils the various religious and historical legends and chants that he knows, elucidating as he does so (and to the extent he wishes) the underlying meaning of the symbols occurring in texts (Holloman 1969: 232–234).

Some of the details of this educational system are particularly interesting. According to Holloman, when Second Cacique Olotepilikina was studying under the famous Nele Kantule between 1910 and 1920, he was one of twenty to thirty pupils seeking instruction from the *nele*. Nordenskiöld notes that at times Nele Kantule had with him as many as forty to fifty young people who "came from all over the Cuna territory" (see 1931: 466). These young men, who aspired to high political offices, often delayed marriage until eighteen or nineteen years of age in order to pursue their studies in residence with various teachers (other young men married just before or at puberty). Even after marrying and becoming a minor leader in his home community, a young man might make frequent weekend trips to a teacher and take a year or more off to study from time to time. The pupils who were resident with a given instructor worked as members of the teacher's household, and, as Holloman notes, the command over manpower that a great chief held because of his twenty or thirty pupils had significant economical potential. Particularly under the slash-and-burn technology of earlier decades, before cash cropping had become as significant as it is today, this extra manpower would have greatly enhanced the major teacher-chiefs' economic position (Holloman 1969: 234–235).

The importance of journeying to distant places to acquire knowledge carries significance beyond that of an individual's quest for a good instructor or even of the expansion of the personal economic-political base of the teacher. Howe explains that the student-teacher relationship also carries with it a distinct context of relative ranking with the student subordinate in status to his instructor. Given the strong tendencies for status competition among village leaders, a man, perhaps already of some prestige, desirous of learning a certain song or chant may not wish to place himself in such a position vis-à-vis a village peer who knows the chant (although village teachers may in fact be consulted at times). Instead, he elects to study with a teacher who lives at a distance and with whom the status relationship may present less of a problem. Indeed, if the teacher is a man of high reputation, association with him may enhance the student's own prestige.

As a man's reputation grows, he seeks ever more prestigious teachers. In Howe's words, "though ideally one should study with whomever has a useful piece of knowledge whatever his position in life, the Cuna in fact take it that learning from someone implies subordination and acknowledgement of relative ignorance, so at each stage of a chief's learning career, he strives to study with teachers who are clearly superior in knowledge and general prestige, and avoid teachers whose prestige is equal or only slightly higher than his own" (1974: 162). Howe further notes that "many chiefs in fact end their studies in middle-age not only because of personal limits to their ambition and interest, but also because after a certain number of years as chief they feel that there is almost no one with whom they can study without loss of face" (ibid., p. 163; see also pp. 160–165). In addition, "learning at a distance has a special prestige . . . and it offers opportunities to acquire specialties unknown in one's own village. . . . Furthermore, by learning a somewhat distinct variant of a chant far from home, one makes it more difficult for local critics to suggest that one has mislearned it" (ibid., pp. 232–233).

Journeying for knowledge carries yet another connotation. The esoteric knowledge that Cuna young men work so diligently to acquire, and that probably was a major source of sacred-secular authority for pre-Columbian priests and chiefs, is itself a form of "journey" leading toward increased understanding of worlds and experiences beyond the ordinary and familiar. Indeed, because a concept of removal from the ordinary (mundane or familiar) to the extraordinary (extraworldly or unfamiliar) is involved, the metaphor of a "journey" is a basic motif in Cuna curing chants and myths. The place journeyed to may be temporally distant, as a trip into the past or a glimpse of a future life, or it may be spatially removed, as a journey upward to the multiple worlds above the terrestrial or downward to levels beneath the terrestrial or horizontally to new terrestrial lands beyond the known territory (see Wassén 1938: 88–98, and 1949; 129–130; Nordenskiöld 1938: 157, 267; Lévi-Strauss 1967; Chapin 1970; Howe 1974: 161).

Comparable "journeys" into extraordinary space-time worlds are found among the experiences of many tropical American religious practitioners and are indicated in the myths of ancient Nuclear America.[20] Among the Desana, to take one example, the world entered by the *kumú* or others via trance is one where time is eclipsed and foreshortened and where, as with the Cuna, space includes additional worlds located in a vertical axis with respect to the earth, some above and some below *terra firma* (Reichel-Dolmatoff 1971: 173–174, 138, 24–25, 43–47). Similarly, Weiss has detailed the extraordinary world conceived by the Campa of eastern Peru where supernatural phenomena have geographical or spatial referents (1972). Not only do spirits inhabit various strata above and below the earth, but they also are resident at the farthest limits of the horizontal or terrestrial domain. The Campa "understand themselves to occupy a definite region on a flat earth extending out in all directions to unknown limits." They are surrounded, first, by known neighboring tribes and peoples, but "the land beyond the circle of neighboring tribes is largely *terra incognita,* until the limits of the conceptualized or 'known' world are reached. Good spirits reside there" (ibid., p. 252).

Weiss' account is significant for its clear depiction of how the Campa have accorded distinct differences to their perception of terrestrial space, explicitly coding horizontal distance as part of the extraordinary world of the unknown. Similar concepts have been recorded for a number of other tropical American indigenies (see Gossen 1974; Mishkin 1940; Wagley 1940 and 1943; Wilbert 1972; Lipkind 1940: 248; cf. Ortiz 1969). Mircea Eliáde discusses this concept of the "sacredness" of space in more general terms. In order to concretize or objectify or "make real" the world about them,

Eliáde says, people seek to "construct" space, to give it shape and meaning. "For religious man, space is not homogeneous; he experiences interruptions, breaks in it; some parts of space are qualitatively different from others" (1959: 20). The basic spatial distinction recognizes, on the one hand, a fixed point, a "central axis," an organized and understood place that becomes a point of orientation. It discerns, on the other hand, increasingly distant frontiers, or "other worlds," that appear less and less organized or understood and that are perceived as places of disorientation and chaos. In Eliáde's view the basic difference between the "known" and "unknown" worlds rests on the belief that the "known" world has become ordered, "humanized," regularized by sacred precepts, while the "unknown," peopled by ghosts, demons, and "foreigners," still lacks these civilizing features and thus lies beyond the "controlled" and "sacred" center (ibid., p. 29).

It follows from this perspective and from the specific world views held by tropical native Americans that the "lands beyond," where dwell foreigners and spirits, are also places of "cosmic" or "universal" or "natural" energy or power. For example, the Chamulas of Highland Chiapas in Mexico believe that the competition between good and evil still continues at the edges of the earth where sun and moon deities plunge into and emerge from the sea (see Gossen 1974: 29). Such power, though chaotic and unregulated, is potentially useful for human life (life at the "center") if it can be controlled and directed by sacred specialists whose responsibility it is to "travel" to these foreign domains.

This line of thought has relevance for our understanding of the nature of Panamanian chiefship and of long-distance exchange networks. The hypothesis I wish to consider proposes that the high elite of ancient Panama, who presumably held the deepest understanding of the most esoteric sacred-secular lore and who were also involved in long-distance contacts, were most familiar with distant geographical regions that were *terra incognita* to the less educated elite and to the "unknowing" commoners. For such "ordinary" persons the "center of the world" was their own domain. Distant geographical realms were extraordinary "foreign" worlds that were as unknown and awesome as were the supernatural nether worlds above and below the earth. To the *quevís* and *tequinas*, however, specialized sacred lore and first-hand knowledge of geographically distant lands "organized" these frontiers into "known" territory, coalesced these "foreign" regions into a very real sociopolitical-religious world.[21]

Among the contemporary Cuna, geographical distance and foreign (non-Cuna) peoples carry a distinct fascination that is explored wherever possible by first-hand contact. Cuna men in particular are known for their penchant for traveling and, as Marshall says, "have never been ignorant of the world around them" (1950: 265). After European contact young men readily took jobs on European sailing vessels traveling worldwide. Some spent many years in residence in Europe or the United States. Cuna young men today readily live and work for extended periods in the cities of Panama and the Canal Zone. These trips may be understood as part of a growing cash economy, but they also reflect an interest in the wider world that goes considerably beyond the desire for money.

We find, for example, that acquisition of foreign languages carries great prestige and is essentially another form of esoteric knowledge (Howe 1974: 229, 258). The experiences of workers and sailors are also seen as a source of special knowledge (*ikar*) for the returned traveler, knowledge of which he is as proud and competitive as any other "knower" of esoterica (ibid., pp. 229, 256). This knowledge is shared with the rest of the men of the village in the evening gatherings, where visitors or local men newly returned from "outside" recount their experiences and provide news of the world beyond the village. By these accomplishments and by short-wave radios and other means (for example, regional chiefs' meetings; see note 25 below), the Cuna "accumulate a general knowledge of the world at large remarkable for such an isolated people" (ibid., pp. 359–360; see pp. 361–362 for examples of such information sharing).

In Cuna myth, in which other aspects of the Cuna study of non-Cuna worlds may be found, concepts associated with travel to places within the natural or geographical landscape are blended with visits to the supernatural. For example, it is by traveling in "ships" that the spirits who live at the four corners of the world are reached. These spirits dwell in the east (the place where the sun rises), in the west (where the sun sets), in the mountains, and in the open sea (Chapin 1970: 57). One fascinating tale recounts how an ancient *nele* visited Europe prior to the conquest and prophesized Columbus' voyage (ibid., p. 58). The various peoples and places he "saw" in Europe are described in the same style as are the human and animal "villages" of the underworld (where dwell, respectively, the dead and the game animals waiting to be released to earth), which *neles* also frequently "visited."

I sense a common denominator in these seemingly disparate bits of data: an impression that for the postcontact Cuna *"distant" supernatural realms coalesce with "distant" geographical realms* and that exploration of any and all distant (that is, nonlocal or non-Cuna) lands by whatever means is a worthy undertaking for all who have the opportunity or the interest (see Holloman 1969: 63, for a comparable view). From such explorations greater knowledge and thus greater power are obtained.

For the contemporary Cuna the European-derived world of conquest is particularly viewed as a "place" of great power and potency, knowledge of which will provide benefits within Cuna society for those able to acquire it. In this context it is noteworthy that knowledge of Hispanic customs and of the behavior of Euro-Americans living in the Canal Zone is now used by chiefs in their chanted admonitions in the *congreso* (Howe 1977: 161). This information, moreover, is used in the same spirit of instruction as are the teachings of such legendary heroes as Tad Ibe! Similarly, the potent, *purba*-filled wooden figurines, or *nuchus,* used by shaman-curers are carved not only in the shapes of animals and birds of nature but also in the form of Europeans clad in suits and uniforms (Stout 1947: 103; Nordenskiöld 1938: 423–426). This fact leads to the obvious conclusion that in the Cuna view Europeans and European domains possess power of the same "cosmic" significance as do other manifestations of the natural-supernatural realms.[22] The use of foreign objects in medicines—for example, bits of sharpened metal or razor blades for rheumatism cures (Stout 1947: 102; Nordenskiöld 1938: 365, 395, 436)—can be understood in the same terms, for we can attribute the use of such objects to the *purba* believed to exist in them. In short, such forms or expressions of "foreign" power can be tapped by sacred-secular leaders and put to "human" (that is, Cuna) use in curing illness (via *nuchus* and medicines) or by directing social behavior (via chiefly admonitions).[23]

To be sure, these data may well be interpreted as indicative of acculturation and of a materialistic desire by the Cuna for Western goods. Yet the data also clearly indicate that the Cuna have incorporated Western (European) material goods and their observations of Western (European) behavior into their own cosmology and have attributed supraordinary or extraordinary powers or significance to at least some of these goods and behavioral observations (see Sherzer and Sherzer 1972: 196–197). In other words, they have found "power" in their knowledge of geographically "distant" places and of culturally distinct peoples and things. They have acquired this knowledge by travel to the places inhabited by these peoples and also by meeting traders, missionaries, Peace Corp representatives, and other agents of change who have traveled to their territory (see Holloman 1969; Sherzer and Sherzer 1976: 34).[24]

There are even a few tantalizing bits of data in the Hispanic records of sixteenth-century Panama suggesting that at that time the newcomers from Europe were similarly viewed as extraordinary beings come from afar bringing exceptional wisdom and power. I referred above to the private, indeed "secret," meetings between Balboa and various *quevís* in which the "secrets of the earth" were discussed. It is easy to imagine the deep curiosity of the native *quevís* as to who the Europeans were, where they came from, and what Europe was like. We read, too, that the intruding Spaniards were virtually equated with the gods by the indigenous Panamanians. Oviedo informs us that the Indians accorded to the Spaniards the same name they gave their deity, *tuira,* believing the Spaniards to be as wise as the deity and thinking to praise and honor them by such a name (1853: bk. 29, chap. 26, p. 127).

This hypothesis concerning the "power" of the European world in Cuna perceptions is strongly supported by the description given by Wassén (1938: 24–45) and Holloman of the training undertaken by a leading Cuna *nele* in preparation for his duties as a religious-political specialist. In this recounting of the education of the famous Nele Kantule we find that the "esoteric knowledge" the *nele* learned included not only traditional Cuna lore but also awareness of the customs, particularly the governmental systems, of non-Cuna peoples, meaning, in today's world, Western European–derived cultures of Colombia, Panama, and the United States. Indeed, Holloman particularly emphasizes the "open" nature of this educational pattern, which encourages a man of knowledge to specifically explore the ways of "foreigners" both by traveling to their realms and by studying with others who have been there. She notes that the ability to deal with foreign, non-Cuna political leaders is a quality, or hallmark, of a good Cuna leader (1969: 63–64, 233, 237, 418, 441).

Nele Kantule was born sometime between 1860 and 1870 at Ustupu. He was the son of a prominent shaman and was marked from birth for his calling, as are all *neles.* These auspicious beginnings, combined with a sharp intelligence, encouraged Nele (as he is known) to begin his education at the early age of nine under the tutelage of his father. His first course of study was of plants and their medicinal uses. When he was twelve, his father took him to Sasardi where he took up residence as a pupil of a curer who was a friend of his father. Later, Nele continued his studies in the interior mainland villages of Sokupti and Kwiti in the Bayano region. At the age of seventeen he traveled to the village of Caiman in northwestern Colombia where he studied medicine and the histories of the great neles under the high chief of the region. This chief later designated Nele as his successor. Traveling next to Arquilla, also in Colombia, he studied additional aspects of chiefship. For three years he lived in the provincial capital of Quidó studying, among other things, "civilization" and the life of Simón Bolivar under an acculturated Cuna who had completed "the highest class" in school in Colombia and who, when a young man, had been a soldier under Bolivar.

Nele then returned to the Bayano region in Panama to study under William Smith, a chief who had been a sailor for many years and who instructed him in European civilization. Further education in "the civilization and customs of North America, the federal system, and democracy" were undertaken with another leader, then living at Akanti in Colombia, who had sailed for thirty years on British and American ships. Nele then went to Paya in Panama where he was instructed for three years in aspects of the Cuna language, particularly the origin of words. In 1908 Nele made several visits to Nargana to learn about Catholicism and to discuss chief Charlie Robinson's program for modernizing Nargana (Holloman 1969: 441–443).

Nele Kantule was probably in his late thirties when he began his political career as an assistant in the local *congresos* of his home village. He appears to have spent approximately twenty-five years acquiring his education. The *nele*'s education clearly emphasizes his study in regions beyond the immediate Cuna territory and his concern about non-Cuna societies. Holloman thinks that Nele's interest in this regard may have been somewhat unusual, but that there was also well-established precedent for this field of inquiry (1969: 441). I would go so far as to suggest that a direct continuum exists between the interest of Cuna political-religious specialists, such as Nele Kantule, in contemporary non-Cuna cultures and the hypothesized interest of pre-Columbian Panamanians, particularly the high elite, in contacts with "distant" spheres. In these earlier centuries, and apparently to some extent still today, "distant" places would include both the mystic levels of the heavens and underworld and the geographically distant places and peoples: domains that could be reached by "long-distance" contacts or "journeys" of several sorts, including trance, probably also dreams, and actual travel to geographically distant regions. All these travels would have yielded various forms and expressions of knowledge essential to chiefship.

In the contemporary Cuna religious-political system, shamanic and chiefly control includes both intervention with supernatural spirits and contacts with foreign governments (for example, with Panamanian officials), as well as admonishment and arbitration within local Cuna villages or in interisland affairs (see Holmer 1951: 185–186; Holloman 1969: 225; Howe 1974). In the ethnohistoric literature pertaining to chiefs, priests, and shamans in early sixteenth-century Panama, references are found to supernatural contacts and to arbitration (and by extension admonition) within the polity, as well as to warfare and chiefly "exchange" activities (these latter having ceased or become greatly attenuated or refocused among contemporary Cuna or Guaymí). We do not find contacts with "foreign" governments or any other interest in geographically foreign (that is, beyond the isthmus) peoples and places specifically designated in the Spanish documents, other than elite conversations with conquistadors such as Balboa. It is the tenor of these pages, however, that this aspect of chiefly rule was present and was a fundamental element legitimizing the leadership of *quevís* and *tequinas*.

The only direct evidence of pre-Columbian elites' interest in and contact with foreign domains exists in archaeological material remains and in the ethnohistoric data concerning "trade" in exotic goods, such as gold, slaves, pearls, textiles, and the like. In Chapter 3, relationships between geographical distance, the acquisition of scarce goods, and chiefly sanctity were briefly discussed. It was further proposed that symbols of high sanctity are depicted iconographically in the elaborate gold pieces worn by the ancient Panamanian elite as evidence of chiefly authority and power. Ethnohistorical and archaeological data strongly suggest that some of these elaborate gold pieces, particularly such cast pieces as effigy pendants and nose clips, were crafted in geographically distant regions, particularly Colombia, and were acquired by some method involving long-distance contacts or exchange. It can now be suggested, in addition, that the fundamental significance of the long-distance contacts by which these symbolic representations of the extraordinary or "distant" supernatural world were obtained is properly understood as part of the search for esoteric knowledge, itself a scarce chiefly "good" combining deep insights into the mysteries of the supernaturally distant world with contacts with powerful sacred-secular rulers and teachers in geographically distant lands.

The personal-knowledge quests of contemporary Cuna sacred-secular leaders suggest at least one mechanism by which contact with distant regions and rulers and the search for esoteric sacred knowledge could have been combined in the pre-Columbian era. It is entirely conceivable that, like Nele Kantule, young members of the elite, future *quevís* and *tequinas,* sought out famous places of traditional learning in the isthmus of Central America or in northern South America where renowned religious and political elites-cum-teachers imparted insights into the mysteries of sacred-secular lore and related political affairs.

Indeed, various levels of "learning networks" can be correlated with the several levels of exchange networks postulated in Chapter 2. It is hypothesized that those *quevís* and *tequinas* (or more likely their sons) associated with the dozen or so regionally influential centers proposed for pre-Columbian Panama were in contact with the most distant learning and exchange centers beyond the isthmus, just as the most promising young leaders of Cuna society, some like Nele Kantule destined to become regional chiefs, seek the most extensive education. On a more restricted level, elites of ancient Panamanian hinterland polities located at greater distance from the regional centers may have sought to study at these regional hubs under the aegis of the religious-political "high chiefs" whose fame as "men of wisdom" reflected their supraisthmian experiences.[25] In such a fashion did Cuna pupils study under Nele Kantule or other great Cuna chiefs of wide experience (see Holloman 1969: 234, 235). Within each polity, on the local level, pre-Columbian village headmen (*çabras*) and district administrators (*sacos*) may have looked to the *quevís* and *tequinas* of their own domain for guidance in matters relating to sacred-secular knowledge. In like manner lesser Cuna chanters and village *congreso* leaders (lesser chiefs, translators) turn at times to more experienced local leaders for direction.[26]

There is only a modicum of ethnographic data to assist in ascertaining how, in pre-Columbian times, such scarce goods as gold pieces may have been obtained or exchanged as part of these "knowledge quests." It appears significant within this context, however, that at least some instruction in the traditional Cuna educational system requires payment of some sort from pupil to teacher. Labor contribution while resident in the teacher's village or home is one mode of traditional payment, but today cash is necessary, too, at least for some forms of knowledge. Various statements regarding the cost of an education can be found in the ethnographic literature. For example, Densmore tells of a chanter who paid fifteen dollars for one of the many songs he had learned from various teachers and who also claimed that a longer course of instruction lasting perhaps ten years could easily result in fees totaling a hundred dollars for the student (1926: 2, 12–13). Howe mentions that the important *Muu Ikar* chant costs six dollars to learn, while, according to Holloman, a chief who studied under Nele Kantule purportedly paid approximately one thousand dollars to the *nele* over the years (1969: 235). Howe reports more generally that when student and teacher have established a close and lasting relationship the student often contributes work, goods, and money on an informal, irregular basis (personal communication).

It is quite likely that in pre-Columbian times esoteric knowledge was similarly "valued" and that religious-political elites visiting regional centers of learning in the isthmus or beyond took valued scarce goods, such as raw gold, pearls, cotton goods, and war captive-slave-bearers, as prestations for those with whom they studied and conferred. In turn they received the knowledge that would eventually bring them power (and material wealth) as chiefly teachers and priestly prognosticators and curers in their own right. Elite scholars also may have received various ornaments or other paraphernalia from their tutors indicating their successful completion of a period of training or mastery of a topic of instruction. Cuna ethnography provides two brief statements that suggest a returning scholar-leader may have brought goods with him either for distribution among his associates or for his own use as evidence of his distant contacts. One example is accorded by Rubén Pérez Kantule who, at the end of a six-month stay in Sweden as the guest of Erland Nordenskiöld, took back to Panama "gifts and articles for bartering" (Nordenskiöld 1938: xvi). The second case is also reported by Nordenskiöld, whom I will quote in full for the general summary concerning the intellectual activities and "aura" of Cuna elites, for the data concerning goods for redistribution, and for the tantalizing suggestion that the experiences of traveling Cuna scholars can be expressed in art, a thought that may have direct significance for our interpretation of the origins and iconographic significance of ancient Panamanian metallurgical pieces and other forms of art. Regarding Cuna "medicine men," whom he terms the "cultivated class" in Indian society, Nordenskiöld says:

> they tend, in order to enhance their position in society, to wrap themselves in a cloak of mystery. They undertake long voyages to broaden their learnings. The old Selimo who traveled with us for a long time had a true passion for self instruction. *When he left us to return home, he carried a whole collection of curiosities with which to impress his clients.* When in his company we visited the Bogotá Indians who live very far from his country, I saw him take infinite pains to study their medical science as much as possible. It is thus quite natural that these medicine men have been able, in the course of their travels *and even in the artistic domain,* to acquire new information which, upon their return, has found its application in their own tribes. (1929: 157; my emphasis)

Nordenskiöld's views on the artistic aspects of long-distance contacts are not clearly expressed in this particular quotation. Considering generally the relationship between art, ideology, and ritual among the Cuna, however, he argues that there is a close connection between contemporary Cuna art forms and techniques (including color symbolism, pictographs on wood or paper, carving of *nuchus,* basket-weaving designs, and probably women's clothing and ornamentation) and shamanic ceremonies (ibid.). He presents by way of example illustrations of "written texts" in which the animals, medicine plants, and culture heroes sung about in chants and "conjurations" are given material representation in polychrome drawings. Such drawings, along with other ornaments and art forms, are in effect material representations of the esoteric knowledge learned at home and abroad by politico-religious specialists.

Nordenskiöld also thought that contemporary Cuna art, though revealing influences from European contact, "has its roots in pre-Columbian art" (1929: 158). These ancient artistic roots also included, I propose, the custom of incorporating in art forms the experiences and knowledge gained by the ancient Panamanian elites on journeys to distant realms, journeys that led via trance to supernatural realms above or below the earth's surface or journeys entailing actual physical travel to elite centers in neighboring countries. These same ancient artistic roots are materially evidenced in the elaborately–and symbolically–decorated golden helmets, breast plates, earrings, nose rings, pendants, and other "ornaments" of the pre-Columbian elites, whose travels have long been over but whose material emblems of chiefly journeys, esoteric knowledge, and rivalrous power remain to us.

The data concerning chiefly travels and the acquisition of prestigeful elite goods symbolic of the knowledge learned in these peregrinations, when combined with the diverse lines of discussion that have been presented so far, allow the suggestion that much (though not necessarily all) of the acquisition and exchange of scarce goods by elites in pre-Columbian Panama may have occurred not as regularized "trade" (though admittedly we have no data on this topic) but as adjunct to other chiefly activities, including knowledge payments and evidence of distant journeys, politically supportive *krun* distributions, and strategic marriage arrangements. All these activities were of a political rather than strictly economic nature and were concerned with the maintenance and expansion of chiefly power in its many dimensions more than with the more specific fueling of the economy per se (see Swartz, Turner, and Tuden 1966: 26; Cohen 1969: 217; Sahlins 1972: 139–141). Such political motives probably underlay the pleased reception of gifts of necklaces, bracelets, mirrors, and other European baubles presented to the chiefs by the Spanish conquistadors—first representatives of another "distant" power domain heretofore unknown to the rulers of the isthmus—who tell us with deceptive simplicity that "the natives cherish these things highly, for whatever comes from abroad is everywhere most prized" (Anghera 1912: I, 283).

5

Perspective from Colombia

Places of Origin and Geographical Distance

There is yet another aspect to the sacredness of geographical distance and to long-range contacts that may be relevant to this analysis. In native American cosmologies space may also be equated with time and with cultural history in the sense that the more distant (and hence unknown) a space or place the older or more ancient it may be thought to be. In the view of the Chamulas of Highland Chiapas, for example, previous "ages of man" that no longer exist among the contemporary Chamula are believed to continue in the unknown distant places that lie beyond the safe Chamula heartland (Gossen 1974: 29–30). Taken to its logical extreme, this aspect of cosmology correlates ultimate spatial distance with the "origins" of human existence.

"Origins" in this context can be interpreted as the genesis of controlled, human, "cultural" life from the chaos of unregulated "nature" (see Gossen 1974). But "origins" may also be interpreted as the uncontaminated font, or pure source, of the regulated, civilized life style valued as the truly human mode of existence. This meaning of "origins" appears, for example, in the cosmology of the Tewa Indians of the southwestern United States, who also associate such "origins" with spatial distance. The Tewa recognize four sacred mountains, located more or less at the cardinal points some fifteen to eighty miles from the village, as the outermost boundary of their world

(Ortiz 1969: 19). The sacredness of these mountains derives from the lakes or ponds associated with each, wherein dwell the most sacred deities of the Tewa world. These deities still reside in the perfectly ordered universe from which the first Tewa emerged. The mountains' sacredness also derives from the "earth navels" located on the top of each, which, like the lakes, are believed to give access to the underworld or extraterrestrial universe and from which beneficial blessings are directed toward the Tewa. The four sacred mountains and the lakes and earth-navel shrines are thus conceptualized as "origin points," as places that identify the source of all the universal powers that can benefit man.

It is the task of Tewa ritual specialists to assure that these benefits will be received and honored by the populace. To this end they hold responsibility for social control and pray to the sacred authority of the mountains and make occasional pilgrimages to the mountain shrines. The Tewa sacred mountains thereby become tangible manifestations of, and wellsprings or points of authority for, both the ritual specialists and the teachings and regulations that this leadership admonishes the members of the polity to believe and to obey.

The travels of contemporary Cuna *neles* and chiefs or of ancient Panamanian *tequinas* and *quevís* to geographically distant centers of teaching may be interpreted as a return to the sources, or origin points, of the system of religious-political beliefs that these scholar-rulers wish to learn and that underwrite their positions of authority within society. (The heavy emphasis in Cuna religious-political education on delving into the "origins" of things and the power that is thought to derive from the exploration of the origin of things is significant here, too.) We previously noted that traditional centers, or "places of origin," of contemporary San Blas Cuna medical knowledge have been located in the headwaters of the Bayano-Chucunaque river systems, while political-religious histories and traditions have centered on or "originated" at Paya, or Pae, situated on the Río Tuira system, and Arquia and Caiman, both located in northwestern Colombia near the Atrato river delta. It was further suggested in previous chapters that at least some of the centers of learning to which ancient Panamanian leaders traveled were also located in Colombia, which implies that religious-political-medical traditions of the Colombian elite may have been the "source" of at least some Panamanian elite traditions and lore. In other words, it is hypothesized that pre-Columbian Panama was, in a sense, a political-religious hinterland of Colombia, by which I mean that ancient Panama shared a common political-religious belief system with Colombian peoples and that the elites of Panama turned to the rulership of select Colombian centers as mentors in the esoteric details of politico-religious traditions.

Goldworking in Panama

There are no primary data that directly refute or substantiate this proposal. In considering its validity we must rely on inferences drawn from archaeological data and from the reports of Hispanic conquistadors, both of which present only the most general evidence of prehispanic Panamanian-Colombian connections. Arguments developed in previous sections also suggest that pertinent data might emerge through consideration of chiefly sumptuary items, such as goldwork, which may have served as material expression of chiefly contacts and conclaves and the political-religious lore learned therefrom.

In Chapter 1 it was noted that, in spite of the conquistadors' avid interest in matters pertaining to gold, there are no sixteenth-century reports of alloying or casting in the Panamanian isthmus, even though one of the best observers of the times, Gonzalo Fernández de Oviedo y Valdés, was resident in Panama as the king's *veedor* of gold assays. To be sure, Pedrarias, governor of the Spanish settlements in Panama after Balboa, declared that the village of Panamá was a center for goldworking. But when the town was visited by Spaniards, this claim proved to be entirely unfounded.[1] The Spanish documents do record that the native population obtained moderate amounts of raw gold from stream beds and ravines or from shallow deposits in savannahs or other cleared land (Oviedo 1959: 107; Balboa in Andagoya 1865: viii, ix, xi; Colón 1959: 241–261 passim; Sauer 1966: 133–134, 244–246, 275–276). They also report that quantities of golden ornaments (many actually made of *guanín* or *tumbaga*, a copper-gold alloy) were taken from the inhabitants. Archaeological excavations and grave robbers have unearthed similar treasure in the isthmus, too. The conquistadors are not known for the thoroughness of their observations in general, but Sauer, for one, has found it significant that there is no ethnohistoric evidence to support the very frequent assumption—repeated for close to a century by anthropologists, historians, and museologists—that the technologically sophisticated casting and alloying skills evidenced by archaeological finds and private collections were practiced by isthmian artisans (see, e.g., Stone 1972: 150, 159–160, 183; Baudez 1963; Lothrop 1937: 74–87 passim, and

1966: 196, 198; Willey 1971: 331; MacCurdy 1911; Jones 1974: 22; Bray 1974*b*: 47; Moriarty 1974; Holmes 1887: 26).[2]

The Spanish documents do imply, however, that simple hammering was known to Panamanian craftsmen, for it is recorded that "hill peoples" of the mountainous interior near Comogre fashioned small gold pieces in the shape of leaves for exchange (Anghera 1912: I, 221) and that the smaller pieces of gold found at the town of Darién were of local origins (Casas 1927: bk. 2, chap. 63, p. 351), as apparently were the golden disks or mirrors of Veragua (Colón 1959: 243). Further confirmation of gold hammering is found in a sixteenth-century Spanish document unearthed from the archives at Cartago, Costa Rica, and published in translation in MacCurdy's *Study of Chiriquían Antiquities* (1911), where we read the report of one Don Diego de Sojo, Captain of the Guard of the Governor of Veragua, who in 1587 traveled through the province of Veragua and reported to his superior regarding the quantity of gold there, "as can be seen from the plates of gold the Indians *beat out,* it not being alloyed with other metals." Don Diego continues that gold is found in the rivers and hills of the area, "and the Indians extract gold with calabashes in very large grains, and a cacique of the same town named Ucani works it into the said pieces" (ibid., pp. 190–191, my emphasis; compare Colón 1959: 243).

The gilding technique of *mise-en-couleur* was also known to pre-Columbian Panamanian craftsmen (Oviedo 1959: 110; Anderson 1914: 320; see also Lothrop and Bergsøe 1960), and Balboa's letter makes mention, with no further elaboration, of gold grains being brought to Comogre "to be melted" (Andagoya 1865: xii). However, these references need not automatically be taken as indicative of local casting. Concerning *mise-en-couleur,* Lechtman argues that surface treatment of alloys by various methods was a separate and specific development in South American metallurgy, particularly in Colombia and Peru where specific modes of surface treatment can also be correlated with distinct metallurgical traditions (1975*a*; see also Lechtman 1973 and 1975*b*). Furthermore, the creation of bright color on the surfaces of alloyed objects by enrichment techniques may have carried distinct socioideological significance (Lechtman 1975*a* and *b*). Possibly, the use of *mise-en-couleur* by Panamanian craftsmen to brighten *tumbaga* objects was a significant aspect of isthmian metalworking in and of itself and should not be interpreted simply as evidence for local casting. With regard to the "melting" of gold grains, in Colombia gold grains and nuggets apparently were sometimes melted into crude lumps or disks, which were then sent to craftsmen elsewhere for manufacture into finished pieces or which served as exchange tokens (Duque Gomez 1965: 318; Wassén 1955: 98–99; Trimborn 1948: 191). It is noteworthy here that Lothrop presents an illustration of several tiny ingots and disks of gold and copper found at the Sitio Conte (1937: 75, fig. 46). The provenience of these objects is not known, however, and Lothrop considers it probable that metal in the form of small ingots was exchanged from one region to another (ibid.).

Tools used in melting and casting have occasionally been found in Colombia, although rarely in controlled archaeological excavations (Bray 1974*a*: 35–36; Emmerich 1965: 87–88, 169–170; Bruhns 1970 and 1972; Bright 1972). To the best of my knowledge, such tools are not known from Panama, although a mold used for casting "Chiriquí" frog figurines has been recently reported by Lange from a Late Polychrome (ca. A.D. 1200–1500) site in Guanacaste, Costa Rica (Cooke 1977). Lothrop makes mention of small ceramic vessels found in Panama at the Sitio Conte that could have been used as crucibles and that show signs of exposure to high heat. But, he cautions, none showed remnants of slag on the walls, so it is not possible to know whether the heat was a functional application or the result of exposure to fires used for another purpose not directly related to the function of the vessels themselves (1937: 77).

In considering the significance of these few data and the assertions based upon them, we should also bear in mind that, if in fact goldworking in Panama at the time of European conquest was limited to hammering and to gilding presumably already-cast *tumbaga* objects via *mise-en-couleur*, it is still logically possible that casting and alloying were practiced in earlier centuries but then abandoned. Some of this uncertainty may be clarified as our archaeological knowledge of ancient Panama deepens. The ethnological and archaeological perspective suggested in the previous sections argues, however, that, while gold pieces, such as nose plates and earrings, worn by all members of Panamanian society as symbols of "humanness" and of membership in ordered society may have been produced in the isthmus by such simple techniques as hammering (as at least some of the hammered and embossed helmets, greaves, and chest plates worn by the elite also may have been), the more elaborate cast gold and *tumbaga* ornaments, particularly effigy pendants and some elaborate nose ornaments, associated with the elite as symbols of sacred-secular power and authority, were manufactured outside the isthmus and were acquired through long-distance contacts that derived at least in part from the obligation of the Panamanian rulership to seek esoteric knowledge of distant places and things. From this perspective it can be argued that there would be good reason NOT to develop alloying and casting skills locally if possession of the exquisite gold pieces crafted by such means were correlated with prestigeful long-distance contacts.

This hypothesis can be amended to the effect that, even if casting and alloying were locally practiced in the early sixteenth century, the association of a particular class or category of gold pieces, such as effigy pendants and elaborate nose pieces, with the rulership could have resulted in acquisition of these pieces from afar, while other ornaments, perhaps indicative of lesser status, were locally produced. It is, in fact, within the collection of cast gold and *tumbaga* effigy pendants and more elaborate nose rings and clips that Lothrop found most of the specimens that he interpreted as "trade" pieces at the Sitio Conte. The great majority of the gold artifacts associated with Veraguas and Chiriquí are also pendants in the form of animal and anthropomorphic figures cast from gold-copper alloys (see Lothrop 1966: 199–200; MacCurdy 1911: 189–226; Holmes 1888: 36, 41–49, 52–53). Reviewing some of the Chiriquí materials, Holmes comments that the relative absence of hammered objects in the collections is rather "extraordinary," since one would expect to find hammered pieces preceding casting in the "normal" developmental sequence of metallurgical skills (ibid., p. 53; see also Root below). This "extraordinary" occurrence makes sense, however, if the predominance of cast effigy figurines is seen to reflect not a stage in the development of local metallurgy but the expression of a system of elite contacts with distant places and peoples.

Yet, again, it is necessary to admit the possibility of the local production of cast figures, this time utilizing data recorded a century after initial European contact. In an *informe* dated 1610 concerning the Talamancan region of eastern Costa Rica and written by a Franciscan missionary, Fray Augustín de Zevallos, regarding what was then a frontier mission district, we find mention of the abundance of gold in this mountainous region and of its use by the native population in barter, as ornaments, and as burial objects. The gold was crafted locally into the form of "eagles," small lizards, and other animals and made into larger *patenas,* or medallions. The animal figurines were crafted by pouring into molds gold that had been melted in crucibles of clay and mixed with copper. The medallions, or *pa-*

tenas, however, were hammered of pure gold (Fernández 1886*b*: 158–159).[3] This report, when taken in conjunction with that of Diego de Sojo regarding gold hammering in Veragua and with Columbus' account concerning the Almirante Bay region as a source of gold ornaments for the people of Cariai (Puerto Limón) in Costa Rica, is highly suggestive of a long-established gold manufacturing region in the general Talamanca-Veragua area of northeastern Costa Rica and northwestern Panama. Goldworking was also reported by the Spaniards from the interior of the Diquis region of southeastern Costa Rica, where the *cacique* of the village of Couto "worked" (*labrava*) gold pieces described as animal figurines and *patenas* (Fernández 1886*a*: 231).

There is no way of knowing how accurately these accounts reflected the pre-European contact situation. Were both casting and hammering practiced prior to as well as after contact or was hammering alone formerly practiced? Was the same range of artifacts still manufactured? Did the collapse of long-distance contacts as a result of European conquest lead to renewed emphasis on local crafting? None of these questions can be answered at this time and all possible interpretations must be considered. It is worth repeating in this context that there is no reason to assume either that *all* cast and alloyed pieces must have been locally produced in pre-Columbian times or that *all* such pieces were acquired by long-distance contacts. Recognition of the various sociopolitical-ideological contexts in which gold pieces may have been used in pre-Columbian isthmian society allows for the possibility that some of these items, particularly those associated with commoners or lower-status elites, were locally produced, while the most prestigeful elite pieces were acquired abroad for reasons hypothesized above.

The Colombian Heartland

Let us leave this point for the moment and turn to Colombia, the purported source of some of these elegant gold pieces and the region where "aboriginal gold-work in the Americas reached its highest development" (Reichel-Dolmatoff 1965: 18). In northwestern Colombia, that portion of the country relevant to this discussion, the Andes break into three large mountain chains separated from each other by deep rift valleys carrying major river systems that drain the mountain slopes and flow into the Caribbean Sea (see Figs. 2 and 23). Moving in cross-section from west to east across this predominantly north-south-trending complex, we first encounter the hot rain forest of the Pacific coastal lowlands and then the mighty Río Atrato, the major waterway connecting the Panamanian isthmus with northern Colombia, which drains the western slopes of the Sierra Occidentalis, or Western Cordillera, of the Colombian Andes.

The eastern slopes of the Western Cordillera are drained by tributaries of the Río Cauca, which flows between the relatively low (altitude about 2,000 meters) western range and the lofty, snow-capped (altitude averaging 3,000 meters) Sierra Centralis, or Central Cordillera. As the Río Cauca emerges from the mountain it flows into the lower reaches of the Río Magdalena. This river separates the Central Cordillera from the Sierra Orientales, or Eastern Cordillera, a broad upland and plateau region averaging from 2,000 to 3,000 meters in altitude.

To the north of the three cordilleras the combined waters of the Río Cauca and the Río Magdalena flow across a region of savannahs and swampy river flood plains that stretches from Venezuela to the Gulf of Urabá. A number of other rivers also cross this Caribbean lowland, including the Río Sinú (see Reichel-Dolmatoff 1965: chap. 2, for a more detailed summary of geography).

At the time of European conquest this ecologically complex land of mountain masses, intermontane valleys, and coastal lowlands was populated by numerous chiefdoms. Some of these rank societies seem to have been coordinated into larger political groupings, or "federations," under the religious-political leadership of a central lord, which suggests that something akin to regional "fields of influence" may have existed. In this respect and in many other customs the structure and organization of the Colombian polities appear generally comparable to those recorded for early sixteenth-century Panama (see Cieza de León 1864; Anghera 1912: I; Oviedo 1852; Aguado 1956–1957; see also Trimborn 1948 and 1960; Reichel-Dolmatoff 1961 and 1965; Duque Gomez 1965, 1967, and 1970). Indeed, some scholars are of the opinion that the linguistic and cultural patterns of the peoples of at least eastern Panama (often termed Cueva in this cultural context) and of the lower and middle Atrato region, the Western Cordillera, and perhaps also the lower to middle Cauca valley could be considered a single cultural sphere (Trimborn 1948: 47, 53, 192–193, 204; Sauer 1966: 238–239). Such cultural similarity is also implied by my hypothesis regarding northwestern Colombia as pos-

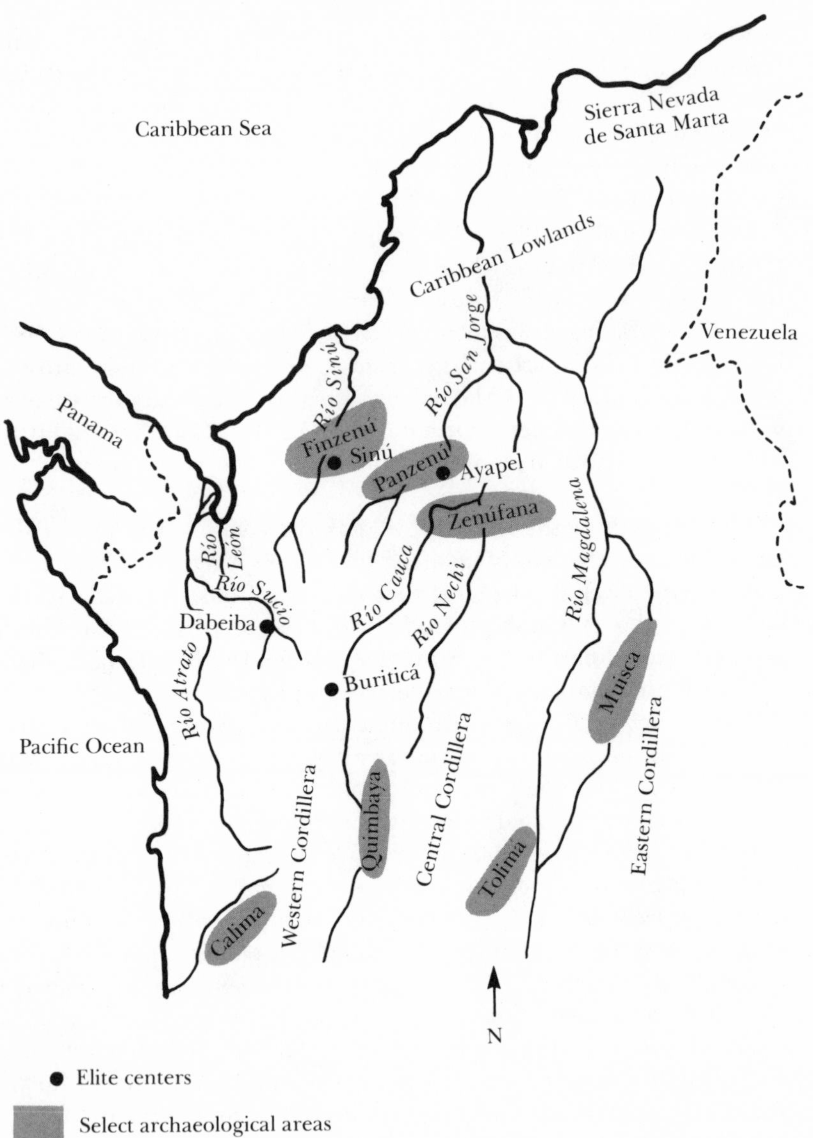

Fig. 23. Northern Colombia.

sible "origin point" in the political-religious world of Panamanian elites and as a region offering important sacred-secular contacts for these elites.

In pre-Columbian times, the indigenous peoples of northern Colombia and neighboring regions were related by marriage, warfare, political alliances, and exchange. With respect to the latter, the goods exchanged are virtually the same as those mentioned for ancient Panama, including salt (prepared from both sea water and interior saline springs), cotton and cotton products, dried fish, game (particularly peccaries), war captive-slaves, raw gold and manufactured gold pieces, ceramics (probably), sea shells, and gemstones. Of these, salt and gold (either unworked or fabricated), cotton products, and slaves appear to have been particularly ubiquitous. Some of this exchange moved between coastal or lowland peoples and groups in the more mountainous interior. Mountain groups also exchanged raw and fabricated mountain and coastal products among themselves (Trimborn 1942: 112–122, and 1948: 121–154; Duque Gómez 1970: 35, 39, 110, 134, and 1965: 311–354; Wassén 1955: 96, 102–104).[4]

Of the various goods mentioned in the literature, the exchange in raw gold and in manufactured gold and *tumbaga* objects is of most interest to us. The ethnohistoric materials make it clear that both unworked and fabricated metals were widely exchanged in rather complicated networks of which only the barest outlines are known. Generally, it appears that, while some Colombian groups both collected raw gold and then crafted gold pieces, others manufactured gold objects from imported raw metal, while still others collected and "exported" the raw gold and then "imported" finished gold products from elsewhere. Still others neither collected nor fabricated metal but acquired finished gold pieces in exchange for other valuables, such as cotton products, slaves, or salt. (See details of exchange in Cieza de Léon 1864: 36, 37, 66; Anghera 1912: 339–340; Vadillo 1884: 406; Trimborn 1942 and 1948; Wassén 1955; Duque Gómez 1970: 24, 39–40, and 1965: 281–330; Markham 1912: 17–18; Gordon 1957: 42–43; Sauer 1966: 171–172.) Extending this perspective to Panama, it is tentatively proposed that the central *quevís* of regional spheres of influence were primarily "exporters" of raw gold to Colombia and "importers" of cast gold and *tumbaga* pieces manufactured in Colombia and perhaps gilded in Panama, although it is probable that they themselves manufactured hammered gold pieces and, possibly, some cast gold pieces.

If, in fact, cast gold and *tumbaga* products were brought into Panama from northwestern South America, where were they initially crafted? Ethnohistoric data point to at least two Colombian gold-crafting centers as relevant for early sixteenth-century Panama—the chiefdoms of Sinú and the elite center of Dabeiba. Much of the Panamanian goldwork actually known to us, however, dates from several centuries before the European conquest. Archaeologists have identified close connections on stylistic grounds between these gold pieces and the goldwork of Sinú, but they do not recognize Dabeiba as one of the "archaeological areas" of Colombia. (Colombian "archaeological areas," of which approximately one dozen are recognized, are best considered as geographical rather than culturally defined regions. See Reichel-Dolmatoff 1965: 39; Jones 1974: 25–26.) Instead, archaeologists and art historians note close relationships between Panamanian gold pieces and those associated with the Colombian region of Quimbaya.

Quimbaya and Dabeiba may have been part of the same exchange network in the early sixteenth century, but there is a definite gap between the historically known Dabeiba, which will be discussed in more detail shortly, and the "archaeological area" of Quimbaya. There is also confusion between the archaeological Quimbaya and the historically known tribe of that name which apparently had no direct connection with most of the archaeological materials now called Quimbaya, too (but see discussion in Duque Gómez 1970). To be sure, at the time of conquest the Quimbaya Indians of the south-central Cauca valley were famous for their elaborate goldwork, and Trimborn discusses their exchange relationships with the mining area of Buriticá farther to the north, which, in his opinion, provided some of the raw gold that the Quimbaya Indians crafted (1942: 117; see also Duque Gómez 1970: 24, 37–38, 85). The Buriticá mining area also provided some, perhaps most, of the raw gold for crafting at Dabeiba, as we shall see, and a busy exchange in cotton products, salt, gold and gold pieces, and other goods may have moved among all three. Hence Quimbaya-Buriticá-Dabeiba ties appear likely in the early sixteenth century. It is because of the goldwork of the sixteenth-century Quimbaya Indians that the term "Quimbaya" has also been adopted archaeologically to identify a rather wide range of ceramic and gold artifacts associated with the Cauca valley and the Central Cordillera, some of which show close stylistic ties to Panamanian gold pieces dating several centuries before the Spaniards' arrival (Reichel-Dolmatoff 1965: 101–109).

The reports of the sixteenth-century conquistadors in Panama, however, say nothing of Quimbaya, although they associate at least some Panamanian gold pieces with Dabeiba. The elite center of Dabeiba has been tentatively located on the western slopes of the Western Cordillera in the middle reaches of the Río Sucio close to the confluence of two major headwater tributaries (the Río Urania and the Río Frontino) that lead into the western mountains, probably to the Boquerón de Toyo, the lowest pass between the Atrato and Cauca drainages in this part of the Western Cordillera (Parsons 1967: 3; Trimborn 1948: 16, 31, 168; Sauer 1966: 227, fig. 26). If this location is approximately correct, Dabeiba was situated in an extremely advantageous location for access, on the one hand, to the Gulf of Urabá (and Panama beyond) via the Atrato and, on the other, to the gold-rich chiefdoms of the middle Cauca valley and the Central Cordillera and, through them, to lands like Quimbaya lying still farther south.

Dabeiba is first mentioned in Balboa's report of his reconnoiter in 1512 of the lower reaches of the Río Atrato and its tributaries. In undertaking this trip, it was his intent to pursue rumors of a great *queví* named Dabeiba who was said to live beyond the lower Atrato lowlands and to be very rich in gold (see Sauer 1966: 223). Although Balboa did not reach Dabeiba on this trip, he became convinced that there was such a lord and land and reported as much to the king of Spain: "From the house of this cacique Dabeiba comes all the gold that goes out through this gulf [of Urabá] and all that the caciques of these surroundings possess. The report is of many pieces of gold in strange forms and of great size" (Balboa quoted in ibid., p. 227).

Balboa's letter continues to describe how Dabeiba acquired raw gold for his craftsmen from more distant peoples who collected it from streams or by burning terrain in the interior of the Cordillera Central. This metal was then brought for smelting and crafting to Dabeiba who "[had] great smelting of gold in his house and a hundred men continually fabricating gold." In exchange for this raw metal Dabeiba provided the collectors with various goods (some of which probably came from the lowlands farther north), including peccaries, fish, salt, cotton, cloth, servants, and objects of fabricated gold. Balboa concluded his report by saying, "All this I know by dependable information because I am never told anything different wherever I go. I have learned thus from many caciques and Indians, as well as from subjects (*vecinos*) of this cacique Dabeiba as from other sources, finding it to be true by many ways, putting some to the torture, treating others with love, and giving to others presents of things from Castile" (Balboa quoted in Sauer 1966: 227–228; see also

Balboa 1864: 532–533; Andagoya 1865: x; Trimborn 1948: 114, 181–185, 189, 191).

Dabeiba, in other words, appears to have acted as a middleman between gold-collecting centers of the Cauca valley, particularly the Buriticá mines in the vicinity of Antioquia if Trimborn's interpretation be accepted (although even more distant sources are implicated), and peoples of the northern lowlands, including, apparently, the eastern Panamanian isthmus, who provided various resources in exchange for the crafted gold pieces that Dabeiba's artists prepared (see Sauer 1966: 228, 258; Trimborn 1948 and 1942; a description of the native gold mines near Antioquia can be found in White 1884: 245; Duque Gómez 1965: 311–314; see also Cieza de León 1864: 57). Trimborn notes that the *queví* Dabeiba would have been in a good position to benefit himself from such exchange, and that some of the cotton goods and other lowland products were kept at his chiefly center where they may have been used to subsidize the gold craftsmen (1948: 208). Trimborn also feels that the *queví* probably acquired some of the raw gold for his crafting from local placer gold sources of the Río Sucio and its tributaries as well as from Buriticá (1942: 114, and 1948: 181–182, 189). I would further suggest that gold grains from Panama were another source of raw material for the Dabeiban smiths.

In light of the above, it is not surprising to find that the *queví* Dabeiba held considerable political influence and was reportedly overlord of many people and of a considerable territory (Trimborn 1948: 180, 186–188; Sauer 1966: 223, 227). Furthermore, and again expectedly, the place called Dabeiba was reportedly a major religious center and "a place of pilgrimage for the inhabitants of the lower Atrato basin" (Trimborn 1960: 103). Indeed, a great many imaginary statements exist in the general literature concerning Dabeiba as a second El Dorado and as the site of a golden temple dedicated to a powerful goddess. Trimborn rightly cautions against uncritical acceptance of such myths. He identifies the "golden temple" as essentially an elaborate *bohío* of the type we have encountered in Panama, but he recognizes that this chiefly compound served as a shrine or holy place of considerable repute (1948: 178–179, 200; see also Vadillo 1884: 407, 408–409). Priests and *caciques* periodically ascended a platform within a walled sanctuary in the *bohío* compound (compare the Panamanian *surba*) to intercede with the deities regarding the weather or some other topic. While the priest and *cacique* were engaged in this secluded task, the people, summoned by trumpets and tinkling bells, ceremoniously assembled outside the enclosure to await the outcome of the rulers' interaction with the gods (compare the Panamanian *nele* demonstrations quoted previously) (Anghera 1912: II, 319–320).[5] The people who attended these sacred activities are said to have come from near and far (Trimborn 1948: 201). Martyr reports that "great popular meetings" were held from time to time and that the *caciques* "of even the most distant countries" sent slaves to be sacrificed at the sacred place at certain times of year (Anghera 1912: II, 318–319). Elsewhere we read that "pilgrims" coming "from afar" brought "costly presents" as well as human sacrifices (see Bancroft 1886: 498–499).

In sum, Dabeiba appears as an elite center of considerable political-religious influence and renown—a center, too, for goldsmiths (and probably other craftsmen) advantageously situated with regard to the movement of resources between the northern Caribbean lowlands of Colombia and the eastern Panamanian isthmus and interior mountainous regions of central Colombia. The *queví* who regulated all this activity must have enjoyed a high and widely respected reputation for both sacred and secular abilities, and it is not surprising that Balboa heard much of him.

The raw gold mined and collected in the Cauca valley also found its way, sometimes via Dabeiba, to Sinú, another center for gold crafting located in the northern Colombian lowlands where the Río Sinú and the Río San Jorge course toward the Caribbean (see Reichel-Dolmatoff 1958 and 1965: fig. 3). As was mentioned above, Sinú is implicated as a source of gold artifacts for Panama by virtue of the so-called Sinú style characteristic of some isthmian gold pieces. This representational style is associated with the "archaeological region" located in the foothills and lowlands north of the Cordillera Occidental.

In the early sixteenth century, Spanish conquistadors encountered three large chiefdoms—Finzenú, Panzenú, and Zenúfana—in this general region, with the rulership of Finzenú, capital of the populous Sinú valley, regarded as primary by the others. The town of Finzenú (or Sinú proper) was a large political-religious elite center associated with an extensive necropolis where natives of different regions were buried and where deceased elites from Zenúfana and Panzenú and probably even from Urabá were interred in large *tumuli*. (Dabeiba may also have served as a necropolis, for *tumuli* with elite burials are reported to have been there. See Trimborn 1948: 187; cf. Coe 1956, and 1975: 102–103.) A "sister city," Ayapel, also with a necropolis, was situated to the east on a tributary of the Río San Jorge in the area called Panzenú. The Spaniards found both communities to be carefully laid out, with house-lined streets surrounding a central plaza. At Finzenú an elaborate temple containing tall wooden idols in human form stood at one corner of the central plaza. A grove of sacred trees stood nearby. Finzenú, Panzenú, and the third polity, Zenúfana (which occupied the valley of the Río Nechi), were ruled by members of a single elite family.[6]

Finzenú was also a center for crafts and exchange. Contacts extended to people of Urabá to the west, to Dabeiba, to Zenúfana to the southeast, and to the Cauca valley. The items sent to these regions from the lowlands included such cotton goods as hammocks and clothing, fish, peccaries, slaves, and salt, the latter prepared in Finzenú, at Urabá, and on the offshore Isla Fuerte. In addition, Finzenú imported raw gold and exported finished gold pieces. Gordon says that "unworked gold reached Finzenú from Dabeiba; the Indians built bridges across the Cauca and carried gold to Finzenú from the Cauca Valley and its affluent the Río Nechi. Gold artifacts were sent in return. Finzenú was a nation of specialists; the Spanish recognized the handicraft of the Finzenú 'maestros' in gold objects found at Dabeiba and Urabá. The movement of finished pieces both southward and northward from the Sinú indicates that the Zenú had developed local styles prized in an area renowned for its goldwork. . . . The Zenú were acquainted with smelting, alloying, hammering, and casting techniques" (1957: 42–43; see also Vadillo 1884: 406, 408; Trimborn 1948: 190).

According to the paradigm developed above, the few Sinú gold pieces that appear in Panamanian archaeological sites (for example, at the Sitio Conte) were obtained by Panamanian elite as a result of political-religious-educational visits, either to intermediate chiefdoms like Urabá, which was situated just across the Gulf of Urabá from Darién, or to Sinú centers themselves. The fact that Finzenú and Ayapel served as necropolis for a wide area suggests that a superior sacredness was associated with these centers, as do the temple and sacred tree grove at Finzenú. It is quite possible, indeed probable, that Panamanian rulers and priests were in contact with such elite centers, as it is also probable that they were in contact with Dabeiba. Indeed, both the Sinú centers, with their craftsmen and elaborate temple-burial complexes, and the craft and religious-political center at Dabeiba may well have been regarded as "places of origins" in Panamanian religious-political elite thought and as educational centers for study of political-religious lore by chiefly "pilgrims" from the Isthmus.[7] I propose that it may have been during such visits that isthmian elites—particularly those from regionally influential centers—acquired the elaborately crafted cast gold and *tumbaga* effigy pendants and nose clips that today testify to ancient contacts with Colombia (see Lothrop 1937: 204). They would have received these goods in return for education and for prestations to the chiefs and priests of these (and perhaps other) sacred Colombian centers of raw gold, war captive-slaves, pearls, and other "costly goods" from Panama.

The implication here, of course, is that ancient Colombian and Panamanian elites shared a common political-religious view. I assume that such a commonality may have existed because of the general similarity between the pre-Columbian societies of the isthmus and those of northern Colombia and because of evidence regarding the preparation for office required of at least some Colombian elites. For example, among the Chibcha, or Muisca, of the Eastern Cordillera, future chiefs and priests, before assuming office, underwent a special training period in which they spent as many as twelve years in seclusion in a certain temple where they endured various abstentions and were taught religious-political history and various esoteric practices of their calling. Furthermore, upon completion of this training period the noses and ears of the "students" were perforated and new ear pieces and nose pieces of gold were given them. They then were officially recognized in their new capacities by the incumbent ruler (Duque Gómez 1967: 481, 505, and 1965: 364–365; Reichel-Dolmatoff 1965: 160; Markham 1912: 27, 41; Oviedo 1852: bk. 26, chap. 31, p. 410).

Generalizing from these brief comments, it is proposed that comparable retreats and specialized intellectual trainings were required of rulers and priests of other Colombian chiefdoms. I know of no further information specifically regarding travel by high-status students to geographically distant places of instruction, although the so-called pilgrimages to such centers as Dabeiba may have included elite students traveling from distant places to spend a period of instruction under the tutelage of famous priests and politically sophisticated chiefs.[8] There is, however, a tantalizing description left by Oviedo concerning pilgrimages apparently made by Chibcha (Muisca) rulers to a sumptuous temple located some fifteen days' travel away from the Chibcha heartland at a place said to be visited by the sun. (The locality may have been in the Aríarí river basin in the foothills of the Eastern Cordillera southeast of Bogotá.) Travelers returning from this place brought back with them small boys dedicated to the sun who were reared with great care and highest respect until they reached puberty, at which time they were sacrificed. No *cacique* was without at least one of these boys (Oviedo 1852: bk. 26, chap. 30, pp. 409–410; Duque Gómez 1967: 509).

It must be emphasized that this concern with elite intellectual quests and the hypothesis that gold pieces and probably other sumptuary goods were exchanged among elites as part of the process of acquiring highly specialized knowledge is not intended to obviate the possibility that other modes of regional and long-distance exchange operated in northern Colombia and in the isthmus (see Lathrap 1973*b*). The records of the Spanish conquest clearly indicate that in Colombia many kinds of resources were exchanged at periodically held events, which the Spaniards called *ferias* or *mercados*. These exchange activities in at least some cases were conducted in border regions between polities in different ecological zones, for example, in territory adjacent to both highland and lowland zones or at major junctions between watersheds. Some of the *ferias* or *mercados* (for example, those held at Tahamí) lasted for several days and attracted persons identified by the Spaniards as long-distance "merchants" who traveled to exchange centers from great distances (see Duque Gómez 1965: 313, 328–329, and 1967: 213; Trimborn 1942: 122; Wassén 1955: 100). The goods exchanged at such places included salt, textiles, fish and peccaries, slaves, and raw gold and gold pieces. These latter are evidenced, for example, by Vadillo's brief mention of the exchange places visited by lowland peoples from the Sinú centers where they obtained raw gold for crafting from interior groups (Vadillo 1884: 406; Duque Gómez 1965: 313; Trimborn 1942: 112, 119). Local people also congregated at *ferias* to exchange their goods, a process suggesting the interdigitation of local or regional production with long-distance exchange activities (see Trimborn 1942: 115–116, 119, 122; Eidt 1959: 384).

It is difficult to know how to construe this information. Trimborn, for example, argues that the data do not support the interpretations of large-scale and all-encompassing (capitalistic) market-based trade that some writers have suggested (1942: 122). In his opinion, the *mercados* involved small-scale exchanges of goods at select localities or exchange centers. Perhaps, however, we can be somewhat more specific about the nature of these centers and the type of activities that were conducted there. In the Spanish reports the so-called market centers, or *mercados*, are also termed *ferias*, that is, market in the sense of "fair" or "bazaar" or "holiday gathering." This implies that the populace engaging in exchange of goods assembled at a given place for reasons other than, or in addition to, the strictly economic—reasons having to do with religious-political holidays or festival celebrations (see, e.g., Castellanos quoted in Trimborn 1942: 122; Wassén 1955: 100).

Of course, since *ferias* of this sort were a part of sixteenth-century European life, the conquistadors may be misleading us with an ethnocentric view. In Spain at this time two distinctive types of town markets were well established: the market, or *mercado,* held more or less on a monthly basis, and the fair, or *feria,* held less frequently and usually in conjunction with the fiesta of the town's patron saint. *Ferias* were particularly significant in towns along the routes followed by pilgrims visiting holy centers, such as at Santiago. *Ferias* were—and still are—also characterized by the presence of itinerant traders who made the rounds from one fair to the next to take advantage of the social holiday atmosphere (Foster 1960: 107–111; Turner 1974: 188; cf. Fogg 1940).

The references in the Colombian conquest literature to "traveling merchants" and to *ferias o mercados* suggest that the Spaniards recognized native gatherings in which a festival atmosphere prevailed as much as a commercial one. Recognition of sacred elite centers to which "pilgrimages" were made and information that pilgrims carried various "costly goods" to the center further suggest that at least some of the "markets" where goods were "bought and sold" may have been conducted as part of public gatherings convened for sociopolitico-religious reasons. It is particularly interesting in this context to find that certain of the exchange sites used by the Chibcha were apparently perceived in somewhat sacred terms, being marked by stones carved in religious symbolism and showing representations of the objects exchanged (Duque Gómez 1967: 468).

It is also clear that the salt, cotton goods, slaves, emeralds, sea shells, and goldpieces which moved through these exchange centers were elite sumptuary goods, which implies that at least some of the *ferias o mercados* observed by the Spaniards were held at locales that were also elite political-religious centers or perhaps recognized places of pilgrimage (compare Comogre and Veragua in Panama). At such centers the exchange of various resources would have had political-religious connotations as much as strictly economic significance (compare the multiple social, political, economic, and religious activities of Aztec "market" places; see Kurtz 1974: 696–699; the term "pilgrimage" is another difficult word fraught with potential European ethnocentrism; see Turner 1974: 178–179, 188, 190). One wonders too, what type of relationships existed between the so-called professional or long-distance merchants and elite rulers who also, I have suggested, dealt with "distances" and the valuable resources obtained therefrom.

The data in general do not allow hard and fast conclusions to be drawn regarding means of exchange of resources in ancient Colombia, but we should guard against too facile a use of such economic concepts as "trade" in discussion of these and other pre-industrial New World societies. Certainly, a number of sumptuary goods, including gold, played little or no part in economic life per se but were associated with the religious-political sphere. As Cieza de León expressed it regarding gold, "If the Spaniards had not come, all the gold in the country would certainly have been offered to the devil, or buried with the dead, for the Indians neither want it, nor seek it for any other purpose. They do not pay any wages with it to their men of war, nor do they want it except as ornaments when alive, and to be placed by their sides when dead" (1864: 77). Indeed, not only in Colombia and the isthmus of Panama but throughout ancient America, gold was looked upon primarily as a sacred element symbolic of rulership and sacred power. As such, gold and other elite sumptuary resources most likely were distributed through activities of a political-religious nature more than by strictly economic mechanisms.

Gold Styles and Cultural Sequences

The spatial distribution and temporal depth of various goldworking techniques and representational styles may assist in an understanding of Panamanian-Colombian contacts. This discussion derives mainly from a paper by Root (1961), which considers the occurrence of gold styles and crafting techniques in what he calls "local cultures" of lower Central America and northwestern Colombia. (Root's "local cultures" are comparable to the "archaeological areas" noted before. It must be emphasized that these regions are probably best considered as geographical rather than cultural areas.) Simply stated, Root proposes several stages in the evolution of metallurgical techniques in which southern regions of Colombia evidence the earliest and simplest metallurgical techniques, while northern areas of Colombia and adjacent lands evidence later and more complex metallurgical skills.

More specifically, the Calima and Tolima areas in the more southern reaches of the Western and Central Cordilleras (Río Cauca and Río Saldana headwaters, respectively) reveal some of the earliest examples of Colombian metallurgy.[9] Ornaments of pure gold made by hammering and annealing and, a little later in time, by open-back casting by the lost-wax process and the use of gold-rich (10–45% copper) *tumbaga* are characteristic. In Root's interpretation, these earliest stages of goldworking may be tentatively dated pre–500 B.C. to about A.D. 100. (These dates and others given below do not necessarily refer to Root's opinion regarding the *duration* of a given style but a given *stage* in the development of metallurgical techniques.)[10] The next major developments took place in the Quimbaya region located in the Central Cordillera and the Cauca valley somewhat north of the Calima and Tolima regions. While the so-called Quimbaya style extended over a long period of time and includes objects of virtually all techniques, Root focuses on the development of hollow casting and, a bit later, of copper-rich (45–90% copper) *tumbaga* and true *mise-en-couleur* gilding. These technological developments may have occurred, according to his chronology, between approximately A.D. 100 and 700. The final developmental level in Root's scheme saw the emergence of distinctive local styles about A.D. 700 in northern Colombia (Muisca, Tairona, Sinú), in Panama, and in Costa Rica. These styles are based on a diversity of well-established metallurgical techniques, including hammering and embossing *tumbaga*, *mise-en-couleur* gilding, casting, and false filigree.

Although cultural sequences are poorly understood for the various regions whose gold styles and technologies are considered by Root, the increased skill in metallurgical techniques and the distribution of gold styles can be provisionally associated with the evolution and spread of chiefdoms, that is, with the rise of the sacred-secular elite leadership of rank societies and with the growth and spread of a more-or-less unified system of elite politico-religious beliefs that were given material representation via gold pieces and other forms of elite goods (see Reichel-Dolmatoff 1972*c*: 132). Satisfactorily dated stratigraphic archaeological sequences that might substantiate or negate this interpretation are particularly lacking for both the southern regions (including Calima-Tolima) and the central Cauca valley (Quimbaya territory). The archaeology of northern Colombia, however, is better known. In broad terms these data reveal a developmental sequence from small Formative villages with a riparian focus and, later, root-crop agriculture to communities based on intensive maize agriculture. Some of these settlements were now located farther inland from the sea and major rivers on the fertile slopes of the more mountainous interior regions. The interior agricultural settlements formed the basis for the emergence of rank societies in northern Colombia, at which time metallurgy also appeared in this region, apparently fully developed and without signs of *in situ* growth (Reichel-Dolmatoff 1958: Reichel-Dolmatoff, however, does entertain the possibility of goldwork at Momil and related sites; see 1965: 77–78).[11] By this time chiefdoms of the sort described by the Spanish conquistadors in the early sixteenth century were in existence not only in northern Colombia but also throughout much of the Colombian Andes (Reichel-Dolmatoff 1961, 1965, and 1972*c*: 132–139; Willey 1971: 280–281, 307–326).

If this pattern of northern Colombian cultural development is compared with Root's analysis of stages in gold technology, and if the appearance of gold pieces and metallurgy is considered broadly associative with the rise of rank societies and a religious-political elite, then I suggest the following sequence of cultural events in pre-Hispanic Colombia:[12]

1. About 1000 B.C. to A.D. 1: development of local egalitarian village societies in northern Colombia; in southern Colombia gold technology introduced and lost-wax casting developed among cultures of unknown sociopolitical form (but see the sequence of development for early San Agustín in Reichel-Dolmatoff 1972*c*).
2. About A.D. 100 to 700 or 1000: development of local rank societies in northern Colombia and a general move inland from the northern lowlands into the north-central mountains of the cordilleras concomittant with a general spread of goldworking techniques from southern Colombian regions to the more central mountains of the cordilleras; distribution may reflect the spread of local rank societies from southern Colombia to the more central regions (see Reichel-Dolmatoff 1965: 109–110).
3. About A.D. 700 or 1000 to 1500: meeting and overlapping of these two lines of cultural and stylistic movement such that elites of the local chiefdoms of the north-central mountains and northern lowlands encounter those of the south-central regions and accept the use of gold as a sumptuary elite item; in some central and northern rank societies metallurgy developed at important political-religious elite centers while elites of other polities received finished gold

> pieces in exchange for other sumptuary goods, including raw gold.

Figure 24 attempts to diagram the situation. As this figure also indicates, the sequence of cultural development known for Panama is broadly comparable with that for northern Colombia. According to a survey by Baudez (1963; see also Lothrop 1966; Linares 1975: 21–25) of developmental stages for the isthmus and Cooke's recent analysis of carbon-14 dates (1976), by the early centuries of the A.D. era (ca. A.D. 150) small, permanent villages and a life style based on fishing, hunting, and agriculture were firmly established. Between approximately A.D. 150 and 500, agriculture intensified and rank societies began to appear. Chiefdoms were fully developed from about A.D. 500 until the European conquest (see Willey 1971: 288–294, 327–338). Baudez notes the sudden introduction in the archaeological record, as rank societies emerged, of highly specialized artifacts, including gold pieces, which appear "in full development" with complex iconographical and artistic styles (see, e.g., Early Coclé phase in Lothrop 1937 and 1942*a*: 198–252). Judging from Cooke's dating sequence, we can suggest a date of ca. A.D. 500 for this introduction.

The appearance of goldwork in the isthmus generally accords chronologically with the introduction of goldwork into northern Colombia and can be considered as part of the spread of goldwork from southern Colombia to northern Colombia and lower Central America. Judging from the approximate dates (and it must be emphasized that they are tentative), however, gold may have appeared in Panama somewhat earlier than in some of the northern Colombian regions (approximately A.D. 500 for the former and A.D. 700 to 1000 for the latter). If this be true, it suggests that Panama's initial metallurgical contacts with northern South America were with gold-producing regions of central Colombia, such as Quimbaya, rather than with northern Colombia, and that comparable association with the Colombian north developed after approximately A.D. 700–1000 as goldworking centers and systems for the circulation of gold pieces developed in this northern region, also via contacts with Quimbaya and other interior centers (see Reichel-Dolmatoff 1958: 82, 89, 90).

The stylistic association of Panamanian gold pieces, particularly the proveniences proposed by Lothrop for the Sitio Conte, supports this interpretation to some extent. Much of the goldwork found in both Early Coclé and Late Coclé phases at the Sitio Conte (A.D. 500–1000) is closely associated with the so-called Quimbaya style. Indeed,

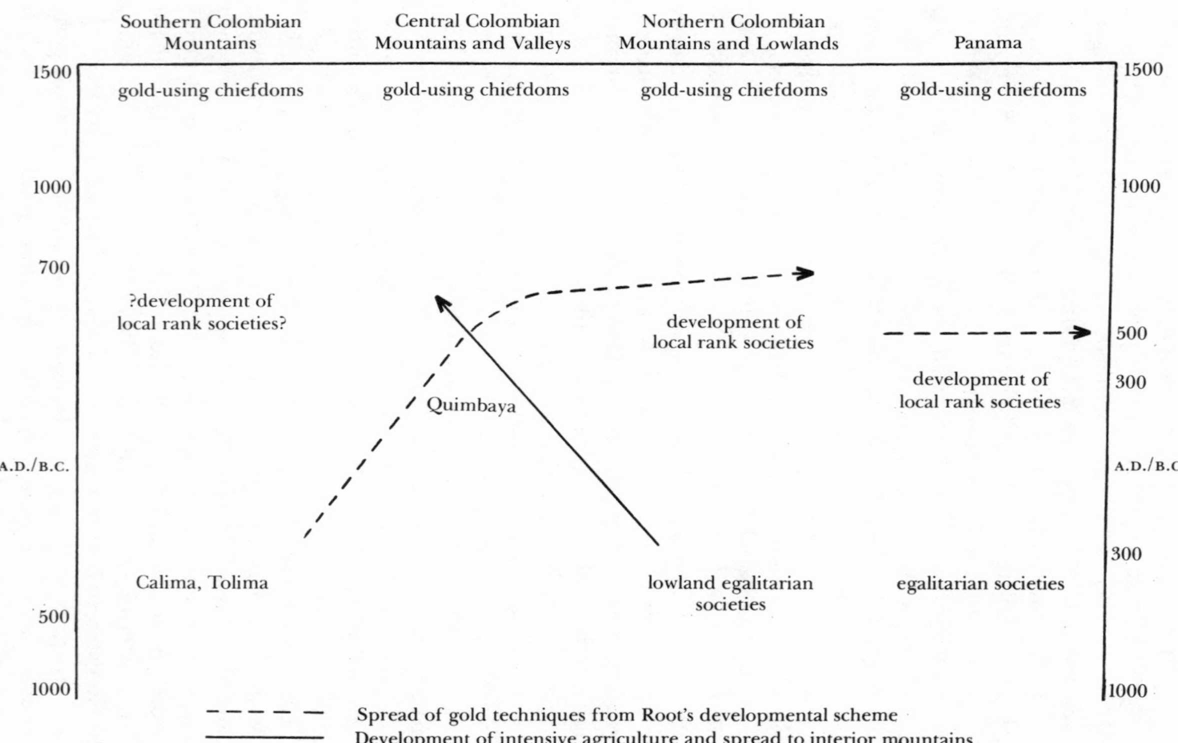

Fig. 24. Proposed patterns of cultural development and spread of gold technology in Colombia and Panama.

in Lothrop's opinion, in both form and technical processes Quimbaya goldwork is more closely related to that associated with Coclé than is the goldwork of any other region (1937: 69, 204). The pieces recognized as probably deriving from Sinú are fewer in number (though Lothrop feels that Sinú had a "definite influence" on Coclé's art) and, in Lothrop's opinion, associate more with Late Coclé (which terminates ca. A.D. 1000) when metallurgical evidence of contact with distant lands (Sinú, Quimbaya, possibly even the Muisca area and Ecuador) is strongest (1937: 70, and 1942*a*: 252). Balboa's reports on the connections between eastern Panama and Dabeiba in the early sixteenth century indicate the continuation of these ties with north-central Colombia during succeeding centuries.

Ideological and Political Systems in the Intermediate Area

The sudden appearance of sophisticated gold pieces when isthmian rank societies were first developing from the Formative base strongly suggests that the elites emerging to prominence in these early Panamanian chiefdoms had effected contact with the elites of rank societies in Colombia (particularly the Cauca valley–Quimbaya region and, later, northern Colombia) and were sharing in a political-religious belief system common to chiefdoms in this wide region—a belief system given material representation by, among other things, gold pieces and involving mutual contacts among elites.[13] In spite of regionalism, the Panamanian isthmus and Colombia (at least central and northern Colombia) continued to form a single, interwoven political-religious (and perhaps also economic) system of beliefs and elite activities during the five hundred to one thousand years prior to European conquest (cf. Reichel-Dolmatoff 1972*c*: 132, 138). This belief system can be assumed to have had its roots in the much more ancient cosmologies developed in Colombia and the isthmus during the millennia of Formative village life that preceded the chiefdom period in both territories, when mutual contacts were already in existence (see Reichel-Dolmatoff 1972*c*: 138; Myers 1973).

The clearest evidence of this shared political ideology may be found in the iconography portrayed on the valued gold pieces that became so widely distributed among all the rank societies of the isthmus and Colombia. To date the iconographic significance of the figures and designs portrayed on this goldwork remains virtually unexplored. Various birds and beasts have been more or less identified (see Lothrop 1937; Duque Gómez 1965: 304–311), but the religious-political metaphors signified by these and other iconographic features have hardly been considered, even though the various felines, raptorial birds, fish, snakes, and other creatures that can be discerned are also common elements in the iconography of other regions of pre-Columbian Nuclear America and feature in the mythology of numerous native peoples of tropical America today (Myers 1973: 6–7; Reichel-Dolmatoff 1972*c* and 1972*b*; Helms 1977).

To date analysis of Colombian and lower Central American goldwork has predominately emphasized "style," which is essentially a classificatory technique (see Perez de Barradas 1954–1966) that groups pieces together on the basis of stylistic similarities (see Reichel-Dolmatoff 1958) and emphasizes differences among style groups. These similarities and differences are then projected onto the geographical and cultural landscape such that a correlation between a given style and a distinct geographical and cultural region is assumed. This has occurred in spite of or, more likely, because of the fact that the provenience of much of the ancient gold of the Intermediate Area is unknown or uncertain. The assumed correlation between a given "style" and a corresponding "culture" has also led to the assumption that the diverse styles were made by different groups of craftsmen resident at the places where the style-associated culture is assumed to have existed.

These correlations and assumptions imply that the particular design contrasts, or "styles," that appear significant to scholarly observers today were recognized as such by pre-Columbian peoples, and that these design packages did in fact identify significant cultural areas to those who crafted and wore the ornaments. Perhaps they did but perhaps they did not. We do not know how the ancient peoples of Colombia and the isthmus conceptualized the designs portrayed on gold pieces, that is, how or what they interpreted as design similarities and differences. Nor do we know how or if patterns of design correlated with cultural or political units. Such insights may always elude us, but we might achieve a higher degree of understanding if we broaden our investigations and interpretations beyond the constraints of the concepts of style.

A few scholars have begun this process, noting the wide distribution of Intermediate Area iconographic motifs and religious concepts within Nuclear America. For example, Lothrop, working with Panamanian materials, recognized symbolic motifs that could be traced north to Mexico and south to Colombia, Ecuador, and Peru (1942*a*: 252, and 1961*b*). Reichel-Dolmatoff, discussing the iconography of

San Agustín, emphasizes the commonality of many ancient ideological themes held by aboriginal peoples of Nuclear America (for example, the concepts of a supernatural Master of Animals, of the significance of the jaguar, of the symbolic value of various minerals, of color symbolism). He then states, with reference to the widespread thematic representations that iconography associates with several ideological spheres of pre-Columbian Nuclear America, including Olmec, Chavín, and San Agustín, that, while these concepts were likely to find quite different stylistic expressions in their respective regions, "the important thing is the verifiable extent of the idea, and not its divergences in detail" (1972*c*: 138). This approach could be modified to apply to the various iconographic representations found within any one ideological sphere, for example, to the goldwork associated with the Intermediate Area itself. Here, too, we may expect to find common symbolic themes among the diversity of so-called styles, although the modes of representation, that is, the details of the "style" of presentation, may be quite divergent.

Bolian has taken an approach similar to this in his stylistic seriation of one Colombian gold style. In analyzing the attributes of the so-called Darién Style anthropomorphic figure, he found that "it was evident that many, but not all, of the attributes were also present in other gold styles and that the Darién anthropomorphic figure was not an isolated phenomenon but, rather, it was one expression of a widespread and long lasting artistic tradition that existed in the northern Andes and Central America. Some of the features which the Darién figure shares with other Colombian and Central American gold styles are general concepts, such as the basic kinds of figures that are represented, while others are more specific, such as particular decorative features or combinations of features" (n.d.: 1–2). A similarly wide-ranging motif, Bolian adds, is the eagle. "Eagle pendants are typically thought of as very representative of the Veraguas Style of gold work. . . . However, eagle pendants have a widespread distribution ranging from Costa Rica to the Sinú, the Cauca Valley, Tierradentro, Popayán and the Muisca area. There are some differences in the pendants from place to place but the basic motif prevails in all of the regions with local decorative elaborations being added" (ibid., p. 2). Other scholars have noted the "interrelatedness" of the various styles characteristic of Colombia and Panama (Lothrop 1937: 204) and have indicated the difficulties of working within the geographical-cultural constraints frequently associated with styles (see Jones 1974: 25–26; Root 1961: 250). It has been suggested that individual goldsmiths could easily have crafted pieces in more than one of the styles as they are currently defined (Bolian n.d.: 1; Bray 1974*b*: 46), or that "styles" attributed to locality might carry chronological significance, at least in part (Cooke 1977).

Why, in fact, were gold pieces crafted with such a range of representational detail, or "stylistic difference"? The great diversity of metallurgical techniques and the variety of modes of representation ("styles") characteristic of Intermediate Area goldwork—a diversity and variety that are greater here than for any other single area of native America—might possibly correlate with the large number of rank societies that evolved in this territory in pre-Columbian times. Did a particular configuration of details (perhaps but not necessarily the same as those used by contemporary scholars to differentiate a particularly "style" today) symbolize or identify membership in a given rank society or regional sphere of influence, as a particular configuration of body ornaments identifies societies in Brazil today (see Seeger 1975)?[14] Did a particular mode of depiction of basic religious-political themes identify a given elite "learning center," perhaps serving as a metallurgical identification symbol or "emblem glyph" for such centers (cf. Berlin 1958; Marcus 1976)?

Whatever the significance of the diversity of gold forms may be, if we look beyond the representational detail and seek basic iconographic motifs, we will likely find a set of common, unifying religious-political themes expressed throughout this body of material. Contrary to Willey's well-known comments (1962: 9 and 1966: 144) on the seeming absence of a "sophisticated, richly iconographic, and widespread art style—of a common ideology or religion uniting other peoples" in the Intermediate Area (in contrast to Mesoamerica and Peru, where such definitely occurred), I propose that the societies of the Intermediate Area did share a common set of beliefs that did promote a widening of the "social field" (Willey 1962: 10) and a unification of sorts, particularly among the elite. This belief system included agreement concerning the political validity of the quest by elites for esoteric knowledge, the specific content of that knowledge, and the means to achieve it (via supernatural contacts and via study at recognized centers).

Primary data to support this hypothesis may be found in the rich, sophisticated but little-understood (by us) iconography expressed in gold and in gilded *tumbaga*. Indeed, the very fact that gold and gold alloys were used throughout the Intermediate Area as a vehicle (though not the only one) for religious-political symbolism may be construed as evidence for widespread agreement concerning the religious-political (power) symbolism attributed to the bright yellow metal. To be sure, Central Andean peoples also used gold widely, and for similar reasons, but it may be significant here that techniques of goldworking differed somewhat between Andean peoples and those of the Intermediate Area who in particular made greater use of *tumbaga* and associated techniques of surface gilding (see Root 1949: 222–224; Lechtman 1975*a*). It is my assumption that the political symbolic use of gold-colored pieces within the Intermediate Area contained internal consistencies that identified an area elite "social field," and that the use of gold among central Andean elites showed a comparable but distinctly different set of internal consistencies.

6

The Interpretation of Long-Distance Exchange

The Ubiquity of "Trade"

The pursuit of esoteric knowledge concerning "distant" places and peoples by the political elite of pre-Columbian Panamanian chiefdoms, as postulated from the pursuit of such knowledge by contemporary Cuna leaders, who may be regarded in their religious-political roles as descendants of these ancient rulers, may carry implications for interpretations of the operation of rank societies elsewhere in pre-Columbian America. Recognition of the significance of esoteric knowledge to the operation of elite sectors may have relevance for our understanding of such phenomena as the spread of Olmec and Chavín art and architectural styles, the operation of lowland Classic Maya society, or the significance of the Hopewellian "interaction spheres."

The archaeologically documented distributions of various elite goods associated with these pre-Columbian chiefdom systems have elicited a number of interpretations that attempt to account for the material evidence of far-flung contacts characteristic of these political systems. For example, a number of scholars have proposed that the wide distribution of Olmec and Chavín stylistic and iconographic features represents the spread of religious traditions, either by the gradual diffusion of beliefs or perhaps by more active proselytizing by missionaries (Willey 1962; Patterson 1971: 41–44; see also Lanning 1967: 98; Grove 1974: 124). Intrusions of colonists or at least visiting heartland emissaries, possibly at times employing militaristic modes of expansion, have also been suggested (see discussion in Lanning 1967: 102; Grove et al. 1976; Coe 1965: 771). In yet another interpretative exercise, Flannery explains the distribution of exotic goods and raw materials between the Olmec heartland and the Valley of Oaxaca as supportive of the status systems and attendant religious concepts in terms of which these ancient chiefdoms were organized (1968; see also Drennan 1976: 355–359).

The major propositions of Flannery's well-known argument state that a flow of luxury goods to the elite centers in the Olmec heartland was important for the maintenance of the Olmec status system, and that those groups who supplied these goods and who were most receptive to Olmec influence were themselves organized into rank societies *almost but not quite* as stratified as the Olmec heartland chiefdoms. Flannery proposes that the entrepreneurs who facilitated the exchange by such mechanisms as ritual visits, intermarriage, or "adoption" of members of the other group would derive from the elite of the societies involved. Furthermore, the initiative to explore Olmec associations would rest with the ruling elite of the slightly less complex societies as much as with the Olmec, for the rulership of those less sophisticated societies would seek to emulate Olmec elite behavior and status trappings, even language forms, in order to increase their own prestige.

The ultimate effect of such contacts, in Flannery's opinion, however, was not only to support elite status systems but also to create a far-reaching economic sphere that linked highland hinterlands and lowland centers into a more unified economic whole. Thus, his insightful religious-political interpretation essentially rests on an economic-ecological foundation (see also Willey 1962: 9–10). Many scholars, in fact, inject an economic factor into their interpretations of the evidence of long-distance contacts among ancient chiefdoms. Some place heavy emphasis on economic models, speaking, for example, of the opening of "trade routes" or "trade networks" by which professional merchants, perhaps operating from strategically placed "gateway communities," sought scarce, rare, and valuable elite goods (see Coe 1965: 771; Hirth 1978). Others soften the economic focus somewhat by postulating social alliances, such as intermarriage, as well as trading partnerships as mechanisms by which economically important goods could be acquired, perhaps in exchange for esoteric or "cult" paraphernalia (Parsons and Price 1971: 178–188; Rathje 1972; Molloy and Rathje 1974). A "pilgrimage-market" model, which integrates an economic-commercial view with the ideological-ceremonial nature of elite centers and sumptuary goods, has also been proposed (Grennes-Ravitz 1974: 107; Grove 1974: 124–125; Grove et al. 1976).

To some extent the ubiquity of economic elements in these and other interpretative exercises may reflect a certain disenchantment among many archaeologists with the usefulness of ethnographic analogies for archaeological research (but see Pires-Ferreira and Flannery 1976) and a tendency to fall back instead on current anthropological "common sense" (see Earle and Ericson 1977: 9–10, 11). One major component of the climate of opinion presently in vogue among many anthropologists stresses the primacy of the natural environmental, technical, or "economic" aspects of cultural systems over the more strictly social structural or ideological. This conceptual framework is particularly enticing for reconstruction of prehistoric cultural systems where the primary data, being composed of material things, lend themselves readily to this perspective. Consequently, the spatial and temporal distributions of material things, even objects of obvious symbolic or ideological significance, are frequently explained as economic phenomena (see Webb 1974: 364, 367; Price 1977: 212–213).

To be sure, as several examples given above of Olmec-Chavín interpretations have shown, pre-Columbian economic systems are interpreted by some investigators in a "substantivist" sense, with sociopolitical and ideological interactions, such as tribute payments, gift giving, marriage alliances, and other diplomatic high-status prestations by priests and chiefs, postulated as predominate modes of exchange or with emphasis on exchange as a form of communication or information flow concerning many social and political matters, including relative social distance and the nature of social relationships (see Flannery 1968; Drennan 1976; Molloy and Rathje 1974; Wilmsen 1972; Renfrew 1975: 22–24; Dalton 1977). All too frequently, however, the activity surrounding ancient exchange has been interpreted not with reference to social (kinship) or political modes of conduct but by reference to economic concepts, most notably "trade."

The concept of trade as it is used in discussion of ancient societies is usually meant to refer to any and all means by which material goods are moved about in a peaceful manner (see Kohl 1975: 43; Clark in Dalton 1975: 114; Adams 1975: 452; Wright 1974). This broad usage, however, renders the term "trade" so generally as to virtually make it meaningless as a definition of activity (see Pires-Ferreira and Flannery 1976: 287). But there is an additional danger in the use of this term, for in the market-based economies in which most anthropologists live it also connotes specifically commercial ventures in commodities (cf. Dalton 1975: 101). Consequently, in those many instances where the term "trade" is used by anthropologists as a general expression simply intending "contact" and "exchange," the implication of commercial events cannot be easily avoided (cf. ibid., p. 123 n. 43). Indeed, "trade" may often be chosen as a catch-all term by archaeologists describing ancient societies precisely because it is a word that focuses on the exchange of material goods as a goal in itself, and thus it is assumed to be fundamentally appropriate to explanatory models utilizing material remains as primary data and concerned basically with economic forms and systems (see Webb 1974).

Esoteric Knowledge as a Scarce Resource

No one would deny that control of material resources is a fundamental requisite of cultural adaptation and, more specifically, of those charged with the leadership of the population living within the cultural system. What is less readily considered by many anthropologists reconstructing ancient societies, however, is the wide range of human interactions, the social setting in its broadest sense, that lead to manipulation of material resources (but see Wilmsen 1972; Dalton 1977). Also lacking is sufficient appreciation of the range of resources other than "material goods" that are fundamental for the survival of a population-cum-cultural system and that must also be controlled by the leadership if the polity is to be maintained in an orderly and "liveable" state (see Kohl 1975).

One of the fundamental resources available to human beings is the capacity for experiencing "the sacred," a capacity associated with the high order of human intelligence and with symbolic communication. As Rappaport has pointed out in an insightful and stimulating paper, the adaptive significance of sanctity and sacredness lies in their affirmation of the "truthfulness" of otherwise unverifiable propositions and in their certification of the reliability of information, so that actors may accept it as such and respond in predictable ways (1971). Thus, the concept of sanctity affirms the propriety of the particular conventions organizing a particular society. In addition, sanctity regulates the special interests of particular subgroups concerned with the government of society.

The importance of sanctity in social control hierarchies is particularly significant in societies where authorities have little secular power to achieve compliance with social norms. In these circumstances, found notably in rank societies, sanctity becomes a vital element of political power since it is largely by virtue of their aura of sanctity, that is, of association with "ultimate truth," that the leaders of such societies control the people and material resources under their charge (Rappaport 1971: 37–39; see also Netting 1972). More specifically, it is largely by virtue of their close association with the most abstract and esoteric concepts and the most sophisticated cognized model available to society that chiefs and priests of rank societies hold their positions of control (ibid., p. 34).

In operational terms this means that those assigned to leadership positions must evidence control of a particular kind of knowledge: knowledge of the nonordinary and of the nonconcrete; knowledge that explains and reaffirms the validity, the truthfulness (the sanctity) of the cognized model in terms of which the rulership claims its powers and position and the members of society are enjoined to act. This esoteric knowledge of that which is most abstract and nonmundane—of the "origins" and "nature" of things (the cosmos), of the fundamental or universal "processes" by which all things (the cosmos) operate, of the place of human society in such a universal system—then becomes a resource itself, a controllable form of "elite goods," a resource that is as important for the operation of society as are the material products of the economy.

In previous chapters the search for, acquisition of, and control of esoteric knowledge as it is defined and expressed by the leadership of the contemporary Cuna of eastern Panama were briefly examined and it was proposed that a similar pattern can be projected onto the political life of their pre-Columbian isthmian ancestors. It was argued by ethnographic analogy that in the ancient rank societies of Panama the search for this "resource" required contact among the various Panamanian elites and between select Panamanian elites and colleagues in northern Colombia, and that select Panamanian rulers or young "leaders in training" actually may have traveled to northern South America to confer with elite leaders of recognized intellectual excellence. I further suspect (borrowing from Flannery's model) that, generally speaking, the rank societies of the Panamanian isthmus were *slightly less complex* than at least some societies of northern and central Colombia (for example, those where temple centers and elite necropolises are documented by the early sixteenth-century conquistadors) and that the rulership of Panama gained in status and prestige through this association with more elaborate Colombian centers.

From the Panamanian perspective, the attraction and significance of Colombian elite centers may have been couched in terms of geographically distant religious-political "places of origin" whence the deepest insights and understanding of the religious-political "nature" of things would be obtained. From the perspective of the Colombian elite, the sacred authority accruing to them as widely respected teachers and "men of wisdom" (truth) to whom others of high status tendered a subordinate position may have constituted a major elite "resource." (The political-economic value derived from the labor of several dozen resident students must not be discounted, either.) A comparable bolstering of sacred authority would accrue to the chiefs and priests of Panamanian regional "fields of influence," from whom other Panamanian elite-trainees would seek to acquire the knowledge requisite for their own position.

By placing emphasis on the acquisition of sacred religious-political lore, this paradigm may appear related to the "diffused cult" or "ecumenical religion" interpretations offered for the Olmec and Chavín phenomena (see Willey 1962). Although a superficial similarity exists in the emphasis on ideological factors, at least two important points of contrast must be noted. First, an ecumenical interpretation implies the teaching of new ideological content to prior nonbelievers, who by definition did not initially share the same cognized model held by the proselytizers. In the model I am suggesting, a shared ideological context is a prerequisite for all those involved, either in teaching or in learning. Agreement as to the basic form and content of the religious-political and cosmological system is assumed to have underwritten the long-distance educational network and to have provided a basic epistemological foundation on which elite students and teachers could build and through which elite rulers and commoners could communicate. Second, the cult or ecumenical religion interpretation assumes an outreach from the "core" area to those in hinterlands beyond. I postulate instead (again following Flannery 1968) that elites in the isthmian "hinterland" actively pursued contacts with the Colombian "heartland" as Panamanian rank societies evolved and as competitive leaders sought ever greater (higher) criteria of sacred credibility.

Since esoteric knowledge, like all aspects of chiefly power, must be activated to be effective, we find that this elite intellectual quest was given material expression through (among other things) material goods. In previous pages I attempted to interpret the goldwork of ancient Panama and Colombia within this paradigm. A similar interpretation may also be directly applicable to the significance and distribution of the artwork and other elite goods associated with other ancient chiefdom systems, including Olmec-Chavín, Hopewell, and the lowland Classic Maya (see Drennan 1976 for a formulation along these lines).

The religious-political realm of leadership, of course, bears directly on the economic-technological affairs of society, and in the emphasis on elite knowledge systems I do not intend to deny the importance of other forms of production and exchange that supplied economically useful goods to the population and politically essential power to the rulership (see Netting 1972). Indeed, it is tempting to speculate as to what economic-technological developments may have been stimulated in Panama and northern Colombia by the elite political-religious system. I infer that in Panama the elite knowledge system was largely, though not entirely, responsible for the development of regional "spheres of influence," but that these widening political spheres need not have included greater economic specialization. Instead, by creating alliances among the elite, the effect of a leader like Comogre or Parita may have been primarily to link more units of like type into a single but potentially "segmentary" political field, one that was not internally more differentiated as a result of such linkages. In Colombia, in contrast, a relatively more differentiated political structure showing increasing complexity in internal political organization through greater occupational and craft specialization may have developed, at least at some polities. (Cf. the contrast between Mixtec kingdoms and Tarascan states posited by Spores 1974: 307.) Such contrasts may account for the presence of distinct temple structures in northern Colombia, as at Sinú, at the time of conquest and for their absence from Panama in the early sixteenth century.

Whatever the degree of economic and social complexity of the pre-Columbian isthmian rank societies, the forces that determined and guided the production and distribution of material resources were defined, supported, and probably enhanced by an ideological system that identified and authenticated the social-political arrangements by which the populace lived; the system also defined and interpreted the natural world whose resources were also essential for life. Such a system can be analyzed from any of several perspectives and with a focus on any of the several major variables involved. However, "the advance of a discipline is as much in the identification and isolation of these variables as in the analysis of their interdependence" (Cohen 1969: 216). Recognition of the significance of esoteric knowledge for the political life of human society is a field of investigation that may cast considerable light on the nature of cultural systems. This analysis of ancient Panamanian rank societies is offered as a step in this direction.

Appendix

The Origins of Fire Tale, or *Iskar y Achu,* is found in several sources. The earliest record, and the shortest version, dates from the mid-seventeenth century (Salcedo 1908: 127). Later collections from the twentieth century record longer and more detailed versions (Wassén 1937: 27–29; Chapin 1970: 32). Although there are some small differences among them, the general outline of the story is consistent over time. The version presented here is paraphrased from Chapin (1970) and Wassén (1937).

Tad Ibe ordered Iskar (Iguana), who could run across the surface of the water, to go to Jaguar's house, which was located on the other side of the river. Jaguar was the only animal-person at this time who possessed fire. The other animal-men wished to have it, but Jaguar, who was strong and whom they feared, had refused to lend it. One rainy night Iguana crossed the river, which was swollen from the storm, went to Jaguar's dwelling, and found Jaguar resting in his hammock with coals burning in a small clay jar beneath to keep him warm. Iguana told Jaguar that he had come to do him the service of tending the fire while Jaguar slept. Jaguar agreed. As soon as Jaguar was asleep, Iguana began to urinate on the coals. Jaguar awoke, looked beneath his hammock, and saw Iguana diligently fanning the coals. He saw, too, that the fire was partly extinguished, but Iguana said that the rain had come through a hole in the roof and he was doing all he could to keep the fire going. Jaguar went back to sleep. Iguana then took a small piece of burning coal and hid it in the crest on the back of his neck. He then extinguished the rest of the fire with his urine and ran out of the house. Jaguar woke up, saw his fire gone, and gave chase, but he could not swim and was unable to pursue Iguana across the rain-swollen river. Iguana gave the coal to Tad Ibe, who distributed fire to the people.

The Evil Ibelele tale, or *Tad Ibe contra Poni Ibelele*, is found in Chapin (1970: 23–27), which should be consulted for the full version. The paraphrase given below does not present a number of details that should be considered by those who might wish to work further with this tale.

Poni Ibelele, who was the chief of the evil spirits and also Master of Fire (that is, celestial fire, the Sun), issued a power challenge to Tad Ibe. Putting on his golden clothes and tying a gold band around his waist, Tad Ibe approached Poni Ibelele as a potential son-in-law would approach a potential father-in-law, offering to work for him cutting wood, sowing the fields, and hunting together and to live in his home (the Cuna are matrilocal). Poni Ibelele challenged Tad Ibe to a work contest in the fields, but when they arrived he suggested a short rest in the sun first. When he believed that Tad Ibe was asleep, Poni Ibelele surrounded him with a ring of fire. Tad Ibe, opening his eyes, called upon Rain to extinguish the fire, which it did. Tad Ibe then escaped home. He soon returned to Poni Ibelele's house and offered again to serve as a helpful son-in-law. Poni Ibelele sent him to hunt game, and while he was gone, Poni Ibelele built a great bonfire. On Tad Ibe's return, he and Poni Ibelele engaged in a competition to see who could withstand the fire longest. Tad Ibe, sustained by great mystical power, endured, but Poni Ibelele eventually lost his power to the fire. His body was consumed by the flames except for his spine. Meanwhile, Tad Ibe's brothers had pushed the rest of Poni Ibelele's family—his wife and daughters—into the flames. Tad Ibe and his brothers then carried Poni Ibelele's spine to the river where it changed into a *taim* or *lagarto* (caiman). "In years to come," Tad Ibe said, "you will stay in the water and serve as a boat to carry evil spirits in their travels across the levels of the underworld." The remains (backbones) of Poni Ibelele's wife and daughters were also thrown into the water where they were transformed into another form of *taim* (*taim ome*—the wife of the *lagarto*) and into three varieties of small *lagartos* (*iskin*, *tir*, and *nonor*), respectively.

The Iguana-Chief tale, or *Tad Ibe contra Olokisbakwalele,* is again found in Chapin (1970: 27–28) and is summarized therefrom. Again, those wishing to appreciate this tale most fully should consult the original version in Chapin.

Iguana-Chief, a very powerful man who had heard of Tad Ibe's conquests of other competitors, promised to give Tad Ibe a difficult time if he (Iguana-Chief) should be challenged, too. Tad Ibe, a man of power who was greatly respected and warmly welcomed in all the region, went with great pomp and ceremony to visit Iguana-Chief, and the two immediately began to quarrel. Iguana-Chief's family joined the fight and, being many, threw Tad Ibe to the ground. Tad Ibe struggled free and went home to prepare himself, by bathing with powerful medicines, for the next encounter. After achieving great strength, he returned to Iguana-Chief's house. He sent some of his men ahead to announce his coming to the people and to divert Iguana-Chief with dancing and clowning, and while Iguana-Chief was helplessly laughing Tad Ibe seized the sons of Iguana-Chief and turned them into species of small lizards (*lagartijas—saegwa, maar, kwamusir, kwamuswili, yalaiskin*). Then he went home again to bathe in medicines and to prepare himself for the next encounter. Tad Ibe returned to visit Iguana-Chief four days later and suggested they go to the river to bathe. At the river they removed the golden clothing they both wore leaving it on the sand. Tad Ibe then proposed that they have a contest to see who could swim farthest underwater. Although Tad Ibe (who swam first) surreptitiously walked a bit farther after his swim so as to increase the distance he apparently had covered underwater, Iguana-Chief swam still farther and easily won. Tad Ibe and Iguana-Chief then went to a cliff where Tad Ibe proposed they see who could jump to the ground and still survive. Tad Ibe went first, but before jumping he called to Cotton, who spread a soft mattress at the foot of the precipice. Tad Ibe, still a little faint-hearted, jumped and landed safely. Picking up the cotton mattress, he substituted many sharp stones in its place. When Iguana-Chief jumped, he hit hard against the stones, leaving much blood from his badly wounded body. Still, lifting his head, he turned to Tad Ibe and said, "See! I still live!" Tad Ibe went home again to bathe in powerful medicines and to gain power and strength anew; then once more he returned to Iguana-Chief's house. This time he proposed an endurance contest in which they would beat their testicles with stones to see who could endure the most pain. Tad Ibe again went first. Sitting on a rock, he prepared to beat his testes with a stone, but before striking he pushed his testes back into his stomach so that he struck only empty skin. When Tad Ibe finished beating himself, Iguana-Chief was quite impressed. Then Iguana-Chief took his turn and, without realizing Tad Ibe's deception, beat his own testes thoroughly and hard—but he felt no pain! Tad Ibe then suggested yet a fourth contest in which they would push thin sticks of gold up their noses to see who had the largest nasal fossa. But before Iguana-Chief took his turn, Tad Ibe filed the stick to a sharp point, and when Iguana-Chief placed it up his nose, Tad Ibe pushed with all his strength and Iguana-Chief fell dead to the ground. Tad Ibe took away Iguana-Chief's golden clothing and announced that henceforth he would serve as food to the populace (the Golden People) when they would come to earth. Iguana-Chief was then changed into an edible iguana (*ari*).

Notes

1. Panama in the Early Sixteenth Century

1. Recognition must be accorded the work of Samuel Lothrop, Carl Sauer, Claudio Baudez, and Doris Stone, among others, who have studied the peoples and cultures of lower Central America in terms of what was, in fact, achieved. A new generation of anthropologists, historians, and geographers is continuing this approach. The papers in Helms and Loveland (1976) and in Young and Howe (1976) provide an introduction to some of this recent work.
2. Anderson (1914: 320) makes a similar statement.
3. Lothrop (1961*a*) and Sauer (1966: 286) discuss the climate and vegetation that might have prevailed in the isthmus when first peopled, as well as the changes that may have occurred in vegetation over millennia of human occupation.
4. A chiefdom, or rank society, "is one in which positions of valued status are somehow limited so that not all those of sufficient talent to occupy such statuses actually achieve them" (Fried 1967: 109). Those leaders who fill these central positions coordinate in varying degrees the economic, social, and religious affairs of the group. Introductions to the structure, organization, and operation of such societies may be found in Fried (ibid.) and Service (1971). Schwerin (1973) discusses the distribution and characteristics of chiefdoms in Middle and South America at the time of European conquest.
5. In 1680–1681, a century and a half after the initial Spanish conquest, the English-speaking surgeon-buccaneer Lionel Wafer spent four months among the natives inhabiting (probably) the headwaters of the Río Bayano. His account (1903, 1934) provides additional

ethnographic information, much of which probably reflects precontact conditions. The description of the Guaymí of western Panama written in the seventeenth century by Friar Adrian de Ufeldre (Santo Tomás) provides additional information (see Young 1971: 52).

6. Wafer notes that "their houses lie mostly thin and scattering, especially in New Plantations, and always by a River-side. But in some Places there are a pretty many together, so as to make a Town or Village, yet not standing close or orderly, in Rows or Streets, but dispers'd here and there, like our Villages on Commons, or in Woodlands" (1934: 89).
7. Wafer provides a description of the settlement of the chief Lacenta in 1680, which was excellently situated for defense: "This House is situated on a fine little Hill . . . [that] contains at least 100 Acres of Land; and is a Peninsula of an Oval form, almost surrounded by two great Rivers, one coming from the East, the other from the West; which approaching within 40 feet of each other, at the front of the Peninsula, separate again, embracing the Hill, and meet on the other side, making there one pretty large River, which runs very swift. There is therefore but one way to come in toward this Seat; which . . . is not above 40 foot wide, between the Rivers on each side: and 'tis fenced with hollow Bamboes, Popes-heads [a variety of cactus] and Prickle-pears, so thick set from side the Neck of Land to the other, that 'tis impossible for an Enemy to approach it" (1934: 17).
8. "*Boiu* means 'house' in the language of Hispaniola" (Anghera 1912: I, 196; see also Sauer 1971: 174).
9. Fernando Colón reports that on the Caribbean Coast of western Panama the Spaniards saw indications "of a structure [masonry], which was a great mass of wall, or imagery, that to them seemed to be of lime and stone" (Anderson 1914: 94; Colón 1959: 243). Note also the rows of stone columns forming an enclosure on the Río Caño in Coclé and at the Sitio Conte (Lothrop 1937: 30–31, 39–40; Verrill 1927). Marshall (1950: 288–289) also summarizes the scant information regarding mounds in western and eastern Panama, some of which stand one hundred feet high.
10. Howe (1974: 83) gives the dimensions of a "small-to-medium" sized Cuna meeting house as 56′ by 28′, much smaller than the ancient *bohíos* described by the Spaniards (see also Stout 1947: 19; Bennett 1962: 37). It is most interesting to learn that in these meeting houses pictures, documents, posters, and the like are prominently displayed, with portraits of dead leaders predominating (Howe 1974: 86, 95). This custom suggests analogy with the pre-Columbian practice of displaying the actual remains of dead leaders in a special chamber of the chiefly *bohío.*
11. *Tiba* and *jura* were other titles used to designate principal lords in some regions, but there is no evidence that these titles and personages differed significantly from *sacos.* I am using *queví* and *saco* for consistency and also because the sum of the evidence suggests that these were the major elite statuses (see Oviedo 1853: bk. 29, chap. 26, pp. 129–130; and chap. 27, p. 131).

12. Bride service may have been seen by Wafer (1934: xviii–xix n. 1) in the late seventeenth century; it is still customary among the San Blas Cuna (Stout 1947: 81; Holloman 1976: 136–137).
13. The men and boys who served this function also assumed women's dress and performed women's customary household chores, suggesting transvestism (Oviedo 1959: 105).
14. Among the contemporary Cuna, in addition to the mastery of highly specialized songs and chants by sacred-secular specialists, a number of other pursuits and skills are given public significance and recognition. Many of these skills can be performed publically, such as playing the panpipes a little or performing animal tales or short songs of various types. But "canoe-building, carpentry, hunting, turtle-fishing, and to a lesser extent, even special skill in tasks all men know such as fire-fan weaving can receive some public recognition, and ultimately almost any special piece of knowledge or experience (such as a trip as a seaman, knowledge of a prediction that came true, or a visit to Colombia) can be considered an *ikar* [special knowledge or skill] of sorts" (Howe 1974: 229).
15. For example, the multiple marriages of the *queví* Comogre, the alliance formed between Careta and Balboa by means of the gift of one of Careta's daughters to Balboa, and the alliance between Escoria and Parita via Escoria's marriage to Parita's daughter.
16. According to Friar Adrian's seventeenth-century account, the deceased was carried in his hammock half a league from his house and placed on a platform (*barbacoa*) along with food and his bows and arrows. Three or four months later, after birds had consumed the flesh, relatives retrieved the bones, washed and wrapped them, and buried them with gold ornaments in a new clay vessel (Salcedo 1908: 135).
17. Oviedo further tells us that, if a chief were lost at sea or in battle so that his body could not be recovered or dessicated, an empty space was left in the row of deceased chiefs in the burial chamber and the sons of the dead *cacique* were required to compose a song commemorating the manner of the death and to sing of it, and of others whose earthly remains were similarly lost, at festivals (1959: 38, and 1853: bk. 29, chap. 31, p. 155).
18. The concept of power as used here and elsewhere in this study refers to the manipulation of situations and people that derives from control over valued things, including persons, natural resources, skills, information, and the like (see Adams 1975: 9–29; Balandier 1970: 34–41). Related concepts of authority and legitimacy follow the definitions by Adams (1975: 30–36) and by Swartz, Turner, and Tuden (1966: 10–12).
19. "El primero hijo que han varon, aquel subçede en el estado; é faltándole hijos, heredan las hijas mayores, é aquellas casan sus padres con los prinçipales vassalos suyos. Pero si del hijo mayor quedaron hijas é no hijos no heredan aquellas, sino los hijos varones de segunda hija, porque aquella ya se sabe ques forçosamente de su generaçion; assi quel hijo de mi hermana indubitadamente es mi sobrino é nieto de mi padre; pero el hijo ó hija de mi hermano

puedese ponder en dubya" (Oviedo 1853: bk. 29, chap. 27, p. 133).

20. When Balboa reached the chiefdom of Chape, he found that Chape himself was dead and a woman served as lord of the land while her brother acted as a sort of "regent-prime minister" (Oviedo 1853: bk. 29, chap. 3, p. 14; see also Romolí 1953: 165). In this situation the "*hermano*" presumably was not a firstborn male of the ruling descent group proper.
21. Malinowsky (1962: 63–64) discussed this role under the rubric "the principle of legitimacy." To be socially legitimate a child must have a sociological father who provides the male link between the child and the rest of the community.
22. See Lathrap (1973: 173) regarding hostilities and periodic trade fairs in northern South America.
23. This emphasis on resource redundancy also reflects the fact that there are no data regarding the extent of variability of basic resource distribution in early sixteenth-century Panama. Probably one of the functions of *krun* lay in providing an opportunity for exchange of local resources, thereby redressing resource imbalances to some extent. Other mechanisms may have existed, too. For a useful discussion of the relationship between resource variability and social organization in rank societies, see Suttles (1962).
24. Conceivably, fishing and hunting were also activities that objectified the role of the chief as a leader of men, and access to fishing and hunting areas was valuable for its political potential as much as (or perhaps even more than) for subsistence benefits.
25. It is noteworthy that in Traditional and, to some extent, Open Polynesian societies, production was mainly the concern of lesser elites rather than of the high chief, who instead dealt with the ritual and religious aspects of production and with exchange of goods (Goldman 1970: 482–486, 508). Similarly, I shall argue that the Panamanian high chiefs' concern was with ideology and exchange systems more than with secular control of production.
26. See Tourtellot and Sabloff (1972) and Rathje (1972) regarding environmental redundancy or uniformity and the sociopolitical significance of centralized control of long-distance exchange in status paraphernalia and utilitarian goods among lowland Maya chiefdoms of Mesoamerica. Details differ between this region and ancient Panama, but some overall analogies are suggested.
27. By way of Colombia, contacts may also have extended east to Venezuela and even to Amazonia (see Lathrap 1973*b*) and south into Ecuador and the central Andean kingdoms, although it may be questioned whether Panamanian chiefs held direct contacts this far afield.
28. Comparable situations can readily be found in the ethnographic literature. For example, Elmendorf (1971) discusses how, among the Coast Salish of the Northwest Coast of North America, a system of intercommunity or regional relationships supported and enhanced social rank and status within villages and groups. Miles' analysis (1957) of the sixteenth-century Pokom Maya in Guatemala proposes chiefly interrelationships expressed by gift giving and warfare, which also may be

similar to those characteristic of sixteenth-century Panamanian society (see also Moore 1969).

2. *Fields of Influence*

1. James Howe discusses analogies sometimes made today by the contemporary San Blas Cuna of northeastern Panama, between chiefs and rivers and between the polity and the river system. In this comparison the chief may be compared with the mainstream, while lesser chiefs, other political assistants, and the young men who are not yet officers are as major tributaries and as the small rivulets and source streams at the headwaters. The river is also a common metaphor for the village (that is, the polity). "This makes sense, given that villages are invariably associated with a mainland river from which they draw their fresh water, many villages take their names from their rivers, and the chiefs frequently allude metonymically to villages as rivers or river mouths in admonishments" (Howe 1977: 156, and personal communication). There is, furthermore, a tendency to locate graves near the principal river associated with a village (Howe 1976*a*: 162 n. 8). Regarding rivers as territorial boundaries, we find that among the San Blas Cuna the territorial limits of mainland villages are frequently expressed in terms of natural features—rivers, mountains, or the sea. Thus, for example, the "geographical limits" of Armila village are given as the Caribbean to the north, Karsip (Sarsip) Mountain to the south, Ipeti Mountain to the east, and the Río Tukti to the west (Wassén 1949: 86–87).
2. In that it involved several geographically adjacent societies that are presumably culturally similar with a central area holding influence over its neighbors, the "field of influence" as I conceive of it may appear similar to the traditional culture area–culture center concept (see Olien n.d.; Newman 1971). However, the "field of influence" is interpreted as an elite phenomenon with associated societies interlinked primarily at the top of the sociopolitical hierarchy. The particulars of such a "field" as I envision it make "field of influence" much more closely related to notions of "social field" and "social network" (see Lesser 1961; Jay 1964) and to the concept of "political fields" as defined by Swartz, Turner, and Tuden (1966: 8, 26–31, 247–253).
3. The name of Darién is used in various ways in the ethnohistoric and scholarly literature. It may refer to a specific native "province" or chiefdom that included territory from the Atrato delta to Cape Tiburón. It is also the name applied by the Spaniards to the entire eastern half of the isthmus of Panama as far as the Atrato basin. Darién was also the name of the major native community within the Indian "province," which was then remade into the Spanish settlement called Santa María la Antigua de Darién.
4. A land, or "Castilian," league equaled 4.4 kilometers, or 2.76 statute miles. A marine, or "Portuguese," league equaled 5.9 kilometers, or 3.68 statute miles (Romolí 1953: 355, and 1960: 22 n. 8).
5. Since Careta's domain also gave ready access across the *serranía* to

Comogrean territory, Careta is placed under Comogre's postulated field of influence, although it is likely that Careta and Darién were involved in various forms of exchange and alliance, too. Careta's border with Darién apparently adjoined a territory of little or no settlement, population being centered in the nucleated town of Darién.

6. Many *caciques' bohíos* were located in foothills near plains or valleys, that is, between upland and lowland resource areas.
7. In 1680–1681, Wafer's host, chief Lacenta, seems to have lived on a north-flowing tributary of the Río Bayano headwaters. Nordenskiöld (1938: 122) suggests a location at the junction between the upper Río Bayano and the Río Cañazas where the village of Pirya stood in contemporary times. With chief Lacenta lived "Fifty Principal Men of the Country, all under Lacenta's Command, who is as a Prince over all the South part of the Isthmus of Darien; the Indians both there and the North side also, paying him great respect" (Wafer 1934: 18).
8. This location is surmised in part because the territory so delineated includes the estuary of the Río Sabana in the east and because Chape was apparently located south of the chiefdom of Cuquera, which may have been situated on the upper Río Congo drainage.
9. Similar pearl fisheries were found at the island of Otoque.
10. The Pearl Islands, in the Gulf of Panama, may also have composed a regional sphere of influence, with the lords of the smaller islands under the direction of the *queví* of the largest. We know very little of this territory, except that game was abundant, as were pearls, and that the chief resident on the largest island had a large and richly appointed *bohío* and claimed dominion over the surrounding islands. For a survey of the Spanish accounts of the Pearl Islands, see Linné (1929: 63–72).
11. Additional chiefdoms are noted for this general area but their locations are not specified. See Oviedo (1853: bk. 29, chap. 5, pp. 18–19).
12. The *bohío* of Cuquera lay about three leagues (eight or nine miles) beyond the head of canoe navigation in the mountains. In terms of Figure 6, this would place it possibly three or four leagues beyond the border of the adjacent lowland chiefdom of Chape, whose domain might have ended, logically enough, at the limit of canoe navigation.
13. Concerning the political significance of distances, it is noteworthy that the leaders of the "hill people" of the north slopes of the Serranía de Cañazas are described by the Spaniards as "of small account," being located "only one or two leagues apart from each other." These data suggest lineage or village headmen who were not co-ordinated into a larger territorial-political entity under the leadership of one chief.
14. Chepo should not be confused with Chepabar, the name of the Spanish settlement established thereabouts. Chepabar was located just west of the lower Río Chepo (Sauer 1966: 280).
15. Another Azuero society, Huera (or Guera), said to be subject to Parita but not listed as one of those conquered (Lothrop 1937: 10), appears to have been situated still farther to the southeast on the Pacific side of the southern Azuera mountains near Tonosí (Espinosa 1864: 503; Sauer 1966: 262). Parita's territory was said to stop near

Pocri, suggesting that Huera lay beyond Parita's area of conquest. There is also mention in the documents of war captives from Chiru and Escoria in the chiefdom of Parita, and Oviedo says that Parita controlled territory as far north as Punta Chame (Oviedo 1853: bk. 29, chap. 13, p. 63; Lothrop 1937: 8). However, war captives could have been received via exchange, and, as Lothrop notes, the validity of the claim to such extensive territorial control is highly questionable (1937: 10).

16. In the ensuing battle (in which Parita was defeated), twenty chiefs were lost. This figure may give us some idea of the number of *quevís* and *sacos* in Parita's field of influence. Elsewhere we learn that Parita could summon as many as 4,000 warriors, a figure roughly in line with Comogre's reported control of 3,000 (Lothrop 1937: 6).
17. In addition to coastal societies, brief mention is made by the Spaniards of interior provinces, for example, Tobre and Trota (see Andagoya 1865: 24; Espinosa 1864: 509, 517), suggesting a pattern of coastal and interior hill polities, which would be in keeping with the distribution of societies elsewhere in the isthmus. See Sauer (1966: 272, 275) regarding the possibility of Mesoamerican peoples in this sector of the isthmus.
18. The chiefdom called Veragua should not be confused with the region also termed "Veragua" by the Spaniards, who rather vaguely applied this name to the region from Almirante Bay to Nombre de Dios (Anghera 1912: I, 205; Sauer 1966: 131, 170).
19. For example, gold objects found by Columbus at Puerto Limón, Costa Rica (Cariai in Columbus' record), were apparently acquired from the peoples of Chiriquí Lagoon (Anghera 1912: I, 323; Anderson 1914: 92; Sauer 1966: 30–31).
20. A small population of Cuna people still reside in the Tuira region at two villages known today as Pucro and Paya, the latter recognized as an ancient place of great traditions. These settlements are situated along the lower courses of the rivers of those names, not far from their confluences with the Río Tuira, more or less where it would be reasonable to find ancient settlements. A comparable continuity of settlement at a place of "great traditions" may be proposed for the Bayano-Chucunaque headwaters where the *bohío* of the *queví* Comogre was located, where Wafer visited chief Lacenta, and where villages of the so-called Bayano Cuna have continued to exist until very recently (see Bennett 1962).
21. Students of Mesoamerican prehistory have postulated similar models of multiple levels of exchange networks involving different types of goods for such groups as the lowland Maya and for peoples of the Valley of Oaxaca (for example, Tourtellot and Sabloff 1972; Pires-Ferreira and Flannery 1976: 287). See also Struever and Houart (1972) for analogous interpretations of Hopewell materials.
22. Consideration of redistribution between chiefs and populace in ancient Panama and any economic effects of this activity (as in diversification and intensification of production) is obviated by the absence of primary data on this subject. I tentatively suggest, however, that, as

in Polynesia, direction of economic production may have fallen more to the hands of lesser elites—*çabras* and *sacos*—than to the *quevís*, whose activities may have been more directed to the regional and long-distance exchange of chiefly valuables.

The association of "chiefship" with "activity" also appears in the political life of the contemporary San Blas Cuna. In some contexts certain political metaphors used by the Cuna note the metaphorical association of the chief with the *movement* of rivers (see note 1 above) in the sense that, as a stagnate or motionless river in dry season has no cleansing effect upon the fallen trees, slimy rocks, and other debris that "soil" or "make unclean" the waterway, so an inactive chief (or a chief whose assistants fail him) has no effect upon the evil behavior that "soils" or "makes unclean" the social world of man. Conversely, as a raging flooding river washes away the clogging tree trunks and other debris and "makes clean" the waterway, so an active chief (with the support of his assistants) rids the community of evil doing and "cleans" the body politic (Howe 1977). Yet again, regarding the multiplicity of lesser chiefs, secretaries, and treasurers who assist the chief in directing the affairs of the community, Howe comments that "it is hard to avoid the conclusion that here the Cuna are to a certain extent interested in creating positions for their own sake, since the offices have multiplied beyond the demands of the tasks themselves" (ibid., p. 34). This statement contains the implication that, as positions of leadership proliferate independently, to some extent, of their need, so a certain amount of work or activity is generated simply to support the political field as much as to accomplish a necessary task.

3. Symbolism and Power

1. This holds true, of course, regardless of the degree of "secularization" and competitiveness found in rank societies, be they Traditional, Open, or Stratified. Indeed, it is a criterion of any reasonably stable political system (see Cohen 1969).
2. This discussion rests heavily on Goldman (1970: 10–13).
3. See Elmendorf (1970) for discussion of comparable phenomena with reference to the Northwest Coast.
4. The goal-motivated behavior proposed here, whereby chiefs would strive purposefully to establish ever wider and more far-flung associations with distant peoples, has been broached before in terms of the value of exchange systems (and warfare) as political situations that heighten the political visibility of ambitious men. In a publication specifically discussing archaeological interpretations of regional exchange systems, Robert Adams (1974) also argues for greater recognition of consciously motivated individual behavior as a processual factor of major importance in the operation of such systems. He notes that if this is not done exchange spheres are given rather broad and abstract functional or "systemic" interpretations in which behavior is viewed as that of the group gradually and unconsciously adapting to

local environmental demands. Swartz, Turner, and Tuden (1966: 8) make a comparable point in support of the study of politics as the investigation of processes and purposes within networks or fields of interaction rather than of structures and of society as an entity.

The motivations and activities of high chiefs of rank societies as they struggle to deal with the problem of scarcity of high-status goods may indeed ultimately serve broad social or group needs and objectives and create local and regional environmental and political effects. However, the specific aspirations of these chiefs express their intense desire to maintain their personal positions of power by actively evidencing their personal capabilities through (among other things) the acquisition of scarce goods, thereby also providing means for rewarding high-status supporters and evincing the strength of their sanctity to potential rivals and to the populace at large.

5. Compare Reichel-Dolmatoff, *Amazonian Cosmos* (1971: 253) regarding a comparable myth in which the Desana culture hero teaches the use of metal earrings.
6. Annealing refers to heating a piece of beaten metal to achieve a restructuring of the crystals, which (depending on the metal) strengthens the piece by reducing the brittleness or relaxing the springiness caused by hammering. Embossing is a technique whereby a design is raised in relief on a flat piece of metal.
7. The mythology of the contemporary San Blas Cuna is far removed temporally from the belief systems of pre-Columbian Panamanian peoples. Yet I think that a careful handling of Cuna myth themes may offer guidelines for the interpretation of ancient symbols and practices. While to date this form of ethnographic analogy lacks vigor and precision, I concur with the "ethnological approach" to the study of ancient imagery as discussed by Grieder (1975). I argue that, in the absence of more direct data, analysis of contemporary myth at least allows some plausible guesses, which are better than "common sense" guesses or none at all. For an opposing argument see Linares (1977*b*: 59).
8. "Se puso zapatos de oro, un sombrero de oro, una camisa de oro, un saco de oro, pantalones de oro y brazales de oro. . . . Finalmente se ciño una banda de oro en la cintura, el extremo de la cual caía hasta sus piés, y se pintó con achiote" (Chapin 1970: 24).
9. This focus on "cosmic energy" and its manifestations is derived largely from the terminology and general approach of Reichel-Dolmatoff, whose study of Desana cosmology in particular (1971) I have found to be an excellent general guide for understanding Panamanian materials. Thompson's interpretation of ancient Maya cosmology (1970) is of interest in the Panamanian context, too.
10. Two major realms are recognized in Cuna cosmology: that of the earth, or the Below, associated with Great Mother, and that of the celestial realm, or the Above, associated with Great Father. The origins of all things can be attributed to sexual acts between Great Mother and Great Father (Howe, personal communication).

11. In Cuna thought Tad Ibe, or Ibelele, was originally a culture hero sent to earth from above by Great Father. He later ascended into the sky where he rides in the sun boat and bears a bright shining disk, the sun as we know it now.
12. Belief in the significance of the medium from which a symbolic object is crafted is clearly evidenced among contemporary San Blas Cuna in woodcarving, particularly in the carving of wooden *nuchus* (*suar nuchus, suar mimmis, sualleles, ukkurwalas*), or "stick dolls," which are believed to derive their curing power from the invisible essence, or *purba*, of the type of wood of which they are made, the most powerful being those carved from balsa (see Stout 1947: 45; Nordenskiöld 1938: 345). Oviedo indicates that wood was also a medium for carving religious figures in his time (1959: 37). The use of various colored jewels and semiprecious stones, bones, and teeth, either in association with gold or alone, in pre-Columbian Panamanian "ornaments" also should be explored further in terms of metaphors for cosmological and mythological themes. For example, Lothrop's excavations at the Sitio Conte have revealed animal forms carved from white or green stone (quartz, emerald, serpentine) and from light-colored bone and teeth (1937: 14). Among the Desana a wide range of objects of whitish color, including quartz, were associated with the sun's energy, while green shades were associated with the paradise of the underworld (Reichel-Dolmatoff 1971: 25, 48; cf. the significance of jade in its various blue-green shades among Mesoamericans).
13. The color of the long feathers in the ancient Panamanian headdresses is not given, but museum specimens from the contemporary Cuna show long feathers of red, yellow, and blue. See figure 13.
14. As we have seen (Chapter 2, note 22), among the Cuna the symbolic identification of the chief with a flooding river is a political metaphor sometimes used in chiefly chants and speeches in contexts of chiefly adjudication. In the Origins of Fire myth an adjudicating aspect is not found, but a comparable concept of mediation seems indicated in that Iguana can "cross" the raging river that separates the natural-supernatural realm from the human realm. (See again the metaphor associating chiefship with the mainstream of the river system as discussed in Chapter 2, note 1.)
15. This image undoubtedly denotes a complex symbolism, which I do not claim to fully explain here by any means. For example, the anthropomorphic being with animals dangling from his belt could also be examined within the richly symbolic context of the hunter with his game. As such, the central figure could represent a short person or a dwarf and could be correlated with the widespread native American beliefs in a Master of the Animals or in diverse spirit "owners" of various animals that sometimes take the shape of dwarfs (see Reichel-Dolmatoff 1971: 80–86). Comparable belief elements occur among the Cuna, where short stature in general is said to be admired and associated with strength (Holloman 1969: 92). The Cuna also believe in spirit-animal "owners" of "spirit abodes" who negotiate

with the *neles* concerning the release of game animals from these abodes for the benefit of hunters (Holmer 1951: 29; Howe 1977: 142, 143 n. 6).

It is also most interesting to find in a Bororo myth imagery that appears closely related to this iconography. In a tale concerning the origin of rain and wind, we find a hero who hunts lizards for food and ties the surplus animals onto his belt (Lévi-Strauss 1969: 36). It is also curious to find that Lévi-Strauss considers the Bororo tale to be structurally very similar to the Cuna myth concerning the origins of fire (ibid., p. 138 n. 15), while the theme of edible lizards associated with heroes is of direct significance for various Cuna tales, such as the Iguana-Chief myth.

16. The two tales concerning Evil Ibelele and Iguana-Chief, respectively, also are surely meant to convey various aspects of affinity and consanguinity in their political contexts. Evidence was presented earlier for the importance of affinal ties as a means of supporting chiefship, for example, as a base of *krun* supporters and as implied in the significance of the term "*saco*," and as a possible source of competitiveness for chiefship, as in the succession to chiefly office. We also noted the role of consanguinity in such political arrangements, as in the preference for direct patrilineal inheritance of chiefly office and in the value of daughters as legitimizing agents if direct patrilineal inheritance is not possible. Extrapolating from these data to myth, we can suggest that by destroying Evil Ibelele's wife and daughters Tad Ibe is destroying one aspect of the evil chief's support system (affinal ties with future sons-in-law; daughters to legitimize an heir). When he destroys Iguana-Chief's sons he is eliminating another source of Iguana's-Chief's support (sons as patrilineal heirs and as supporters in *krun*). In this context, then, the two tales appear complementary in theme.

17. This figure is the most naturalistic of the designs that I have studied and, indeed, is the only one that portrays the details of dentition that I find so compelling as identification markers. Other portrayals are invariably more stylized. Since I think that the clue to the iconographic identification rests largely on zoological data, I find this one naturalistic depiction most useful even if stylistically it is a rarity.

18. In myth and metaphor the Cuna also compare their elite leaders ("big people," people with "names"), with "toothed" animals, in contrast to unimportant people (those "without names"), who correspond to animals without teeth (see Howe 1977: 146–147).

19. Iguana is but one of many creatures depicted in Panamanian iconography, all of which surely carried metaphorical significance within the cosmology and political history of ancient Panama. Following Grieder (1975), I consider it appropriate to reconsider the identities and significance of many of these forms within the context of contemporary Cuna belief systems, which, though removed from the pre-Columbian era by hundreds of years, may still incorporate similar themes. The Cuna are at least as close to pre-Columbian Panamanian culture as are

contemporary Euro-American anthropologists, and, by virtue of their familiarity with the same tropical habitat as their ancestors knew, the Cuna may understand better than temperate-zone scholars what fauna are available for symbolic use. For a somewhat different approach to the problem of interpreting ancient Panamanian iconography see Linares (1976).

20. The early sixteenth-century Spanish accounts indicate that iguanas were one of several foods, including fish, crabs, and venison, that were frequently offered to Spanish leaders by *caciques'* representatives as a gesture of peace (see, for example, Espinosa 1873: 85, 98, 107, 109). It is also mentioned that the *cacique* and principal lords of Parita and their warriors ate only fish and iguanas (ibid., p. 32, and 1864: 485; Andagoya 1865: 31). Military leaders of Yucatecan polities were also fed fish and iguanas, according to Bishop Landa (Tozzer 1941: 122).

4. Ideology and Exchange

1. The documents indicate that the term *tequina* was applied to anyone who was "master" of a particular skill. *Tequina* as used in the context of this chapter in reference to high sacred officials of pre-Columbian society may be interpreted as referring to a "supreme master" of the sacred arts.
2. Wafer relates (1903: 62) that all transpired exactly as the Indian seers foretold. The term "Pawawers" may refer to a particular ritual specialist named Pawa, whose exploits are remembered in Cuna legend today (see Wassén 1938: 72–75).
3. Probably Pacific western Panama (see Salcedo 1908: 98, 128).
4. One implication of this statement, to be developed below, is that the various creatures portrayed on gold pieces or on wood are also representations of animals seen in trance.
5. For example, the chosen person, or *tecuria*, after consulting with the supernatural in the *surba* (the small hut or enclosure), "told the chief what he pleased" (Andagoya 1865: 14).
6. For additional information regarding the sacred uses of pepper, see Cooper (1949: 565) and Karsten (1926: 5, 40). The burning of cacao beans also has great magical and ritual importance (see Holmer and Wassén 1953: 91). Among the Rama of southeastern Nicaragua a boiled infusion of cacao beans and chili peppers (cayenne with achiote) is drunk by the *sukya*, or shaman, to induce severe sweating and then trance, during which the shaman communicates with his jaguar counterpart and learns of future events. The pepper-cocoa, which represents fire and water, also is said to symbolize the shaman's power to cure (Loveland 1975: chap. 8).
7. See Cooper (1949: 555) regarding concoctions of *Datura*, tobacco, and chicha. Wassén and Holmstedt (1963: 41) also note that alcoholic beverages, when consumed during snuffing ceremonies, may be a factor in achieving a narcotic effect.
8. Howe suggests, however, that *warso* might refer instead to the short

splints of wood with a lighted ember at one end with which tobacco-blowing ritualists revive their long cigars.

9. The nature and use of the *nia arsan*, or "spirit ladder," briefly discussed by Wassén (1964: 113) is intriguing in this context and should be investigated further. The "spirit ladder" is a type of liana identified by Wassén as a "species of the genus Bauhinia," used by some South American groups (particularly in Brazil and Guiana—see Heizer 1949: 278) as a piscicide or taken as an emetic by the shaman as a means of reaching the supernatural. Wassén suggests the possibility of a comparable shamanistic use among the Cuna.

   It would be appropriate also to examine archaeological materials from the Isthmus of Panama for evidence of paraphernalia associated with the use of hallucinogens or other trance-producing materials in pre-Columbian times. For example, the elaborately carved jaguar *metates* of Central America have been tentatively associated with the preparation of narcotic agents (Furst 1968: 345). Could those found in western Panama be similarly construed (see Lothrop 1937: 95–96)? The hemispherical headdress ornaments on certain gold pendants of northern Colombia and of Panama have been interpreted as mushrooms, perhaps hallucinogenic ones (Furst 1976: 82). What of the curiously spouted jars from the Sitio Conte (Lothrop 1942*a*: 9–10, 65–73; see especially fig. 118) that resemble so strongly snuffing pipes from Mesoamerica and South America (see illustrations in Furst 1974 and in Wassén 1965)? These topics fall beyond the scope of this study but could be fruitful lines for further investigation.

10. This point is obliquely examined in the classic writings by Radin (1957) and Redfield (1964) on the significance of esoteric knowledge in "primitive" societies and the "thinkers" and "intellectuals" who work with this knowledge. Redfield briefly notes that there are ways in which intellectual activities associated with "hidden" or esoteric knowledge are "carried on in statuses and roles, in institutions and perhaps offices, that are parts of the social organization and structure of the society" (1964:40), and that those who deal with these matters frequently "stand-apart" from the majority of the populace, but he does not explore further implications of this line of thought.

11. The "ancient Indian Text" referred to here is the *Códice Matritense de la Real Academia*. There are many similarities in content between myths and tales relating to Quetzalcoatl as culture hero and wise leader and those dealing with the exploits of Tad Ibe.

12. "Origins" refers basically to the sexual interpretation of the creation of the cosmos (see Chapter 3, note 10) and probably carries concepts of a ritual return to, or evocation of, the universal creative energy that was originally expended at the first time of origins, or creation (see Eliáde 1959: 80–85, 97). "Origins" can also be understood as an emphasis on "total knowledge." In an oral-aural culture, with no way to store quantities of knowledge in written records, "man knows what he can recall—all else is so ephemeral as to be negligible" (Ong 1969: 640). The more that can be recalled, the more complete the store

of (mentally held) knowledge available to society. The *most* that could be recalled would be "everything" since the "beginning of things," and the most knowledgeable person would know "everything" back to the "beginning of things," in other words, would know of "origins," which, in effect, means attribution to some culture hero or other form of cosmic or "divine" creativity. Such tremendous knowledge then becomes insight into the nature of man's place and participation in the world. This insight, in turn, becomes a form of "power."

13. As Holloman notes (1969: 336), traditional Cuna communities were loosely associated in regional groupings, which, during the nineteenth and early twentieth centuries, formed the level of Cuna response to activities of the governments of Colombia and Panama. The high chiefs of these regional associations were also accorded recognition as such by chiefs of the local Cuna communities.

14. ". . . oral cultures consider words more powerful than we do, probably in the last analysis because whereas we interpret movement [the inherent mobility of sounds; they cannot be 'fixed' or 'stopped'] as instability, they are keenly aware of the movement of sound as signaling use of power. Words fly, which means that they not only move, but do so energetically" (Ong 1969: 638). It is apparent that chiefly speech in this context becomes another mode of "chiefly action" or the "activating" of political events.

15. Suttles (1958) has discussed a similar association between social rank, esoteric knowledge, and concepts of morality among the Coast Salish, and many of his points probably apply both to ancient Panamanian society and to the contemporary San Blas Cuna.

16. The two distinctive speech formats followed by chanter-curers and *kantules* and by chiefs appear to be directly specified in the two modes of approach shown by the mythological Tad Ibe in his contacts with Evil Ibelele, chief of evil spirits, and with the strong Iguana-Chief. In defeating Evil Ibelele, Tad Ibe relied on the mystical strength he derived from specific herbal "medicines" to overcome his opponent (that is, to defeat illness and the disruptions of undirected sexuality as implied in the underlying female theme of the myth), thereby in the mythological dawn of time making these "medicines" available to human society. So the Cuna shaman-curers and *kantules* emphasize the time-honored, unchanging nature of their curing chants and their ceremonial songs, and perhaps also of their medicines, seeking to continue the direct, unbroken contact with the guidelines of the past. In his contests with the rivalrous Iguana-Chief, however, Tad Ibe relied on his more nimble intellectual abilities to outwit and out-maneuver his physically superior (that is, antisocial) rival. So the Cuna chief is honored for his ability to speak creatively and to deal adroitly and skillfully with troublesome (that is, antisocial) persons and situations.

17. A brief statement by Andagoya is particularly intriguing here. He says that the "devil" took the form of a beautiful boy "in order

that the people, *being simple,* might not be terrified and might believe him" (1865: 14; my emphasis).

18. See Katz (1972: 63, 65, 155), Métraux (1969: 131–132), Soustelle (1961: 119), Morley (1956: 155–157, 183), Krickeberg et al. (1960), and Mishkin (1940) regarding the more complicated ideology and esoteric knowledge of the priesthoods of other ancient Nuclear American societies.
19. Some of these places, particularly Paya, Arquia, and Caiman but also Carti and Sasardi-Mulatupo, are cited in Cuna myths, which attribute their origins to various animal-human ancestors in the mythological past (Chapin 1970: 45). In actuality, the Colombian centers of Arquia and Caiman were apparently settled by Cuna peoples from Darién in the decades following the Spanish conquest, while the centers in the Bayano-Chucunaque headwaters are the home of a very small group of very traditional and conservative Cuna who did not move to the San Blas Archipelago (see Wassén 1949: 28–31, 32). Regarding Paya and the Tuira system, see Chapter 5, note 5.
20. For example, briefly discussing one aspect of the Toltec philosophical system, León-Portilla notes (1969: 58) the Toltec belief that, in order for their epoch to be maintained, each man must journey to the region of wisdom, "the Land of Black and Red Color," as Quetzalcoatl formerly had done.
21. I see the situation as somewhat analogous to that discussed by Mishkin for Incaic Peru, in which differences in social status correlated with differences in world view, including the extent of knowledge concerning geographically distant regions: "It appears that the Incas possessed more knowledge of the extent of the world than the commoners. . . . Their actual horizons . . . [went] as far as northern Argentina and Chile on the one side to the middle of Ecuador on the other and from the sea to the Amazonian jungle. . . . The common people, except those who served in the army or as colonists, had apparently very little idea of the extent even of the Empire except from hearsay and kept to their own small world—their village, puna or bit of table-land" (1940: 232, 233).
22. I further suggest that the depiction of Western material goods on the appliqued women's blouses (*molas*) for which the Cuna are famous also carries this significance. This interpretation is based upon the hypothesis that *mola* designs—whether depicting geometric patterns, flora and fauna, or Campbell soup cans—are not just aesthetically pleasing secular decorations, as is usually said (see, for example, Sherzer and Sherzer 1976), but are symbols of, or metaphors for, aspects of "cosmic energy," such as life, sexuality, fertility, and the growth of people, plants, and animals (see Nordenskiöld 1929).
23. Cuna curers, whose stock in trade includes a vast knowledge of jungle plants, have also explored the power of European flora. Nordenskiöld's informant, Ruben Pérez, who accompanied Nordenskiöld to Sweden for some months, was asked by Cuna curers to bring back with him on his return seeds from Sweden to plant in their gardens (Marshall 1950: 211–212). In like fashion, the furnishings of the underworld, as

described in various myths, include street lights, power boats, telephones, elevators, and shiny knives and tools. Descriptions of heaven are similarly filled with Western (European) products (Stout 1947: 100, 106).

24. Howe, briefly discussing journeys for the purpose of learning, sees a relationship among a chief's travels to learn, a culture hero's mystical (and mythical) visits to different parts (levels) of the universe, supernatural travels by spirits as recounted in chants, and voyages of Cuna sailors. He thinks that "the voyages of Cuna sailors and the knowledge they brought back of distant countries were probably structurally equivalent to traditional learning trips, as perhaps journeys outside San Blas for work or school are today" (1974: 161 and n. 4).
25. Periodic regional meetings of Cuna leaders still take place at the home village of a high chief. These meetings, ostensibly dealing with chants and ritual, are also forums for political matters. The meetings may convene every few weeks for up to six days at a time and every village within the region or sector should send a delegation of chief, *arkar* (translator), and others to the sessions, which are spent in lengthy chanting and in informal but serious political discussions (Howe 1974: 132, 134–137). These gatherings, Howe notes, are a variation on the general pattern of chiefly visiting, for it is deemed appropriate that village chiefs individually (but with a small retinue) should travel about from place to place teaching and admonishing, keeping abreast of recent events, cementing political ties, and conveying requests of his own constituents. Since a chief frequently gains in deference and privilege the farther he goes from his home community, such trips are very popular (ibid., pp. 110, 125–130 passim, 176, 189).
26. The prestigeful political-ideological journeys of the Cuna and the suggestions regarding comparable travels by pre-Columbian elites contain many elements characteristic of pilgrimages. See Turner (1974) for discussion of "pilgrimages as social processes."

5. Perspective from Colombia

1. The statement was apparently part of Pedrarias' political strategem for discrediting Balboa. See Sauer (1966: 276).
2. Sauer summarizes this argument succinctly, noting first that the goldwork of lower Central America and Colombia was made by master craftsmen who knew "smelting, casting, alloying, soldering, plating, gilding, and wire-drawing." He then asks, "Intent as the Spaniards were on getting gold, would they have failed to mention artificers of gold objects if they had found any? They knew that gold was collected in many mountain streams and was carried to a few places to be manufactured and that these centers were not located where the placer gold was found. They knew . . . that such a manufactory might point to the desired source of gold. The absence of notice of any such local industry for . . . the Isthmus suggests that none was found" (1966: 276).

3. ". . . pieças de oro, águilas, lagartillos, sapos, arañas, medallas, patenas y otras hechuras, que de todos géneros labran, vaciando en sus moldes el oro derretido en chrisoles de barro. Y estos yndios cristianos que rrescatan, . . . el día de oy . . . sólo traen oro en las pieças que e dicho, algo baxo de quilates porque su poco artificio les obliga e echarle liga de cobre para poder fundirle, con que le hazen de menos ley; pero en las patenas, como no hazen más que batirlas y estenderlas sin necesidad de liga, se muestra la fineça del oro que sube de veynte y dos quilates."
4. White makes an interesting comment regarding salt and gold, noting that, wherever in the mountains the natives worked salt springs, there the burial places have proved to be richer in gold ornaments than elsewhere (1884: 244). This observation suggests that salt, like gold, was a valued elite exchange item.
5. The documents of the Spanish conquest report that "Dabeiba" was the name of a *queví*, a province, a sanctuary, and a divinity, as well as a river (Anghera 1912: II, 318–319). We further read that in native language the word "Cauca" was designative of a *cacique*'s elite center and of the sacred shrine of an important deity, also called Cauca, which stood on the shores of a river that, as a result, was also named Cauca, as it is still known today (Trimborn 1948: 51–52). According to the conquistadors who first entered Panama, the name of the chief deity of the isthmian natives was Tuira (Tuyra), as is the name of a major river that the myths of the contemporary San Blas Cuna also identify as a "place of origin" (see Wassén 1949: 128). One wonders, again, if somewhere on the Río Tuira in pre-Columbian times a major political-religious center once stood. It is likely, as I have argued in Chapter 2 that, on the evidence of travel routes, one or more major elite centers were located here. The absence of ethnohistorical documentation for this region is indeed unfortunate.
6. These descriptions are from Gordon (1957: 33–45), who compiled them from the Spanish primary sources. Due to Spanish looting and burning, the population of the large centers was quickly scattered and the sites abandoned within a few years of Spanish contact. Reichel-Dolmatoff (1965: 125–128) provides archaeological background and summary of the sites.
7. This supposition rests not only on the ethnohistoric evidence of the political-religious importance of these sites, but also on the more tentatively offered observation that Sinú lies almost directly to the east of Panama. East is the direction of the rising sun, and the solar-celestial affinities of Panamanian rulers have been discussed previously. We also find in the Spanish accounts and in archaeological surface survey that Colombian temples, idols, and the entrances to chiefly burial tombs faced east (see, for example, Cieza de León 1864: 51, 60, 75; Gordon 1957; White 1884: 242). At least some traditional Cuna burials were also aligned east-west (Linné 1929: 12, 247–248), and the majority of the burials at the ancient elite center excavated at the Sitio Conte also faced east (Lothrop 1937: 52, 58, 61). Given the apparently sacred significance of the east and of the sun that rises, or

"originates," there, it would seem plausible that chiefs associated with solar-celestial phenomena and with intellectual interests in cosmological "origins" would focus on lands lying to the geographical-cosmological east. From the Panamanian perspective this direction would focus readily on the political-religious centers of Sinú.

8. Note that, while gold pieces of Colombian "styles" appear in Panamanian sites, pieces in the purportedly lower Central American gold styles (Coclé, Veraguas) do not appear, so far as I know, in Colombian sites. The implications are that Panamanian elites may have visited Colombian religious-political centers, but that Panamanian elite centers may have been considered of a "lesser order" in the Colombian view and were not visited as much by Colombians.
9. Root bases this opinion in part on the generally accepted supposition that the stimulus to Colombian metallurgy derived from Peruvian antecedents to the south. For an introduction to Peruvian metallurgy, see Lothrop (1937: 66–72, and 1967), Root (1949), and the forthcoming volume on South American metallurgy to be published by Dumbarton Oaks.
10. Root's analysis is not the only periodization of these data, but there is general agreement among scholars concerning the broad outlines of the development of metallurgical techniques and styles and of the temporal periods involved (see Emmerich 1965; Perez de Barradas 1954–1966: I, 330).
11. Reichel-Dolmatoff (1958: 79–82) has associated the appearance of metallurgy in northern Colombia with the Tairona II phase and the Betancí complex, which date after A.D. 1000 (see also Reichel-Dolmatoff 1965: 45). Given the absence of evidence for *in situ* development, he deems it likely that metallurgy was introduced to these northern lowlands from the interior to the south, noting particularly close association between metallurgical pieces in the so-called Sinú style and those of the Quimbaya style (1958: 89, 90, and 1965: 127).
12. This tri-partite division roughly follows Reichel-Dolmatoff's "Early Horticulturalist," "Rise of Sub-Andean," and "Sub-Andean" levels or stages in Colombian prehistory (1965) and the latter part of Willey's (1971: 255–261) proposed Intermediate Area developmental period sequence (that is, Formative, Regional, and Late periods). The dates follow Root's scheme, which varies somewhat from those used by Reichel-Dolmatoff and Willey.
13. The process involved may have been somewhat like that of Sanskritization, whereby local castes rising to power in traditional India attempted to acquire the symbols of high status associated with Brahman elites. In Srinivas' words, "When a caste or section of a caste achieved secular power it usually also tried to acquire the traditional symbols of high status, namely the customs, ritual, ideas, beliefs, and life style of the locally highest castes. It also meant obtaining the services of a Brahmin priest at various *rites de passage*, performing Sanskritic calendrical festivals, visiting famous pilgrimage centers, and, finally, attempting to obtain a better knowledge of the sacred litera-

ture. . . . In the traditional setup, the desire to possess the symbols of high rank assumed that the aspiring caste was aware of a wider social horizon than the purely local one. This, in turn, implied contact with centers of pilgrimage and urban capitals, . . . when, for instance, the dominance of a caste extended only to a few neighboring villages, there was frequently no opportunity for it to seek to legitimize its position by resort to Sanskritization. But when that power extended over a wider area, it was likely to come up against the might of the Great Tradition of Hinduism" (1966: 28–29).

I am suggesting with respect to Panama that emerging local elites of the various small chiefdoms strove to associate with wider social and political horizons, which first affiliated them with regional "spheres of influence" in the isthmus and ultimately with those political-religious beliefs and activities common to the Intermediate Area elite as a whole. From the Panamanian perspective, perhaps we can talk of a "Colombianization" process by which *quevis* of isthmian regional spheres of influence strove to participate in a wider network of political-religious contacts with northern South America by means of "pilgrimages" to traditional centers of learning in Colombia, use of common ideological symbolism and iconography, exchange of elite goods, and related forms of contact.

14. Both Holmes (1888: 38) and MacCurdy (1911: 194) note that Chiriquí effigy pendants of cast gold or *tumbaga* are frequently characterized by having the figures' extremities (feet or wings) beaten into flat sheets. Was this hammering done locally in Panama after the cast objects were received via exchange networks in order to give a local or regional stamp or style to these gold pieces? The query is not entirely fanciful. Adams illustrates a vessel from the Maya Lowlands "probably exported from Teotihuacan as a blank and carved by a Maya artist" (1977: 173). Similarly, Duque Gómez mentions that the Muisca imported partially finished gold pieces from the Tolima area to the south (1965: 329).

Bibliography

Adams, Richard E. W.
1977 *Prehistoric Mesoamerica.* Boston: Little, Brown & Co.

Adams, Richard N.
1975 *Energy and Structure: A Theory of Social Power.* Austin: University of Texas Press.

Adams, Robert McC.
1974 "Anthropological Perspectives on Ancient Trade." *Current Anthropology* 15: 239–258.
1975 "The Emerging Place of Trade in Civilizational Studies." In *Ancient Civilization and Trade,* ed. Jeremy A. Sabloff and C. C. Lamberg-Karlovsky, pp. 451–466. Albuquerque: University of New Mexico Press.

Aguado, Pedro de
1956–57 *Recopilación historial con introducción, notas y comentarios de Juan Friede.* 4 vols. Biblioteca de la Presidencia de Colombia, vols. 31–34. Bogota.

Alonso, Martín
1958 *Eciclopedia del idioma.* Vol. I. Madrid: Aquilar.

Alphonse, Ephraim S.
1956 *Guaymí Grammar and Dictionary.* Smithsonian Institution, Bureau of American Ethnology, Bulletin, no. 162. Washington, D.C.: Government Printing Office.

Andagoya, Pascual de
1865 *Narrative of the Proceedings of Pedrarias Davila.* Trans. and ed. Clements R. Markham. London: Hakluyt Society.

Anderson, C. L. G.
1914 *Old Panama and Castilla del Oro.* Boston: Page Co.

Anghera, Peter Martyr d' (Pietro Martire d'Anghiera)
1912 *De Orbe Novo: The Eight Decades of Peter Martyr D'Anghera.* Trans. Francis Augustus MacNutt. 2 vols. New York: G. P. Putnam's Sons.

Balandier, Georges
1970 *Political Anthropology.* Trans. A. M. Sheridan Smith. New York: Pantheon Books.

Balboa, Vasco Núñez de. See Núñez de Balboa, Vasco.

Bancroft, Hubert Howe
1886 *The Works of Hubert Howe Bancroft.* Vol. 3, *The Native Races* (Vol. 3, *Myths and Languages*). San Francisco: History Co.

Baudez, Claude F.
1963 "Cultural Development in Lower Central America." In *Aboriginal Cultural Development in Latin America: An Interpretative Review,* ed. Betty J. Meggers and Clifford Evans, pp. 45–54. Smithsonian Miscellaneous Collections, vol. 146, no. 1. Washington, D.C.: Smithsonian Institution.

Bell, Eleanor Yorke
1910 "The Republic of Panama and Its People." In *Annual Report, Smithsonian Institution, 1909,* pp. 607–637. Washington, D.C.: Government Printing Office.

Bellairs, Angus
1970 *The Life of Reptiles.* Vol. 1. New York: Universe Books.

Bennett, Charles F.
1962 "The Bayano Cuna Indians, Panama: An Ecological Study of Livelihood and Diet." *Annals of the Association of American Geographers* 52: 32–50.
1968 *Human Influences on the Zoogeography of Panama.* Ibero-Americana, no. 51. Berkeley: University of California Press.

Benson, Elizabeth P., ed.
1968 *Dumbarton Oaks Conference on the Olmec.* Washington, D.C.: Dumbarton Oaks Research Library and Collections.
1971 *Dumbarton Oaks Conference on Chavín.* Washington, D.C.: Dumbarton Oaks Research Library and Collections.
1972 *The Cult of the Feline.* Washington, D.C.: Dumbarton Oaks Research Library and Collections.

Berlin, H.
1958 "El glifo 'emblema' en las inscripciones mayas." *Journal de la Société des Americanistes* 47: 111–119.

Bolian, Charles E.
1973 "Seriation of the Darien Style Anthropomorphic Figure." In *Variations in Anthropology: Essays in Honor of John C. McGregor,* ed. Donald W. Lathrap and Jody Douglas, pp. 213–232. Urbana: Illinois Archaeological Survey.
N.d. "Similarities in the Pre-Columbian Gold Work of Colombia and Central America." Paper read at the XXXIX Congreso Internacional de Americanistas, Lima.

Bourguignon, Erika
1974 *Culture and the Varieties of Consciousness.* Addison-Wesley

Module in Anthropology, no. 47. Reading, Mass: Addison-Wesley Publishing Co.

Bray, Warwick

1974*a* "Gold Working in Ancient America." In *El Dorado: The Gold of Ancient Colombia,* pp. 33–39. New York: Center for Inter-American Relations and The American Federation of Arts.

1974*b* "The Organization of the Metal Trade." In *El Dorado: The Gold of Ancient Colombia,* pp. 41–52. New York: Center for Inter-American Relations and The American Federation of Arts.

Bright, A. L.

1972 "A Goldsmith's Blowpipe from Colombia." *Man* 7: 311–313.

Bruhns, Karen Olsen

1970 "A Quimbaya Gold Furnace?" *American Antiquity* 35: 202–203.

1972 "Two Prehispanic *Cire Perdue* Casting Moulds from Colombia." *Man* 7: 308–311.

Burling, Robbins

1974 *The Passage of Power.* New York: Academic Press.

Casas, Bartolomé de las

1927 *Historia de las Indias.* ed. M. Aguilar. 3 vols. Madrid: J. Pueyo.

Caso, Alfonso

1961 "El glifo 'Ojo de Reptil.' " *Ethnos* 26: 167–171.

Chapin, Mac

1970 *Pab Igala: Historias de la tradición kuna.* Universidad de Panamá, Centro de Investigaciones Antropológicas. Panama City.

Cieza de León, Pedro de

1864 *The Travels of Pedro de Cieza de León, A.D. 1532–1550, Contained in the First Part of His Chronicle of Peru.* Trans. and ed. Clements R. Markham. London: Hakluyt Society.

Clewlow, Carl, Jr.

1974 *A Stylistic and Chronological Study of Olmec Monumental Sculpture.* Contributions of the University of California Archaeological Research Facility, no. 19. Berkeley: University of California.

Coe, Michael D.

1956 "The Funerary Temple among the Classic Maya." *Southwestern Journal of Anthropology* 12: 387–394.

1965 "The Olmec Style and Its Distribution." In *Handbook of Middle American Indians,* ed. Robert Wauchope. Vol. 3, *Archaeology of Southern Mesoamerica, Part 2,* ed. Gordon R. Willey, pp. 739–775. Austin: University of Texas Press.

1975 "Death and the Ancient Maya." In *Death and the Afterlife in Pre-Columbian America,* ed. Elizabeth P. Benson, pp. 87–104. Washington, D.C.: Dumbarton Oaks Research Library and Collections.

Cohen, Abner

1969 "Political Anthropology: The Analysis of the Symbolism of Power Relations." *Man* 4: 215–235.

Colón, Fernando

1959 *The Life of the Admiral Christopher Columbus by His Son,*

Ferdinand. Trans. and annot. Benjamin Keen. New Brunswick, N.J.: Rutgers University Press.

Conzemius, Eduard

1932 *Ethnographical Survey of the Miskito and Sumu Indians of Honduras and Nicaragua.* Smithsonian Institution, Bureau of American Ethnology Bulletin, no. 106. Washington, D.C.: Government Printing Office.

Cooke, Richard G.

1976 "Nuevos analisis de carbona-14 para Panamá, al este de Chiriquí: Una actualización de los cambios culturales prehistoricos." *La Antigua* (Panama) 5: 88–111.

1977 "Current Research—Lower Central America." *American Antiquity* 42: 281–282.

Cooper, John M.

1949 "Stimulants and Narcotics." In *Handbook of South American Indians,* ed. Julian H. Steward. Vol. 5. *The Comparative Ethnology of South American Indians,* pp. 525–558. Smithsonian Institution, Bureau of American Ethnology Bulletin, no. 143. Washington, D.C.: Government Printing Office.

Dalton, George

1975 "Karl Polany's Analysis of Long-Distance Trade and His Wider Paradigm." In *Ancient Civilization and Trade,* ed. Jeremy A. Sabloff and C. C. Lamberg-Karlovsky, pp. 63–123. Albuquerque: University of New Mexico Press.

1977 "Aboriginal Economies in Stateless Societies." In *Exchange Systems in Prehistory,* ed. Timothy K. Earle and Jonathon E. Ericson, pp. 191–212. New York: Academic Press.

Densmore, Frances

1926 *Music of the Tule Indians of Panama.* Smithsonian Miscellaneous Collections, vol. 77, no. 11. Washington, D.C.: Government Printing Office.

Dobkin de Rios, Marlene

1973 "Curing with *Ayahuasca* in an Urban Slum." In *Hallucinogens and Shamanism,* ed. Michael J. Harner, pp. 67–85. London: Oxford University Press.

1974 "The Influence of Psychotropic Flora and Fauna on Maya Religion." *Current Anthropology* 15: 147–164.

1975 "Man, Culture and Hallucinogens: An Overview." In *"Cannabis" and Culture,* ed. Vera Rubin, pp. 401–416. The Hague: Mouton Publishers.

Drennan, Robert D.

1976 "Religion and Social Evolution in Formative Mesoamerica." In *The Early Mesoamerican Village,* ed. Kent V. Flannery, pp. 345–368. New York: Academic Press.

Duque Gómez, Luis

1965 *Prehistoria.* Vol. 1, *Etnohistoria y arqueología.* Historia Extensa de Colombia, vol. 1. Bogota: Academia Colombiana de Historia.

1967 *Prehistoria.* Vol. 2, *Tribus indígenas y sitios arqueológicos.*

Historia Extensa de Colombia, vol. 1. Bogota: Academia Colombiana de Historia.

1970 *Los Quimbayas*. Bogota: Instituto Colombiano de Antropología.

Earle, Timothy K., and Jonathon E. Ericson

1977 "Exchange Systems in Archaeological Perspective." In *Exchange Systems in Prehistory*, ed. Timothy K. Earle and Jonathon E. Ericson, pp. 3–14. New York: Academic Press.

Easby, Elizabeth, and John F. Scott

1970 *Before Cortes: Sculpture of Middle America*. New York: Metropolitan Museum of Art.

Eidt, Robert C.

1959 "Aboriginal Chibcha Settlement in Colombia." *Annals of the Association of American Geographers* 49: 374–392.

Eliáde, Mircea

1959 *The Sacred and the Profane*. New York: Harper & Row.

Elmendorf, William W.

1970 "Skokomish Sorcery, Ethics and Society." In *Systems of North American Witchcraft and Sorcery*, ed. Deward E. Walker, Jr., pp. 147–182. Anthropological Monographs of the University of Idaho, no. 1. Moscow: University of Idaho Press.

1971 "Coast Salish Status Ranking and Intergroup Ties." *Southwestern Journal of Anthropology* 27: 353–380.

1974 "A Structural Comparison of Coastal and Interior Salish Power Concepts." Paper presented at the 73rd annual meeting of the American Anthropological Association, Mexico City.

Emmerich, André

1965 *Sweat of the Sun and Tears of the Moon*. Seattle: University of Washington Press.

Enciso, Martín Fernández de. *See* Fernándo de Enciso, Martín.

Espinosa, Gaspar de

1864 "Relacion hecha por Gaspar de Espinosa, Alcalde Major de Castilla del Oro, dada á Pedrárias de Avila, lugar Teniente General de aquellas provincias, de tota lo que le sucedió en la entrada que hizo en ellas, de órden de Pedrárias." In *Colección de documentos inéditos, relativos al descubrimiento, conquista y colonización de las posesiones españolas en América y Oceanía*, vol. 2, comp. Joaquin F. Pacheco et al., pp. 467–522. Madrid.

1873 "Relacion e proceso quel Licenciado Gaspar Despinosa, Alcalde Mayor, hizo en el viaje que por mandado del muy magnifico Señor Pedrarias de Avila, Teniente general en estos Reynos de Castilla del Oro por Sus Altezas, fue desde esta ciudad de Panamá a las provincias de Paris e Nata, e a las otras provincias comarcanas." In *Colección de documentos inéditos relativos al descubrimiento, conquista y organización de las antiguas posesiones españolas de América y Oceanía*, vol. 20, comp. Joaquin F. Pacheco et al., pp. 5–119. Madrid.

Fernández, León

1886*a* *Colección de documentos para la historia de Costa Rica*. Documentos especiales sobre los límites entre Costa Rica y Colombia, vol. 4. Paris: Imprenta Pablo Dupont.

1886*b* *Colección de documentos para la historia de Costa Rica.* Documentos especiales sobre los límites entre Costa Rica y Colombia, vol. 5. Paris: Imprenta Pablo Dupont.

1889 *Historia de Costa Rica durante la dominación Española, 1502–1821.* Madrid: Tipografía de Manuel Ginés Hernández.

Fernández de Enciso, Martín

1932 *Suma de Geographia: A Brief Summe of Geographie.* Trans. Roger Barlow and ed. E. G. R. Taylor. London: Hakluyt Society.

Fernández de Oviedo y Valdés, Gonzalo

1852 *Historia general y natural de las Indias.* Vol. 2 (part II, vol. 1). Madrid: La Real Academia de la Historia.

1853 *Historia general y natural de las Indias.* Vol. 3 (part II, vol. 2). Madrid: La Real Academia de la Historia.

1959 *Natural History of the West Indies.* Trans. and ed. Sterling A. Stoudemire. Chapel Hill: University of North Carolina Press.

Fernández Guardia, Ricardo

1913 *History of the Discovery and Conquest of Costa Rica.* Trans. Harry Weston Van Dyke. New York: Thomas Y. Crowell.

Firth, Raymond

1940 "The Analysis of Mana: An Empirical Approach." *Journal of the Polynesian Society* 49: 483–510.

Flannery, Kent

1968 "The Olmec and the Valley of Oaxaca: A Model for Inter-regional Interaction in Formative Times." In *Dumbarton Oaks Conference on the Olmec,* ed. Elizabeth P. Benson, pp. 79–110. Washington, D.C.: Dumbarton Oaks Research Library and Collections.

Fogg, Walter

1940 "A Moroccan Tribal Shrine and Its Relation to a Nearby Tribal Market." *Man* 40 (124) : 100–104.

Fortes, Meyer

1973 "The Problem of the First-born." Lecture presented to the Chicago Anthropological Society in Chicago, November 16, 1973.

Foster, George M.

1960 *Culture and Conquest.* Viking Fund Publications in Anthropology, no. 27. New York: Wenner-Gren Foundation for Anthropological Research.

Fried, Morton H.

1967 *The Evolution of Political Society.* New York: Random House.

Furst, Peter T.

1968 "The Olmec Were-Jaguar Motif in the Light of Ethnographic Reality." In *Dumbarton Oaks Conference on the Olmec,* ed. Elizabeth P. Benson, pp. 143–174. Washington, D.C.: Dumbarton Oaks Research Library and Collections.

1972 *Flesh of the Gods.* New York: Praeger Publishers.

1974 "Hallucinogens in Pre-Columbian Art." in *Art and Environment in Native America,* ed. Mary E. King and Idris R. Traylor, Jr.,

pp. 55–101. The Museum, Special Publication, no. 7. Lubbock: Texas Tech Press.
1976 *Hallucinogens and Culture*. San Francisco: Chandler and Sharp Publishers.

Geertz, Clifford
1957 "Ethos, World-View and the Analysis of Sacred Symbols." *Antioch Review* 17: 421–437.
1966 "Religion as a Cultural System." In *Anthropological Approaches to the Study of Religion*, ed. Michael Banton, pp. 1–46. A.S.A. Monographs, no. 3. London: Tavistock Publications.

Goldman, Irving
1970 *Ancient Polynesian Society*. Chicago: University of Chicago Press.

Gordon, B. LeRoy
1957 *Human Geography and Ecology in the Sinú Country of Colombia*. Ibero-Americana, no. 39. Berkeley: University of California Press.

Gossen, Gary H.
1974 *Chamulas in the World of the Sun*. Cambridge, Mass.: Harvard University Press.

Grennes-Ravitz, Ronald A.
1974 "The Olmec Presence at Iglesia Vieja, Morelos." In *Mesoamerican Archaeology: New Approaches*, ed. Norman Hammond, pp. 99–108. Austin: University of Texas Press.

Grieder, Terence
1975 "The Interpretation of Ancient Symbols." *American Anthropologist* 77: 849–855.

Grove, David C.
1974 "The Highland Olmec Manifestation: A Consideration of What It Is and Isn't." In *Mesoamerican Archaeology: New Approaches*, ed. Norman Hammond, pp. 109–128. Austin: University of Texas Press.

Grove, David C.; Kenneth G. Hirth; David E. Bugé; and Ann M. Cyphers
1976 "Settlement and Cultural Development at Chalcatzingo." *Science* 192: 1203–1210.

Haberland, Wolfgang
1957 "Black-on-Red Painted Ware and Associated Features." *Ethnos* 22: 148–161.

Harner, Michael J.
1968 "The Sound of Rushing Water." *Natural History* 77 (June–July): 28–33, 60–61.
1973 "Common Themes in South American Indian *Yagé* Experiences." In *Hallucinogens and Shamanism*, ed. M. J. Harner, pp. 155–175. London: Oxford University Press.

Haviland, William A.
1977 "Dynastic Genealogies from Tikal, Guatemala: Implications for Descent and Political Organization." *American Antiquity* 42: 61–67.

Hayans, Guillermo
1952 "New Cuna Myths, According to Guillermo Hayans." Trans. S. Henry Wassén. *Etnologiska Studier* (Göteborg) 20: 85–105.
Heizer, Robert F.
1949 "Fish Poisons." In *Handbook of South American Indians,* ed. Julian H. Steward. Vol. 5, *The Comparative Ethnology of South American Indians,* pp. 277–281. Smithsonian Institution, Bureau of American Ethnology, Bulletin, no. 143. Washington, D.C.: Government Printing Office.
Helms, Mary W.
1977 "Iguanas and Crocodilians in Tropical American Mythology and Iconography with Special Reference to Panama." *Journal of Latin American Lore* 3: 51–133.
N.d. "Succession to High Office among Circum-Caribbean Chiefdoms: Tikal, Panama, Northern Colombia, and the Greater Antilles." Files of the author.
Helms, Mary W., and Franklin O. Loveland, eds.
1976 *Frontier Adaptations in Lower Central America.* Philadelphia: Institute for the Study of Human Issues.
Hirth, Kenneth G.
1978 "Interregional Trade and the Formation of Prehistoric Gateway Communities." *American Antiquity* 43: 35–45.
Holdridge, L. R., and Gerardo Budowski
1956 "Report of an Ecological Survey of the Republic of Panama." *Caribbean Forester* 17: 92–110.
Holloman, Regina E.
1969 "Developmental Change in San Blas." Ph.D. dissertation, Northwestern University.
1976 "Cuna Household Types and the Domestic Cycle." In *Frontier Adaptations in Lower Central America,* ed. Mary W. Helms and Franklin O. Loveland, pp. 131–150. Philadelphia: Institute for the Study of Human Issues.
Holmer, Nils M.
1951 "Cuna Chrestomathy." *Etnologiska Studier* (Göteborg) 18.
Holmer, Nils M., and S. Henry Wassén
1953 "The Complete Mu-Igala in Picture Writing." *Etnologiska Studier* (Göteborg) 21.
Holmes, William H.
1887 *The Use of Gold and Other Metals among the Ancient Inhabitants of Chiriqui, Isthmus of Darien.* Smithsonian Institution, Bureau of American Ethnology Bulletin, no. 3. Washington, D.C.: Government Printing Office.
1888 "Ancient Art of the Province of Chiriqui." In *Smithsonian Institution, Bureau of American Ethnology 6th Annual Report, 1884–1885,* pp. 13–186. Washington, D.C.: Government Printing Office.
Howe, James
1974 "Village Political Organization among the San Blas Cuna." Ph.D. Dissertation, University of Pennsylvania.

1975 "The Consejo as an Aspect of San Blas Cuna Culture." Files of the author.

1976 "Smoking Out the Spirits: A Cuna Exorcism." In *Ritual and Symbolism in Native Central America,* ed. Philip Young and James Howe, pp. 67–76. University of Oregon, Anthropological Papers, no. 9. Eugene: Department of Anthropology, University of Oregon.

1977 "Carrying the Village: Cuna Political Metaphors." In *The Social Use of Metaphor,* ed. C. Crocker and J. D. Sapir, pp. 132–163. Philadelphia: University of Pennsylvania Press.

Janiger, Oscar, and Marlene Dobkin de Rios

1973 "Suggestive Hallucinogenic Properties of Tobacco." *Medical Anthropology Newsletter* 4.

Jay, Edward J.

1964 "The concepts of 'Field' and 'Network' in Anthropological Research." *Man* 64: 137–139.

Jones, Julie

1974 "Precolumbian Gold." In *El Dorado: The Gold of Ancient Colombia,* pp. 21–31. New York: Center for Inter-American Relations and The American Federation of Arts.

Kan, Michael

1972 "The Feline Motif in Northern Peru." In *The Cult of the Feline,* ed. Elizabeth P. Benson, pp. 69–84. Washington, D.C.: Dumbarton Oaks Research Library and Collections.

Karsten, Rafael

1926 *The Civilization of the South American Indians.* London: Kegan Paul, Trench, Trubner and Co.

Katz, Friedrich

1972 *The Ancient American Civilizations.* Trans. K. M. Lois Simpson. New York: Praeger Publishers.

Keeler, Clyde E.

1960 *Secrets of the Cuna Earthmother.* New York: Exposition Press.

Kohl, Philip L.

1975 "The Archaeology of Trade." *Dialectical Anthropology* 1: 43–50.

Kramer, Fritz W.

1970 "Literature among the Cuna Indians." *Etnologiska Studier* (Göteborg) 30.

Krickeberg, Walter, et al.

1960 *Pre-Columbian American Religions.* London: Weidenfeld and Nicolson.

Kroeber, A. L.

1946 "The Chibcha." In *Handbook of South American Indians,* ed. Julian H. Steward, Vol. 2, *The Andean Civilizations,* pp. 887–909. Smithsonian Institution, Bureau of American Ethnology Bulletin, no. 143. Washington, D.C.: Government Printing Office.

Kurtz, Donald V.

1974 "Peripheral and Transitional Markets: The Aztec Case." *American Ethnologist* 1: 685–705.

LaBarre, Weston
1972 "Hallucinogens and the Shamanic Origins of Religion." In *Flesh of the Gods,* ed. Peter T. Furst, pp. 261–278. New York: Praeger Publishers.

Ladd, John
1964 *Archaeological Investigations in the Parita and Santa María Zones of Panama.* Smithsonian Institution, Bureau of American Ethnology Bulletin, no. 143. Washington, D.C.: Government Printing Office.

Lanning, Edward P.
1967 *Peru before the Incas.* Englewood Cliffs, N.J.: Prentice-Hall.

Las Casas, Bartolomé. *See* Casas, Bartolomé de las.

Lathrap, Donald W.
1973*a* "Gifts of the Cayman: Some Thoughts on the Subsistence Basis of Chavín." In *Variations in Anthropology: Essays in Honor of John C. McGregor,* ed. D. W. Lathrap and Jody Douglas, pp. 91–105. Urbana: Illinois Archaeological Survey.
1973*b* "The Antiquity and Importance of Long-Distance Trade Relations in the Moist Tropics of Pre-Columbian South America." *World Archaeology* 5: 170–186.

Lechtman, Heather
1973 "The Gilding of Metals in Precolumbian Peru." In *Application of Science in Examination of Works of Art,* ed. William J. Young, pp. 38–52. Boston: Museum of Fine Arts.
1975*a* "Issues in Andean Metallurgy." Paper read at the Conference on South American Metallurgy, Dumbarton Oaks, Washington, D.C.
1975*b* "Style in Technology—Some Early Thoughts." In *Material Culture: Styles, Organization, and Dynamics of Technology,* ed. Heather Lechtman and Robert S. Merrill. 1975 Proceedings of the American Ethnological Society. St. Paul: West Publishing Co.

León-Portilla, Miguel
1960 "The Concept of the State among the Ancient Aztecs." *Alpha Kappa Deltan* 30: 7–13.
1969 *Pre-Columbian Literatures of Mexico.* Norman: University of Oklahoma Press.

Lesser, Alexander
1961 "Social Fields and the Evolution of Society." *Southwestern Journal of Anthropology* 17: 40–48.

Lévi-Strauss, Claude
1967 "The Effectiveness of Symbols." In *Structural Anthropology,* pp. 181–201. Garden City, N.Y.: Doubleday & Co.
1969 *The Raw and the Cooked.* New York: Harper & Row, Publishers.
1973 *From Honey to Ashes.* New York: Harper & Row, Publishers.

Linares, Olga F.
1975 "Plantas y animales domesticados en la América precolombiana." *Revista Panameña de Antropología* 1: 8–28.

1976 "Animals That Were Bad to Eat Were Good to Compete with: An Analysis of the Conte Style from Ancient Panama." In *Ritual and Symbol in Native Central America,* ed. Philip Young and James Howe, pp. 1–20. University of Oregon Anthropological Papers, no. 9. Eugene.

1977*a* "Adaptive Strategies in Western Panama." *World Archaeology* 8: 304–319.

1977*b* *Ecology and the Arts in Ancient Panama.* Studies in Pre-Columbian Art and Archaeology, no. 17. Washington, D.C.: Dumbarton Oaks Research Library and Collections.

Linares de Sapir, Olga

1968 *Cultural Chronology of the Gulf of Chiriquí, Panama.* Smithsonian Contributions to Anthropology, vol. 8. Washington, D.C.: Government Printing Office.

Linné, Sigvald

1929 *Darien in the Past.* Kungl. Vetenskapsoch Vitterhets-Samhälles Handlingar. Femte Följden. Ser. A, band I, no. 3. Göteborg.

Lipkind, William

1940 "Carajó Cosmography." *Journal of American Folk-Lore* 53: 248–251.

Loveland, Franklin O.

1975 "Dialectical Aspects of Natural Symbols: Order and Disorder in Rama Indian Cosmology." Ph.D. dissertation, Duke University.

Lothrop, Samuel K.

1937 *Coclé, an Archaeological Study of Central Panama. Part I.* Memoirs, Peabody Museum of Archaeology and Ethnology, vol. 7. Cambridge: Harvard University.

1942*a* *Coclé, an Archaeological Study of Central Panama. Part II.* Memoirs, Peabody Museum of Archaeology and Ethnology, vol. 8. Cambridge: Harvard University.

1942*b* "The Sigua: Southernmost Aztec Outpost." In *Proceedings of the 8th American Scientific Congress,* 2: 109–116. Washington, D.C.: Department of State.

1950 *Archaeology of Southern Veraguas, Panama.* Memoirs, Peabody Museum of Archaeology and Ethnology, vol. 9, no. 3. Cambridge: Harvard University.

1961*a* "Early Migrations to Central and South America: An Anthropological Problem in the Light of Other Sciences." *Journal of the Royal Anthropological Institute of Great Britain and Ireland* 91: 97–123.

1961*b* "Peruvian Stylistic Impact on Lower Central America." In *Essays in Pre-Columbian Art and Archaeology,* ed. S. K. Lothrop, pp. 258–265. Cambridge: Harvard University Press.

1966 "Archaeology of Lower Central America." In *Handbook of Middle American Indians,* ed. Robert Wauchope. Vol. 4, *Archaeological Frontiers and External Connections,* ed. Gordon R. Willey and Gordon F. Ekholm, pp. 180–207. Austin: University of Texas Press.

1967 "Peruvian Metallurgy." In *Peruvian Archaeology,* ed. John H.

Rowe and Dorothy Menzel, pp. 258–263. Palo Alto, Calif.: Peek Publications.

Lothrop, Samuel K., and Paul Bergsøe

1960 "Aboriginal Gilding in Panama." *American Antiquity* 26: 106–108.

MacCurdy, George G.

1908 "The Alligator in the Ancient Art of Chiriqui." In *Actas, 16th International Congress of Americanists,* pp. 311–312. Vienna.

1911 *A Study of Chiriquian Antiquities.* Memoirs, Connecticut Academy of Arts and Sciences, vol. 3. New Haven.

McKim, Fred

1947 "San Blas." *Etnologiska Studier* (Göteborg) 15.

Mahler, Joy

1961 "Grave Associations and Ceramics in Veraguas, Panama." In *Essays in Pre-Columbian Art and Archaeology,* ed. S. K. Lothrop, pp. 218–228. Cambridge, Mass.: Harvard University Press.

Malinowsky, Bronislaw

1962 "Parenthood—the Basis of Social Structure." In *Sex, Culture, and Myth,* ed. B. Malinowsky, pp. 42–88. New York: Harcourt, Brace & World.

Marcus, Joyce

1976 *Emblem and State in the Classic Maya Lowlands.* Center for Pre-Columbian Studies. Washington, D.C.: Dumbarton Oaks Research Library and Collections.

Markham, Clements

1912 *The Conquest of New Granada.* New York: E. P. Dutton & Co.

Marshall, Donald Stanley

1950 "Cuna Folk: A Conceptual Scheme involving the Dynamic Factors of Culture . . ." Honors thesis, Department of Anthropology, Harvard University. Reprinted in Human Relations Area File, Code SB5, vols. 5 and 6.

Mason, J. Alden

1931–39 *Archaeology of Santa Marta, Colombia: The Tairona Culture.* Field Museum of Natural History Publications, nos. 304, 358, 446. Anthropological Series, vol. 20, nos. 1, 2, 3. Chicago.

Maturana, Humberto R.

1962 "A Study of the Species of the Genus *Basiliscus.*" *Bulletin of the Museum of Comparative Zoology* 128: 1–34.

Mendoza, Néstor Uscátequi

1956 "El tabaco entre las tribus indígenas de Colombia." *Revista Colombiana de Antropología* 5: 11–52.

Métraux, Alfred

1969 *The History of the Incas.* Trans. George Ordish. New York: Schocken Books.

Miles, S. W.

1957 "The Sixteenth Century Pokam Maya: A Documentary Analysis of Social Structure and Archaeological Setting." *Transactions of the American Philosophical Society* 47: 733–781.

Mishkin, Bernard

1940 "Cosmological Ideas among the Indians of the Southern Andes." *Journal of American Folk-Lore* 53: 225–241.

Molloy, John P., and William L. Rathje

1974 "Sexploitation among the Late Classic Maya." In *Mesoamerican Archaeology: New Approaches,* ed. Norman Hammond, pp. 431–444. Austin: University of Texas Press.

Montanucci, Richard R.

1968 "Comparative Dentition in Four Iguanid Lizards." *Herpetologica* 24: 305–315.

Moore, Alexander

1969 "The Aztec 'Empire' as a Federative Monarchy." Files of the author.

Moriarty, James R., III

1974 "Early Metallurgical Techniques in Southern Meso-America." *Katunob* 8 (4): 15–24.

Morley, Sylvanus

1956 *The Ancient Maya.* 3d ed. Stanford: Stanford University Press.

Myers, Thomas P.

1973 "Formative Period Interaction Spheres in the Intermediate Area." Paper read at the IXth International Congress of Anthropological and Ethnological Sciences, Chicago.

Netting, Robert McC.

1972 "Sacred Power and Centralization: Aspects of Political Adaptation in Africa." In *Population Growth: Anthropological Implications,* ed. Brian Spooner, pp. 219–244. Cambridge, Mass.: MIT Press.

Newman, James L.

1971 "The Culture Area Concept in Anthropology." *Journal of Geography* 70: 8–15.

Nordenskiöld, Erland

1929 "The Relationship between Art, Religion, and Magic among the Cuna and Chocó Indians." *Journal de la Société des Américanistes,* n.s. 21: 141–158.

1930 "Cuna Indian Religion." *Proceedings, International Congress of Americanists* 23: 668–677.

1931 "Faiseurs de Miracles et Voyants chez les Indiens Cuna." *Revista del Institute de Etnología de la Universidad Nacional de Tucumán* 2: 459–469.

1938 *An Historical and Ethnological Survey of the Cuna Indians.* Comparative Ethnographical Studies, no. 10. Göteborg: Etnografiska Museum.

Núñez de Balboa, Vasco

1864 "Carta del Adelantado Vasco Núñez de Balboa, sobre descubrimientos y otros asuntos en el Darien, y dando quejas del Gobernador Pedrárias Dávila (16 de Octubre de 1515)." In *Colección de documentos inéditos, relativos al descubrimiento, conquista y colonización de las posesiones españolas en América y Oceanía,* vol. 2, comp. Joaquín F. Pacheco et al., pp. 526–538. Madrid.

Olien, Michael D.
N.d. "Is There a Latin America?" Files of the author.
Ong, Walter J.
1969 "World as View and World as Event." *American Anthropologist* 71: 634–647.
Ortiz, Alfonso
1969 *The Tewa World.* Chicago: University of Chicago Press.
Oviedo y Valdés, Gonzalo Fernández de. See Fernández de Oviedo y Valdés, Gonzalo.
Parsons, James J.
1960 "Santa María la Antigua del Darién." *Geographical Review* 50: 274–276.
1967 *Antioquia's Corridor to the Sea.* Ibero-Americana, no. 49. Berkeley: University of California Press.
Parsons, Lee A., and Barbara J. Price
1971 "Mesoamerican Trade and Its Role in the Emergence of Civilization." In *Observations on the Emergence of Civilization in Mesoamerica,* ed. R. F. Heizer and John Graham, pp. 169–195. Contribution of the University of California Archaeological Research Facility, no. 11. Berkeley.
Patterson, Thomas C.
1971 "Chavín: An Interpretation of Its Spread and Influence." In *Dumbarton Oaks Conference on Chavín,* ed. Elizabeth P. Benson, pp. 29–48. Washington, D.C.: Dumbarton Oaks Research Library and Collection.
Perez de Barradas, José
1954–66 *Orfebrería prehispanica de Colombia.* 6 vols. Madrid: Talleres Gráficos "Juna."
Pires-Ferreira, Jane W., and Kent V. Flannery
1976 "Ethnographic Models for Formative Exchange." In *The Early Mesoamerican Village,* ed. Kent V. Flannery, pp. 286–292. New York: Academic Press.
Price, Barbara
1977 "Shifts in Production and Organization: A Cluster-Interaction Model." *Current Anthropology* 18: 209–233.
Radin, Paul
1957 *Primitive Man as Philosopher.* New York: Dover Publications.
Rappaport, Roy A.
1971 "The Sacred in Human Evolution." In *Annual Review of Ecology and Systematics* 2: 23–43. Palo Alto, Calif: Annual Reviews.
Rathje, William L.
1972 "Praise the Gods and Pass the Metates: A Hypothesis of the Development of Lowland Rainforest Civilizations in Mesoamerica." In *Contemporary Archaeology,* ed. Mark P. Leone, pp. 365–392. Carbondale: Southern Illinois University Press.
Redfield, Robert
1964 "Thinker and Intellectual in Primitive Society." In *Primitive Views of the World,* ed. Stanley Diamond, pp. 33–48. New York: Columbia University Press.

Reichel-Dolmatoff, Gerardo
1958 "Notas sobre la metalurgia prehistórica en el litoral Caribe de Colombia." In *Homenaje al Profesor Paul Rivet,* pp. 69–94. Bogota: Academia Colombiana de Historia.
1961 "The Agricultural Basis of the Sub-Andean chiefdoms of Colombia." *Antropológica.* Suppl. no. 2, *The Evolution of Horticultural Systems in Native South America,* ed. Johannes Wilbert, pp. 83–89.
1965 *Colombia.* London: Thames and Hudson.
1971 *Amazonian Cosmos.* Chicago: University of Chicago Press.
1972a "The Cultural Context of an Aboriginal Hallucinogen: *Banisteriopsis Caapi.*" In *Flesh of the Gods,* ed. Peter T. Furst, pp. 84–113. New York: Praeger Publishers.
1972*b* "The Feline in Prehistoric San Agustín Sculpture." In *The Cult of the Feline,* ed. Elizabeth P. Benson, pp. 51–64. Washington, D.C.: Dumbarton Oaks Research Library and Collections.
1972*c* *San Agustín.* New York: Praeger Publishers.
1975 *The Shaman and the Jaguar.* Philadelphia: Temple University Press.

Renfrew, Colin
1975 "Trade as Action at a Distance: Questions of Integration and Communication." In *Ancient Civilization and Trade,* ed. Jeremy A. Sabloff and C. C. Lamberg-Karlovsky, pp. 3–60. Albuquerque: University of New Mexico Press.

Robe, Stanley L.
1960 *The Spanish of Rural Panama.* University of California Publications in Linguistics, vol. 20. Berkeley: University of California Press.

Roberts, Orlando
1827 *Narrative of Voyages and Excursions on the East Coast and in the Interior of Central America.* Edinburgh: Constable & Co.

Rodríguez Freile, Juan
1961 *The Conquest of New Granada.* Trans. William C. Atkinson. London: Folio Society.

Romolí, Kathleen
1953 *Balboa of Darién.* New York: Doubleday & Co.
1960 "De Darién a la Mar del Sur." *Boletin de Historia y Antiqüedades* (Bogota) 47: 16–35.

Root, William C.
1949 "Metallurgy." In *Handbook of South American Indians,* ed. Julian H. Steward. Vol. 5, *The Comparative Ethnology of South American Indians,* pp. 205–225. Smithsonian Institution, Bureau of American Ethnology Bulletin, no. 143. Washington, D.C.: Government Printing Office.
1961 "Pre-Columbian Metalwork of Colombia and Its Neighbors." In *Essays in Pre-Columbian Art and Archaeology,* ed. S. K. Lothrop, pp. 242–257. Cambridge, Mass.: Harvard University Press.

Rowe, John H.
1967 "Form and Meaning in Chavín Art." In *Peruvian Archaeology,* ed. John H. Rowe and Dorothy Menzel, pp. 72–104. Palo Alto, Calif.: Peek Publications.

Ruiz Blanco, Fray Matías
1892 *Conversión en Píritú de Indios Cumanagotas y Palenques.* Madrid.

Sahlins, Marshall D.
1958 *Social Stratification in Polynesia.* Seattle: University of Washington Press.
1972 *Stone Age Economics.* Chicago: University of Chicago Press.

Salcedo, Don Juan Requejo
1908 "Relación histórica y geográfica de la Provincia de Panamá." In *Relaciones históricas y geográficas de America Central.* Colección de Libros y Documentos Referentes á la Historia de América, vol. 8. Madrid.

Sanders, William T., and Barbara J. Price
1968 *Mesoamerica.* New York: Random House.

Sauer, Carl Ortwin
1966 *The Early Spanish Main.* Berkeley: University of California Press.
1971 *Sixteenth Century North America.* Berkeley: University of California Press.

Sawyer, Alan R.
1972 "The Feline in Paracas Art." In *The Cult of the Feline,* ed. Elizabeth P. Benson, pp. 91–112. Washington, D.C.: Dumbarton Oaks Research Library and Collections.

Schmidt, Karl P., and Robert F. Inger
1957 *Living Reptiles of the World.* Garden City, N.Y.: Doubleday & Co.

Schwerin, Karl H.
1973 "The Anthropological Antecedents: Caciques, Cacicazgos and Caciquismo." In *The Caciques,* ed. Robert Kern, pp. 5–17. Albuquerque: University of New Mexico Press.

Seeger, Anthony
1975 "The Meaning of Body Ornaments: A Suya Example." *Ethnology* 14: 211–224.

Service, Elman R.
1971 *Primitive Social Organization.* 2d ed. New York: Random House.

Sherzer, Dina, and Joel Sherzer
1972 "Literature in San Blas: Discovering the Cuna *Ikala.*" *Semiotica* 6: 182–199.
1976 "*Mormaknamaloe:* The Cuna Mola." In *Ritual and Symbol in Native Central America,* ed. Philip Young and James Howe, pp. 21–42. University of Oregon Anthropological Papers, no. 9. Eugene: Department of Anthropology, University of Oregon.

Sherzer, Joel
1974 "*Namakke, Sunmakke, Karmakke*: Three Types of Cuna Speech Event." In *Explorations in the Ethnography of Speaking,*

ed. Richard Bauman and Joel Sherzer, pp. 263–282. London: Cambridge University Press.

Soustelle, Jacques

1961 *Daily Life of the Aztecs on the Eve of the Spanish Conquest.* Stanford: Stanford University Press.

Spores, Ronald

1974 "Marital Alliance in the Political Integration of Mixtec Kingdoms." *American Anthropologist* 76: 297–311.

Srinivas, M. N.

1966 *Social Change in Modern India.* Berkeley: University of California Press.

Stern, Theodore

1945 *The Rubber-ball Games of the Americas.* Seattle: University of Washington Press.

Stone, Doris Z.

1958 *Introduction to the Archaeology of Costa Rica.* San Jose, C.R.: Museo Nacional.

1962 *The Talamancan Tribes of Costa Rica.* Papers, Peabody Museum of Archaeology and Ethnology, vol. 42. Cambridge, Mass.: Peabody Museum.

1972 *Pre-Columbian Man Finds Central America.* Cambridge, Mass.: Peabody Museum Press.

1977 *Pre-Columbian Man in Costa Rica.* Cambridge, Mass: Peabody Museum Press.

Stout, David B.

1947 *San Blas Cuna Acculturation: An Introduction.* Viking Fund Publications in Anthropology, no. 9. New York: Wenner-Gren Foundation for Anthropological Research.

Struever, Stuart, and Gail L. Houart

1972 "An Analysis of the Hopewell Interaction Sphere." In *Social Exchange and Interaction,* ed. E. W. Wilmsen, pp. 47–79. Museum of Anthropology, University of Michigan, Anthropological Papers, no. 46. Ann Arbor: University of Michigan.

Suttles, Wayne

1958 "Private Knowledge, Morality, and Social Classes among the Coast Salish." *American Anthropologist* 60: 497–507.

1962 "Variation in Habitat and Culture on the Northwest Coast." *Proceedings of the 34th International Congress of Americanists.* Horn-Vienna: Verlag Ferdinand Berger.

Swartz, Marc J.; Victor W. Turner; and Arthur Tuden

1966 *Political Anthropology.* Chicago: Aldine.

Thompson, J. Eric S.

1970 *Maya History and Religion.* Norman: University of Oklahoma Press.

Torres de Araúz, Reina

1974 *Etnohistoria Cuna.* Panama: Instituto Nacional de Cultura.

1977 "Las culturas indigenas Panameñas en el momento de la conquista." *Hombre y Cultura* 3: 69–96.

Tourtellot, Gair, and Jeremy A. Sabloff
1972 "Exchange Systems among the Ancient Maya." *American Antiquity* 37: 126–135.
Tozzer, Alfred M., ed.
1941 *Landa's Relación de las cosas de Yucatán*. Papers of the Peabody Museum of American Archaeology and Ethnology, Harvard University, vol. 18. Cambridge, Mass.: Peabody Museum.
Trimborn, Hermann
1942 "Der Handel im Caucatal." *Zeitschrift für Ethnologie* 74: 112–126.
1948 *Vergessene Königreiche: Studien zur Völkerkunde und Altertumskunde Nordwest-Kolumbiens*. Kulturgeschichtliche Forschungen, vol. 2. Brunswick, Ger.: Albert Limbach Verlag.
1952 "Pascual de Andagoya on the Cueva of Panama." In *Indian Tribes of Aboriginal America: Selected Papers of the 29th International Congress of Americanists*, vol. 3, ed. Sol Tax, pp. 254–261. Chicago: University of Chicago Press.
1960 "South Central America and the Andean Civilizations." In *Pre-Columbian American Religions*, ed. Walter Krickeberg et al., pp. 83–146. London: Weidenfeld and Nicolson.
Turner, Terence S.
1969 "Tchikrin: A Central Brazilian Tribe and Its Symbolic Language of Bodily Adornment." *Natural History* 78: 50–59, 70.
Turner, Victor
1974 *Dramas, Fields, and Metaphors*. Ithaca: Cornell University Press.
Vadillo, Juan de
1884 "Carta del Lycenciado Xoan de Vadillo a Su Magestad, dándole quenta de su vysita a la Gobernación de Cartagena." In *Colección de documentos inéditos relativos al descubrimiento, conquista y organización de las antiguas posesiones españolas de América y Oceanía*, vol. 41, ed. Alfonso Torres de Mendoza, pp. 397–420. Madrid.
Verrill, A. Hyatt
1927 "Excavations in Coclé Province, Panama." *Indian Notes* 4: 47–61.
Villamarin, Juan A., and Judith E. Villamarin
1975 "Kinship and Inheritance among the Sabana de Bogotá Chibcha at the Time of Spanish Conquest." *Ethnology* 14: 173–179.
Wafer, Lionel
1903 *A New Voyage and Description of the Isthmus of America*. Ed. George Parker Winship. Cleveland: Burrows Brothers Co.
1934 *A New Voyage and Description of the Isthmus of America*. Ed. L. E. Elliott Joyce. Oxford: Hakluyt Society.
Wagley, Charles
1940 "World View of the Tapirapé Indians." *Journal of American Folk-Lore* 53: 252–260.
1943 "Tapirapé Shamanism." *Antropologia* 3: 61–92.
Wagley, Charles, and Eduardo Galvao
1949 *The Tenetehara Indians of Brazil*. New York: Columbia University Press.

Wagner, Erika, and Carlos Schubert
1972 "Pre-Hispanic Workshop of Serpentinite Artifacts, Venezuelan Andes, and Possible Raw Material Source." *Science* 175: 888–890.

Wardwell, Allen, et al.
1968 *The Gold of Ancient America.* Greenwich, Conn.: New York Graphic Society for Museum of Fine Arts, Boston; Art Institute of Chicago; Virginia Museum.

Wassén, S. Henry
1937 "Some Cuna Indian Animal Stories with Original Texts." *Etnologiska Studier* (Göteborg) 4: 12–34.
1938 "Original Documents from the Cuna Indians of San Blas Panama." *Etnologiska Studier* (Göteborg) 6.
1949 "Contributions to Cuna Ethnography: Results of an Expedition to Panama and Colombia in 1947." *Etnologiska Studier* (Göteborg) 16: 7–139.
1955 "Algunos datos del comercio precolombino en Colombia." *Revista Colombiana de Antropología* 4: 87–110.
1964 "Some General Viewpoints in the Study of Native Drugs Especially from the West Indies and South America." *Ethnos* 1–2: 97–120.
1965 "The Use of Some Specific Kinds of South American Indian Snuff and Related Paraphernalia." *Etnologiska Studier* (Göteborg) 28.

Wassén, S. Henry, and Bo Holmstedt
1963 "The Use of Paricá, an Ethnological and Pharmacological Review." *Ethnos* 28: 5–45.

Webb, Malcolm C.
1974 "Exchange Networks: Prehistory." In *Annual Review of Anthropology,* vol. 3, ed. B. J. Siegel, A. R. Beals, S. A. Tyler, pp. 357–383. Palo Alto, Calif.: Annual Reviews.

Weiss, Gerald
1972 "Campa Cosmology." *Ethnology* 11: 157–172.
1973 "Shamanism and Priesthood in Light of the Campa *Ayahuasca* Ceremony." In *Hallucinogens and Shamanism,* ed. Michael J. Harner, pp. 40–47. London: Oxford University Press.

West, Robert C., and John P. Augelli
1966 *Middle America: Its Lands and Peoples.* Englewood Cliffs, N.J.: Prentice-Hall.

White, Robert B.
1884 "Notes on the Aboriginal Races of the North-Western Provinces of South America." *Journal of the Anthropological Institute of Great Britain and Ireland* 13: 240–258.

Whitten, Norman E., Jr.
1976 *Sacha Runa: Ethnicity and Adaptation of Ecuadorian Jungle Quichua.* Urbana: University of Illinois Press.

Wilbert, Johannes
1972 "Tobacco and Shamanistic Ecstacy among the Warao Indians of Venezuela." In *Flesh of the Gods,* ed. Peter T. Furst, pp. 55–83. New York: Praeger Publishers.

1975 "Magico-Religious Use of Tobacco among South American Indians." In *"Cannabis" and Culture,* ed. Vera Rubin, pp. 439–461. The Hague: Mouton Publishers.

Willey, Gordon

1962 "The Early Great Styles and the Rise of the Pre-Columbian Civilizations." *American Anthropologist* 64: 1–14.

1966 "New World Archaeology in 1965." *Proceedings of the American Philosophical Society,* 110: 140–145.

1971 *An Introduction to American Archaeology.* Vol. 2, *South America.* Englewood Cliffs, N.J.: Prentice-Hall.

Wilmsen, Edwin N., ed.

1972 *Social Exchange and Interaction.* Museum of Anthropology, University of Michigan, Anthropological Papers, no. 46. Ann Arbor: University of Michigan.

Wright, Gary A.

1974 *Archaeology and Trade.* Addison-Wesley Module in Anthropology, no. 49. Reading, Mass.: Addison-Wesley Publishing Co.

Young, John Z.

1962 *The Life of Vertebrates.* 2d ed: Oxford: Oxford University Press.

Young, Philip D.

1971 *Ngawbe: Tradition and Change among the Western Guaymí of Panama.* Illinois Studies in Anthropology, no. 7. Urbana: University of Illinois Press.

1976 "The Expression of Harmony and Discord in a Guaymí Ritual: The Symbolic Meaning of Some Aspects of the Balsería." In *Frontier Adaptations in Lower Central America,* ed. Mary Helms and Franklin Loveland, pp. 37–53. Philadelphia: Institute for the Study of Human Issues.

Young, Philip, and James Howe, eds.

1976 *Ritual and Symbol in Native Central America.* University of Oregon Anthropological Papers, no. 9. Eugene: Department of Anthropology, University of Oregon.

Index

J